THE PETERBOROUGH CHRONICLE

THE PETERBOROUGH CHRONICLE

1070-1154

Edited by

CECILY CLARK

SECOND EDITION

OXFORD
AT THE CLARENDON PRESS
1970

Oxford University Press, Ely House, London W. 1

GLASGOW NEW YORK TORONTO MELBOURNE WELLINGTON
CAPE TOWN SALISBURY IBADAN NAIROBI DAR ES SALAAM LUSAKA ADDIS ABABA
BOMBAY CALCUTTA MADRAS KARACHI LAHORE DACCA
KUALA LUMPUR SINGAPORE HONG KONG TOKYO

PRINTED IN GREAT BRITAIN
AT THE UNIVERSITY PRESS, OXFORD
BY VIVIAN RIDLER
PRINTER TO THE UNIVERSITY

PREFACE TO THE SECOND EDITION

IN the first place, my thanks are due to the Secretary and Delegates of the Oxford University Press, not only for inviting me to prepare this second edition, but also for permitting me to make such extensive changes and additions; in the second place, to the Principal and Fellows of Newnham College, who, having elected me to the Mary Bateson Research Fellowship for quite a different programme of research, in the event most generously allowed me to devote the major part of my tenure of this Fellowship to the present work.

Revision has impinged unevenly on the different sections of the book. The text has seen only the minimum changes needed to correct former errors. The commentary has been completely rewritten, partly in response to suggestions made by reviewers, partly because my own maturer judgement now regards content as more important than philological detail. The introduction, although thoroughly revised, does not differ drastically from that of the original edition, except for the new chapter on style.

In carrying out this work, I have been fortunate enough to have much help and guidance. It is once again a great pleasure to thank Professor Whitelock, who not only gave me support and encouragement throughout but generously read and criticized most of the book in draft, thus saving me from many inaccuracies. I must also thank Professor Clemoes, who has helped me to clarify my ideas on prose style, and Professor Cheney, who, by showing me how to trace the career of Henry of Angély, did much to mitigate my historical incompetence. I am also indebted to Mr. F. W. Bateson for allowing me freely to re-use material first published in *Essays in Criticism*. To my husband, who allows one room of our house to revert to the twelfth century, my debt is incalculable.

C. C.

Cambridge
March 1969

PREFACE TO THE FIRST EDITION

THE excuse for presenting this partial edition of one text of the *Anglo-Saxon Chronicle* is that the chosen annals are of exceptional interest, both to the linguist and to the historian, and are therefore worthy of special study.

My primary intention in embarking on this study was to demonstrate the importance of these annals for the history of the English language. And what emerged from this study was that the First Peterborough Continuation (1122–1131) deserves far more attention than it has hitherto been given by scholars engrossed in the Final Continuation. For in some ways, as I hope I have shown, the First Continuation is much the richer source of information about early Middle English, as it allows us to trace the processes by which some of the typically Middle-English forms arose.

Although the primary purpose of this edition is philological, the other aspects of the text have not been ignored. In particular I have tried to show how intimately these English annals are linked with the contemporary Latin histories. No one is more aware than I of the incompleteness of this aspect of my work. In particular I regret that my ignorance of diplomatic studies has prevented me from dealing adequately with the Interpolations; I hope that the very inadequacy of my treatment may inspire someone better qualified to do for these fascinating documents what I cannot.

In editing the annals themselves the aim has been to provide a readable text rather than a pedantic one. The punctuation is deliberately used as an interpretative instrument and therefore bears little relation to the pointing of the manuscript; where, however, it runs directly counter to the latter, this is discussed in the Notes. Regrettably, perhaps, there is no Glossary: an

Index Verborum, the only kind of glossary of real value to scholars, would have been too bulky and expensive to include in this edition. I hope this lack will not prove too distressing to any users of this book, and would mention that an Index Verborum is available for consultation in the copy of my thesis deposited in the English Faculty Library at Oxford.

Throughout the preparation of this book I have benefited immensely from the advice and help of many scholars, and I am glad to have here the opportunity of expressing my gratitude to them: to Professor C. L. Wrenn, without whose guidance I might never have embarked upon this work; to the General Editors of this Series, for thinking my book worthy of inclusion in it, and in particular to Miss Helen Gardner for her advice on many points of presentation; to Mr. A. Campbell and Mr. G. V. Smithers, whose expert criticism has rescued me from many blunders; to Mr. N. R. Ker, for his unfailingly generous help to a novice in palaeography; to Professor V. H. Galbraith, for explaining history to a philologist; to Professor Dorothy Whitelock, who has discussed many *Chronicle* problems with me and given me the benefit of her wise advice on innumerable details; to Mr. R. W. Burchfield, for his unflagging kindness in helping with East-Midland dialect problems; and to all the friends who have borne with me through typescript and proof.

C. C.

October 1957

CONTENTS

ABBREVIATIONS

A	Corpus Christi College, Cambridge, MS. 173 (the Parker Chronicle).
CMH	*Cambridge Medieval History.*
D	Cottonian MS. Tiberius B iv.
Eadmer	*Eadmeri Historia Novorum in Anglia*, ed. M. Rule, R.S., 1884.
EETS	Early English Text Society.
EGS	*English and Germanic Studies.*
EHD	D. C. Douglas and G. W. Greenaway, eds., *English Historical Documents, 1042–1189*, 1953.
EHR	*English Historical Review.*
EPNS	English Place-Name Society.
ES	*English Studies.*
F	Cottonian MS. Domitian A viii.
Florence	*Florentii Wigorniensis Monachi Chronicon ex Chronicis*, ed. B. Thorpe, 2 vols., 1848–9. (Compare *infra*, 'John of Worcester'.)
Garmonsway	G. N. Garmonsway, trans., *The Anglo-Saxon Chronicle*, Everyman's Library, 1953.
Gest. Pont.	*Willelmi Malmesbiriensis Monachi de Gestis Pontificum Anglorum libri quinque*, ed. N. E. S. A. Hamilton, R.S., 1870.
Gest. Reg.	*Willelmi Malmesbiriensis Monachi de Gestis Regum Anglorum libri quinque*, ed. W. Stubbs, 2 vols., R.S., 1887–9.
Gest. Steph.	*Gesta Stephani*, ed. and trans. K. R. Potter, 1955.
Hen. Hunt.	*Henrici Archidiaconi Huntendunensis Historia Anglorum*, ed. T. Arnold, R.S., 1879.
Hist. Eccl. Dun.	*Historia Ecclesiæ Dunhelmensis*, in vol. i. of *Symeonis Monachi Opera Omnia*, ed. T. Arnold, 2 vols., R.S., 1882–5.
Hist. Nov.	*The Historia Novella by William of Malmesbury*, ed. and trans. K. R. Potter, 1955.
Hist. Reg.	*Historia Regum*, in vol. ii. of *Symeonis Monachi Opera Omnia*, ed. T. Arnold, 2 vols., R.S., 1882–5.

Hugh the Chantor	*Hugh the Chantor: The History of the Church of York, 1066–1127*, ed. and trans. C. Johnson, 1961.
Hugo	*The Chronicle of Hugh Candidus, A Monk of Peterborough*, ed. W. T. Mellows, Oxford, 1949.
JEGP	*Journal of English and Germanic Philology*.
John of Worcester	*The Chronicle of John of Worcester, 1118–1140*, ed. J. R. H. Weaver, Anecdota Oxoniensia, Mediaeval and Modern Series xiii, 1908. (Compare *supra*, 'Florence'; Weaver's text is preferred for the years it covers.)
MÆ	*Medium Ævum*.
(e)ME	(early) Middle English.
MLN	*Modern Language Notes*.
MLR	*Modern Language Review*.
(l)OE	(late) Old English.
ON	Old Norse.
Ordericus	*Orderici Vitalis . . . Historiæ Ecclesiasticæ libri tredecim*, ed. A. Le Prévost, 5 vols., Paris, 1838–55.
Plummer	C. Plummer and J. Earle, eds., *Two of the Saxon Chronicles Parallel*, 2 vols., Oxford, 1892–9.
PMLA	*Publications of the Modern Language Association* (of America).
RES	*Review of English Studies*.
Rich. Hex.	*Historia Ricardi, Prioris Ecclesiæ Haugustaldensis, de Gestis Regis Stephani*, in vol. iii of *Chronicles of the Reigns of Stephen, Henry II, and Richard I*, ed. R. Howlett, 4 vols., R.S., 1884–9.
R.S.	Rolls Series.
Stenton	F. M. Stenton, *Anglo-Saxon England*, 2nd edn., Oxford, 1947.
Suger	*Suger: Vie de Louis VI le Gros*, ed. and trans. H. Waquet, Classiques de l'histoire de France au Moyen Age, Paris, 1929.
TRHS	*Transactions of the Royal Historical Society*.
VCH	*Victoria County History*.
WA	*Waverley Annals*, in vol. ii of *Annales Monastici*, ed. H. R. Luard, 5 vols., R.S., 1864–9.
WG	West Germanic.

Whitelock, *Facsimile*	D. Whitelock, ed., *The Peterborough Chronicle (The Bodleian Manuscript Laud Misc. 636)*, Copenhagen, 1954.
Whitelock, *Translation*	D. Whitelock *et alii*, ed. and trans., *The Anglo-Saxon Chronicle: A Revised Translation*, 1961.
William of Poitiers	*Guillaume de Poitiers: Histoire de Guillaume le Conquérant*, ed. and trans. R. Foreville, Classiques de l'histoire de France au Moyen Agc, Paris, 1952.
(l)(n)WS	(late) (non) West Saxon.

INTRODUCTION

MANUSCRIPT

THIS text of the *Anglo-Saxon Chronicle* (known as E) is preserved in Bodleian MS. Laud Misc. 636. Since the history and the palaeographical features of this manuscript have been fully described both in the introduction to the published facsimile and in Dr. Ker's *Catalogue*,[1] only the minimum account of it need be given here.

It is a parchment manuscript, now interleaved with paper, of ninety-one folios in quires of ten, except that f. 81 is an odd leaf added after the eighth quire.[2] The original size of the leaves is probably shown by ff. 86–90, which are $9\frac{1}{2}\times6\frac{1}{2}$ in. (24×17 cm.) and bear on their wide margins (the original written space is $6\frac{3}{4}\times4$ in.) a thirteenth-century Anglo-Norman chronicle.[3] Ff. 1–85 and 91 have been cut down to $8\frac{1}{4}\times5\frac{1}{2}$ in. (21×14 cm.), with the result that many old marginal notes have been cut through. Since the uncut folios are creased all round as if they had been folded down to the smaller format, the cutting must have taken place some time before the interleaving with seventeenth-century paper $12\frac{1}{4}\times8$ in. ($31\times20{\cdot}5$ cm.). The binding is (in spite of modern rebacking) still substantially the seventeenth-century Laudian one.

Palaeographically, the text of the *Chronicle* falls into three sections.

1. The entries up to 1121, ending on the odd leaf f. 81, are all in a homogeneous hand and ink.

[1] *The Peterborough Chronicle* (*The Bodleian Manuscript Laud Misc. 636*), ed. Dorothy Whitelock, with an appendix by Cecily Clark, Copenhagen, 1954, 13–26; N. R. Ker, *Catalogue of Manuscripts Containing Anglo-Saxon*, Oxford, 1957, 424–6.

[2] See 'Notes on MS. Laud Misc. 636', *MÆ* xxiii. 72.

[3] See C. Clark, in Whitelock, *Facsimile*, 39–43.

2. From 1122 to 1131 frequent changes appear both in the ink and also in the appearance of the writing, the impression being that the annals were written up in six blocks: 1122; 1123; 1124; 1125–1126/11; 1126/12–1127; 1128–1131. The differences between the styles of writing are not, however, absolute: thus, on f. 83ᵛ (1124) a finer style, rather like that of 1122, can be seen gradually coarsening to one like that of the opening of 1123, presumably owing to blunting of the quill. In spite of differences not only in appearance but also in layout and use of abbreviations, Dr. Ker believes that the whole of this section was written by the original scribe, the variations being due to lapse of time. This agrees with the *a priori* supposition that the *Chronicle* would have been entrusted to one man rather than to an ever-changing succession of scribes.[1]

Attribution of all the annals up to 1131 to a single scribe is confirmed by study of the letter-forms. It is true that the annals after 1122 show certain forms not found in the entries immediately preceding. For instance, Caroline *g* is used in *engleland*, *lange* 1122, *englalande* 1125; the straight Caroline *r* in *geare* 1122, *rotbert* (2nd *r*) 1124, *æsterne* 1130; and the bowed *r* in *priores* 1130. And, as Professor Whitelock has pointed out, Caroline a and *d* are used in this second section alongside the insular *a* and *ð* previously regular.[2] This need not, however, mean a difference of scribe, for all these forms are to be found in the first section, mostly at the very beginning of the manuscript; it is as if the scribe, coming fresh to the *Chronicle* or

[1] The *locus classicus* for the way in which a monastic chronicle should be kept is the Preface to the thirteenth-century *Worcester Annals* (for a reconstruction of the history of this Preface, see N. Denholm-Young, 'The Winchester–Hyde Chronicle', *Collected Papers on Mediaeval Subjects*, Oxford, 1946, 89): 'Nec mirandum, si liber annuatim augmentatur, ac per hoc a diversis compositus, in alicujus forte manus inciderit, qui proloquens fecerit barbarismum. Vestri itaque studii erit; ut in libro jugiter scedula dependeat, in qua cum plumbo notentur obitus illustrium virorum et aliquod de regni statu memoriale, cum audiri contigerit. In fine vero anni non quicunque voluerit, sed qui injunctum fuerit, quod verius et melius censuerit ad posteritatis notitiam transmittendum, in corpore libri succincta brevitate describat; et tunc veteri scedula subtracta, nova imponatur.' [*Annales Monastici*, iv. 355.]

[2] Whitelock, *Facsimile*, 5.

resuming it in the intervals of other work, probably Latin, kept the habit of using the Caroline letters. On the other hand, this section shows a great increase in the frequency of the insular forms of *s*.[1]

Since the annals 1122–1131 thus appear all to be written by the same scribe, they may be regarded as a single unit for linguistic study. And they may be considered together with the Peterborough Interpolations made in the first section by the same hand.[2]

3. The last section, 1132–1154, is in a hand completely different from the preceding one, much narrower and more pointed. This scribe never uses the insular forms of *a*, *f*, and *r*, or the low insular *s*; everywhere replaces insular ȝ by *g*; and, although sometimes using *þ*, *ð*, *ƿ*, replaces these signs by the substitutes *th*/*t*/*d*, *uu*/*u*, very much more frequently than the former scribe did.

That this is, as tradition claims, a Peterborough book is beyond question, in spite of its apparent omission from the medieval Peterborough catalogues (unless indeed it is disguised as *Elfredi regis liber anglicus* in the twelfth-century booklist in MS. Bodley 163). The older part of the *Chronicle* (to 1121) is freely interspersed with detailed accounts of episodes in the history of that abbey,[2] and the later additions are so full of Peterborough material that their provenance can hardly be questioned. This is confirmed by the handwriting. The first hand resembles that of MS. Harley 3667 and of Cottonian MS. Tiberius C. i, ff. 2–42, fragments of a scientific manuscript whose origin is proved by the Peterborough obits entered by the original hand in the margins of the Easter Table;[3] and the last hand resembles those of two other Peterborough books, Corpus Christi College, Cambridge, MS. 134 (the correcting

[1] Whitelock, *Facsimile*, 16.

[2] See Appendix, 115–27 *infra*.

[3] *MÆ* xxiii. 71–2; Ker, *Catalogue*, 259–60, 425, and idem, *British Museum Quarterly*, xii (1937–8), 132.

hand) and Society of Antiquaries MS. 60 (The Black Book of Peterborough), ff. 6–71.[1]

TEXT

The text falls, then, into two main parts: (*a*) the annals up to 1121, which are all written in a uniform hand and ink; and (*b*) the various continuations, which were apparently added at Peterborough from time to time as occasion arose and which themselves fall into two main subdivisions, 1122–1131 and 1132–1154. These divisions prove a convenient basis for textual analysis.

The Annals to 1121

Although all except the first few of the annals included in this edition are unique as vernacular records, investigation of their textual relations is neither impossible nor unprofitable. Indeed, much of their interest stems from their place in the *Anglo-Saxon Chronicle* tradition.

Of the seven principal surviving texts of the *Chronicle*,[2] those most closely related to the Peterborough version are D, B.M. Cottonian MS. Tiberius B iv, and F, B.M. Cottonian MS. Domitian A viii, 'the Domitian bilingual'. Between E and F the relationship is fairly straightforward.[3] F is an abbreviated

[1] T. A. M. Bishop, 'Notes on Cambridge Manuscripts', *Trans. Camb. Bibl. Soc.* i (1949–53), 440. Although in general appearance less compressed, the Black Book hand uses letter-forms in much the same way as our last hand does, including *g* for all the functions of ȝ. The chief differences are regular use of *þ* (*þæt*) where Laud has ð and greater rarity in the Black Book of substitutes for *þ*, *ð*.

[2] For a brief but authoritative account of these, see Whitelock, *Translation*, xi et seq. Note that the two twelfth-century fragments, H (f. 9^{v} and 9^{r}, bound back to front, of Cottonian MS. Domitian A ix; printed by Zupitza, *Anglia*, i (1878), 195–7, and by Plummer, i. 244–5) and I (ff. 132^{v}–7 of Cottonian MS. Caligula A xv; printed by F. Liebermann, *Ungedruckte Anglo-Normannische Geschichtsquellen*, Strasbourg, 1879, 1–8; see also Ker, *Catalogue*, 175), are unrelated to E: H, consisting of undated ecclesiastical notes for 1113 and 1114, is mainly important for showing that vernacular annals independent of the E tradition were still being produced at that time; I is an Easter table with bilingual notes, the English ones, from 925 to 1130, being brief and dealing mainly with Christ Church, Canterbury.

[3] For F, see Ker, *Catalogue*, 187–8, and three articles by F. P. Magoun,

bilingual version of the *Anglo-Saxon Chronicle*, written at Christ Church, Canterbury, and based on a pre-E type of text already incorporating some entries from the *Annales de Rouen* but still free of Peterborough interpolations; it makes some Canterbury interpolations of its own, e.g., at 694, 744, 796, 870, and 995. But, although written about 1100 or even later, it breaks off at 1058 and is not, therefore, directly relevant to the annals printed here. Between D and E relationships are more complex, shifting from period to period.[1] D, which continues to 1079, appears to be, as it stands, a post-Conquest compilation, and, with its strong interest in St. Margaret of Scotland and probable debt to a *Life* of her, is perhaps to be dated after her death in 1093.[2] In spite of a great deal of extra material in the former, D and E agree in general as far as the entry for 1031, together representing what is called 'the Northern recension'; this Professor Whitelock believes to have been based at York. After 1031 the two versions D and E are independent for over twenty-five years; but from 1057 onwards D again shares some entries with E, and is apparently derived from conflation of a pre-E type of text (earlier than the version behind F, since it lacks the entries taken from the *Annales de Rouen*) with one of a C-type. In spite of D's often fuller details,[3] the resemblance between the two texts D and E persists until D ends in 1079.

The extant text most closely related to E is not a vernacular but a Latin one: the early-thirteenth-century *Waverley Annals*.[4] From 1000 to 1121 these annals consist mainly of translation

'The Domitian Bilingual of the *Old-English Annals*: Notes on the *F*-Text', *Modern Language Quarterly*, vi (1945), 371–80, 'The Domitian Bilingual of the *Old-English Annals*: The Latin Preface', *Speculum*, xx (1945), 65–72, and '*Annales Domitiani Latini*: An Edition', *Mediaeval Studies*, ix (1947), 235–95; and compare Whitelock, *Facsimile*, 27–8.

[1] See Whitelock, *Facsimile*, 28–31, and *Translation*, xiv–xviii. D has been edited separately by E. Classen and F. E. Harmer, *An Anglo-Saxon Chronicle*, Manchester, 1926.

[2] See Whitelock, *Translation*, xvi; but compare Classen and Harmer, op. cit. xii, and Ker, *Catalogue*, 253–5. See also *infra*, 1093/26 n.

[3] See, for instance, 1074/2 n., 1075/11 n., 1079/6 n. and 8 n.

[4] Ed. H. R. Luard, *Annales Monastici*, ii, R.S., 1865.

from the *Anglo-Saxon Chronicle*, and the surviving version they most resemble is E;[1] but in several places, most notably at 1070, *WA* agrees with D against E, thus showing that it cannot be derived from E itself but must go back independently to a common source.[2] Mostly, however, agreement between E and *WA* is so close as to suggest that E, apart from its interpolations of local material, is reproducing the common original faithfully.[3] The resemblance between the texts ends at 1121; after this, although they share some records and even at times some phrasing, the likeness is no greater than might occur by chance in any parallel sets of annals. Since it coincides with the first break in the hand of the Laud manuscript, the end of the resemblance with *WA* may mark the point where E ceased to copy from the common source.

A similar break at 1121 also marks the relationship between E and another Latin text, the *Historia Anglorum* of Henry of Huntingdon.[4] This work, usually dated from about 1125 onwards, shares much of E's material, although handling it more independently than *WA* does; this free treatment makes the exact relationship more difficult to determine. The absence from the *Historia* of all the interpolated Peterborough material need not mean that Henry did not use E itself (he claims to have known many of the abbots of Peterborough[5] and so would have been well placed for borrowing such a book); but the sparseness of resemblances between the two texts after 1121[6] suggests that, like *WA*, Henry of Huntingdon was probably using not E itself but a parallel version, possibly E's archetype for the entries to 1121.

[1] See Luard, op. cit. xxxiii–xxxv, and Plummer, ii, pp. lii–liii.

[2] See Plummer, loc. cit., and compare 1075/32 n.

[3] This is borne out by the consistent linguistic differences between the copied annals and the Peterborough interpolations in the same hand, see *infra*, xlii.

[4] Ed. T. Arnold, *Henrici Archidiaconi Huntendunensis Historia Anglorum*, R.S., 1879; compare Plummer, ii, p. lv.

[5] Hen. Hunt. 318 (*Epistola de Contemptu Mundi*).

[6] These are almost confined to notices of the annual courts, which, as Hen. Hunt. has them even when E does not, cannot be derived by him from E, see Plummer, ii. p. lvi.

The archetype of the E annals to 1121 thus played a great part in early-twelfth-century historiography. Unfortunately, nothing is known about its provenance or its authorship.

As for date, most of the annals may have been composed soon after the events they describe, for they show little such anticipation of future events as is found even in the near-contemporary entries of the First Continuation (that is, the annals 1122–1131). Such apparent examples of anticipation as do occur, as when in 1077, 1091, and 1093, for instance, various agreements and grants are said to have been speedily revoked ('hit heold litle hwile'; 'ac þet he syððan ætbræd, þa him gebotad wæs'), prove to refer to reversals happening so soon that they could well have been known to anyone writing up the annals within a year or so. Contemporary composition is also implied both by interjected prayers (1086 'ac se ælmihtiga God him gife wurðscipe on þam toweardan!') and also by regular references to such things as weather, epidemics, and crop-failures, which might be expected to fade from memory with the passing of years.

Provenance, however, is indeterminate. The E annals from 1023 to 1061 have been held to originate from St. Augustine's, Canterbury.[1] And in consequence the rest of the annals to 1121 are also sometimes localized there.[2] Certainly the E-archetype must have been available in Canterbury in the late twelfth century, when the F scribe, working at Christ Church, used it not only as the basis for his bilingual epitome but also as a source for his interpolations in the Parker text of the *Chronicle* (A, Corpus Christi College, Cambridge, MS. 173).[3]

[1] See Plummer, ii, pp. xlviii–l, liii, and Whitelock, *Facsimile*, 30, and *Translation*, xvi.

[2] Levison, for instance, took this view, linking the borrowing of the archetype by Peterborough with the evident dependence of one of the spurious Peterborough charters on an equally spurious piece from St. Augustine's (*England and the Continent in the Eighth Century*, Oxford, 1946, 200–1).

[3] See Plummer, ii, pp. xcvii-xcviii, and compare Whitelock, *Facsimile*, 27, and *Translation*, xii.

Yet the late-eleventh-century annals hardly read like Canterbury work. A generally southern bias they do show, with the Glastonbury affair of 1083 treated much more fully than Walchere's murder in 1080 and with the risings of 1088 in Kent and in the West given far more attention than that in the North; minor events, such as the bloody wells in Berkshire and the drying-up of the Thames, are invariably southern. But specifically Canterbury material is rare here. There is no mention of the Pennenden Heath trial of 1075/6, or of the details of the investiture dispute so strongly affecting Anselm, or of the struggle between York and Canterbury for primacy. In 1087/60 the abbot of St. Augustine's is left nameless, and the troubles following his death are ignored. Nor is the notice on Lanfranc in 1089 as full as might be expected from a Canterbury monk, even though not a Christ Church one.

If anything, the minor notices, in some of the annals at least, suggest a slight Westminster (or London) bias. National events happening at Westminster, such as the execution of the Breton rebels in 1075, Rufus's coronation, Henry I's coronation and marriage, and Queen Edith's burial there in 1075 and Queen Matilda's in 1118, must, of course, be left out of account; but even when this is done there remain a good number of Westminster/London notices. Under 1072 (=1073 D) there is the notice of Ægelric's burial at Westminster 'innon Sanctes Nicholaus portice'; under 1076 (=1077 D), the appointment of Vitalis of Bernay as abbot of Westminster; under 1077 (no equivalent in D), the fire at London; under 1087, the burning of St. Paul's and of the best part of London. In 1097 the sufferings of Londoners are given special prominence:

> Eac manege sciran þe mid weorce to Lundenne belumpon wurdon þærle gedrehte þurh þone weall þe hi worhton onbutan þone Tur 7 þurh þa brycge þe forneah eall toflotan wæs 7 þurh þæs cynges heallegeweorc þe man on Westmynstre worhte.

Under 1105 and 1106 there is mention of an otherwise unrecorded visit by Robert of Bellême to the king at Westminster. In 1114 the great ebb-tide along the whole east coast is noted only for its effects on the Thames at London.[1] On the other hand, the church councils held at Westminster in 1102 and 1107 are not treated with any special amplitude, and that of 1108[2] is not mentioned at all. And, although the appointment of Abbot Vitalis is given, neither his death nor the appointment of his successor, Gilbert Crispin, is noted. So provenance remains indeterminate.

With provenance unknown, authorship can hardly be established. The 1087 annalist speaks of himself as one who had lived at the Conqueror's court, and this suggests a retired chaplain; but without localization no attempt to identify him is possible.[3] This annalist does, however, offer a distinctive style;[4] and, as similar if less marked emotive and rhetorical features occur also in some of the neighbouring annals, it seems tempting to attribute the whole group to one author: but this is mere conjecture. At all events, annals such as those for 1080, 1081, 1082, are, in spite of no less promising material (Walchere's murder, Odo's arrest), so much balder that we hesitate to ascribe them to the 1087 writer; and the entries for the 1090s, although full enough, lack his passion.[5]

Apart from style, certain other features mark off groups of annals. Thus, the annals 1083 to 1088 show the only examples in this part of the text of *þe* for the nominative singular of the definite article.[6] From 1091 to 1121 the annals have a similar structure, beginning with the three annual crown-wearings whenever these took place.[7] None of these features need,

[1] Compare Florence, ii. 67. [2] See Eadmer, 193–4.

[3] Even though a Westminster localization were established, and it is not, this would avail little: the only writer known there at the relevant time is the 'Sulcardus' who wrote a Latin history of the abbey (see J. Armitage Robinson, ed., *The History of Westminster Abbey by John Flete*, Cambridge, 1909, 3 et seq., and E. H. Pearce, *The Monks of Westminster*, Cambridge, 1916, 39–42), and, although W. G. Searle, *Onomasticon Anglo-Saxonicum*, Cambridge, 1897, does refer his name to Old-English *Sulcheard*, evidence for his nationality does not seem conclusive.

[4] See *infra* lxxv–lxxix.

[5] Note the cross-references at 1087/9, 'swa we beforan tealdon', referring to 1086, and at 1090/2, 'eallswa wæ ær abufan sædan', referring to 1088.

[6] At 1083/8; 1087/6, 23, 32, 160, 163; 1088/21 (*þeo*), 27, 35, 38, 72.

[7] See Plummer, ii, p. liv.

however, have any bearing upon authorship. At first sight changes in spelling might seem more significant, as when *Rodbriht* (not after 1070) and *Rodbeard* (not after 1096) give place to *Rotbert* (first in 1095; after 1101 almost invariable); but how irrelevant this is appears from the use in 1095 of *Rodbeard*, *Rotbeard*, and *Rotbert* all to refer to the same man. Lexical distributions might afford no firmer grounds for argument. So far, then, no certain means can be found of distinguishing any of the changes of annalist that must have taken place between 1070 and 1121.

The Continuations

With the Continuations, on the other hand, provenance at least is simpler. The book comes from Peterborough. The First Continuation, and the Interpolations incorporated into the copied text, are so dominated by local interests that they could have originated nowhere else; and this Peterborough bias persists to the last entry of all. Peterborough provenance is confirmed by dialect.[1]

Some of the material is, however, still shared with parallel records. Professor Whitelock has pointed out a resemblance between part of the E annal for 1130 and the corresponding entry in 'Florence of Worcester'.[2] Likewise, parallels are to be found between the Final Continuation, 1132–1154, and some of the Latin histories of the time, such as *Gesta Stephani* and William of Malmesbury's *Historia Novella*.[3] In general, however, these late annals seem neither to be a source for the parallel records extant nor to be derived from them, and so may provisionally be considered as independent.

The first break in the handwriting, at 1121, corresponds to a change in the relationships between E and the other histories

[1] See *infra*, xlv–li.

[2] Ed. B. Thorpe, *Florentii Wigorniensis Monachi Chronicon ex Chronicis*, 2 vols., 1848–9, ii. 91–2, also ed. J. R. H. Weaver, *The Chronicle of John of Worcester, 1118–1140*, Oxford, 1908, 30; see Whitelock, *Facsimile*, 31–2, and *Translation*, xvii; also *infra*, xxxii.

[3] See *infra*, Commentary on 1137 *passim*; compare Whitelock, *Translation*, xvii, n. 2.

of the period; it corresponds also to a change in manner. Whereas the annals for the previous decade had been terse, those from 1122 onwards are full and lively. Moreover, from the spirited and half-cynical account of the 1123 archiepiscopal election to the eloquent tale of the pluralist Henry of Angély, whose character is one of the most memorable in the whole *Chronicle*, all the annals from 1122 to 1131 read like the work of one man.[1] The several changes of ink here, most of which coincide with the end of annals, suggest that this First Continuation was written up in six blocks, 1122, 1123, 1124, 1125–1126/11, 1126/12–1127, 1128–1131, presumably as events took place.[2] Contemporary composition is further suggested not only by formal professions of ignorance of the future, as in 1127 'þis was his ingang: of his utgang ne cunne we iett noht seggon', but also by some silent failures to foresee it, as when in 1123 Henry of Angély is introduced as a defender of monastic interests, without a hint of what he was later to mean for Peterborough. At this point the *Chronicle* is being composed before our eyes.

With the section written by the last hand, the annals from 1132 to 1154, comes an abrupt and drastic change in the chronicler's method. The uniformity of the hand shows that these annals were entered into the Laud manuscript as a single block; and their structure shows that they were likewise composed as a single block, probably when the entry was made about 1155.[3] The annalistic form is almost completely abandoned. There are only six headings: 1132, 1135, 1137, 1138, 1140, and 1154. And the material is arranged with a minimal regard for date: under 1137 the story reaches forward to 1144 (St. William of Norwich) and even to 1155 (the end of Martin's abbacy); then it reverts to 1138; then under 1140 is unfolded without reference to date, and not always in true order, an epitome of the military and political history of nearly fifteen years. The total effect is of history written topic by topic, with social and ecclesiastical matters gathered under 1137

[1] See *infra*, lxxix–lxxxii. [2] See *supra*, xvi. [3] See *infra*, lxxxvii.

and military and political ones under 1140, rather than of annals kept year by year: certainly St. William of Norwich is more aptly placed in his present context than he would have been in his true chronological position, among the skirmishing of the Civil War. Even on these terms, however, this section is not wholly successful: so completely has the chronicler failed to thread any kind of path through the 'inextricabilem laberinthum rerum et negotiorum' that was the Anarchy,[1] that without help from other sources the list of events under 1140 can hardly be made to yield sense.

In these Peterborough Continuations, to which the main *Chronicle* tradition is barely relevant and to which none of the Latin national chronicles is at all closely parallel, the chief interest lies in the local material which they offer so plentifully and in its affiliations.

First of all, several so-called 'Peterborough chronicles' have to be dismissed. The first two folios of the Peterborough MS. Harley 3667, of which the hand so closely resembles the first hand of E,[2] contain an Easter table from 1074 to 1181 with royal movements and abbey affairs briefly noted in the margins in Latin;[3] but these notes are brief and unrelated to the corresponding entries in E. Equally irrelevant to E is the Latin *Chronicon Petroburgense* (1122–1295) preserved in the Black Book;[4] in spite of the curious coincidence of its opening date with that of the First Continuation, the earlier entries here too are brief and quite unrelated to those of E. Nor is the *Chronicon Angliæ Petriburgense* in B.M. Cottonian MS. Claudius A v any more relevant,[5] being in any case a late fourteenth-century compilation; in spite of a few coincidences, its annals have little in common with those of E.

The Peterborough work which is important for comparison with our *Chronicle* is the mid-twelfth-century Latin *History*

[1] *Hist. Nov.* 46. [2] See *supra*, xvii.

[3] Printed by Liebermann, *Ungedruckte Anglo-Normannische Geschichtsquellen*, 13–14.

[4] Ed. T. Stapleton, Camden Society, 1849.

[5] Ed. J. A. Giles, Caxton Society, 1845.

of Hugo Candidus.[1] In many places this corresponds with E word for word, a striking instance being the telescoping into one year of events belonging to 1133 and 1135.[2] The *Chronicle* can scarcely be indebted to Hugo's work, at least in the latter's present form: for, if the usual dating of the latter during the abbacy of William of Waterville (1155–75) is correct, then even the Final Continuation, apparently written in 1155, could hardly have drawn from it. Conversely, Hugo's *History* could have drawn from E, and can be shown at times to have done so, as when his reference to Bishop Ægelric's abortive appointment to York depends upon the error shared by 1072 E with the corresponding D annal.[3] In the account of Henry of Angély's career vernacular place-name forms, *Cluni*, *Sauenni*, *Besenscun*, *Seintes*, instead of the normal Latin ones,[4] show that Hugo's source here must have been a vernacular one, but it need not have been English, and cannot have been E itself, which in several places has less information. Elsewhere also Hugo often has information which E lacks, especially about local affairs, as in his more detailed versions of Hereward's raid on Peterborough and of the 1116 fire.[5] Hugo's *History* cannot be based on E supplemented solely by personal reminiscence, for no one still alive in 1155 (when Hugo played a leading role in the abbatial election) could have clear memories of events in 1070; it might, however, have been drawing also upon stories told him by his seniors when he was a boy, as indeed the description of the sources given in one text of the *History*—'quod in ueteribus scriptis scriptum reperi uel antiquorum et fidelium narracione didici'—implies that it was.[6] But, since E is unlikely to be derived from Hugo's work, dependence of both on local oral tradition is not enough to explain the almost verbal

[1] Ed. W. T. Mellows, Oxford, 1949. The account of textual relations at xx–xxix is somewhat oversimplified; compare Whitelock, *Facsimile*, 33–4.

[2] See 1135/6 n.; Hugo's use of a written source at this point is suggested by his note, *sicut scriptum est in pluribus locis* (104).

[3] Hugo, 73–4; see 1070/61 n.

[4] Hugo, 100.

[5] See Commentary 1070 *passim* and 1116/17 n.

[6] Hugo, 3–4.

correspondences between the two works. Clearly, the 'ancient writings' Hugo mentions were a genuine source, not just a figure of speech; but what they consisted of remains partly conjectural. Certainly there were abbey deeds, both genuine and spurious, available to both of them;[1] Hugo's independent use of these is demonstrated when, for instance, he quotes verbatim the spurious bull of Pope Agatho and the spurious charter of Edgar, of which 675 E and 963 E offer only English paraphrases;[2] and his independence of E for the early part of his *History* is further emphasized by his lack of anything corresponding to the charter-based interpolations at 777 E and 852 E. As well as the charters, there might also have been some earlier history of the abbey, on which both Hugo and E drew; this seems necessary to explain the relationship between their versions of such events as Hereward's raid, but it remains a mere supposition. Thus, the relationship between the two works is both complex and variable, with Hugo occasionally using E but more often making independent use of materials available to both of them.

A small point remains: the suggestion that Hugo compiled not only the Latin *History* that goes by his name, but also E itself.[3] This hardly needs formal refutation. If Hugo were indeed, as his name suggests to some, at least half Norman,[4] then he would hardly be likely to have compiled an *Anglo-Saxon Chronicle*: with Latin the fashionable language for historiography, no one but an Englishman would have had any motive for writing annals in English. Besides, with all the earlier chroniclers anonymous, there is no need to demand a name for either of these late continuators.

[1] See *infra*, 115.

[2] Hugo, 16–19, 33–42.

[3] See H. H. Howorth, 'The Anglo-Saxon Chronicle, its Origin and History', *Archaeological Journal*, lxv (1908), 203–4.

[4] Occasional *N*-forms for Lincoln, if indeed they are original, would suggest that the writer of Hugo's *History* was more at home in French than in English.

HISTORICAL VALUE

The Annals to 1121

For most historians the *Anglo-Saxon Chronicle* takes pride of place among records surviving from the early twelfth century.[1] As this period saw not only the compilation of these annals but also the rise of the great school of Anglo-Latin historians, this may seem a large claim. The prime advantage of the annals 1070–1121 over the corresponding passages from the Latin historians is priority in time: as we have seen, these annals were probably written up contemporaneously, whereas, apart from Eadmer of Canterbury, the first draft of whose *Historia Novorum* may have been finished about 1109,[2] none of the Latin historians seems to have been writing until after 1120. Their second advantage is in representing one of the main sources on which most of the Latin historians, not only Henry of Huntingdon and the *Waverley Annals*, were relying.

Thus, Eadmer's work is the only one to dispute with our text near-contemporaneity of record; it is, further, not only a contemporary record but also, unlike the *Chronicle*, an eye-witness one, for Eadmer is relating 'ea quæ sub oculis vidi vel audivi'.[3] Sometimes Eadmer notes events ignored by E, such as Lanfranc's appointment (passed over by D also), and throughout he gives detailed accounts, with citation of documents and reconstructed *oratio recta*, of all the early Norman ecclesiastical controversy which the *Chronicle* deals with so allusively; it is his evidence which explains, for instance, the import of Anselm's journeys.[4] Concentration on church matters, and especially on those in which Anselm was concerned, does, however, unbalance the *Historia Novorum*, so that it is far from

[1] See, for instance, *EHD* 9, 97; compare Stenton, 679–84.

[2] Ed. M. Rule, *Eadmeri Historia Novorum in Anglia*, R.S., 1884; trans. G. Bosanquet, *Eadmer's History of Recent Events in England*, 1964 (the first four books only). See also the references given at 1093/7 n.

[3] Eadmer, 1.

[4] See, for instance, 1095/62 n., 1097/23 n., 1100/41 n., 1103/6 n.

presenting a view of Anglo-Norman society and its doings as comprehensive as that of the *Chronicle*.

Hugh the Chantor's *History of the Church of York* resembles Eadmer's work both in independence and in concentration on ecclesiastical affairs.[1] It does not, however, quite share the eyewitness quality of his work, for the author, working apparently in the late 1120s, is dealing with events up to eighty years old; and its extreme Yorkist partisanship further reduces its stature. So, although supplementing both Eadmer and the *Chronicle*, Hugh the Chantor cannot compete with either of them; his main merit is in reminding us that there were points of view other than the southern ones represented by most extant works.

By contrast with these specialized histories, the *Historia Ecclesiastica* of Ordericus Vitalis[2] offers a view of Anglo-Norman society far wider than that of the *Chronicle*, let alone that of Eadmer or of Hugh the Chantor. Not only does it keep a balance between ecclesiastical and secular affairs but also, without neglecting insular history, it keeps in view (naturally enough, considering that the author was a monk of Saint-Evroult) the Continental background and interests of both king and baronage—interests which the *Chronicle* hardly acknowledges except when they lead to war. Moreover, being a full-scale history, with character sketches and reconstructed dialogue, Orderic's work gives a picture of medieval men and manners far livelier than that of any annalist. Yet the very profusion of detail, and especially the fondness for *oratio recta*, cannot but render parts of the work a little suspect. For this is not an eyewitness account like Eadmer's; Orderic was not present at the events he describes so vividly; nor, since he was not born until 1075,[3] is his record contemporary throughout, as we believe the *Chronicle* to have been. Thus, although

[1] Ed. C. Johnson, *Hugh the Chantor: The History of the Church of York, 1066–1127*, 1961.

[2] Ed. A. Le Prévost, *Orderici Vitalis . . . Historiæ Ecclesiasticæ libri tredecim*, 5 vols., Paris, 1838–55. A new edition and translation by Mrs. M. Chibnall is in progress; vol. ii (the first published) appeared in 1969.

[3] Ordericus, ii. 301.

often supplementing the English annals most richly, Orderic's work does not supersede them.

Apart from his own *Historia Ecclesiastica*, Orderic was also responsible, like Robert of Torigny later, for additions to the *Gesta Normannorum Ducum* of William of Jumièges.[1] This fills in the background of the magnates so tersely mentioned by the *Chronicle*, but, with its Continental standpoint, adds little to our knowledge of English affairs.

Their independence of the *Chronicle* makes Eadmer and Orderic specially valuable, for most of the other historians of this period are largely dependent on it. The debts of Henry of Huntingdon and of the *Waverley Annals* to the E archetype we have already noted.[2] Even William of Malmesbury, the most scholarly as well as the most ambitious of the early-twelfth-century historians, produced in those parts of his *Gesta Regum*[3] dealing with the first three Norman reigns what Stubbs called 'a résumé, and commentary on the narrative, of the Chronicle';[4] it is, however, a commentary that adds flesh to the sometimes skeletal annals, as when Malmesbury explains ecclesiastical appointments by referring to the Conqueror's refusal to promote native clergy.[5] His *Gesta Pontificum*[6] rather than his *Gesta Regum* is Malmesbury's most original contribution to the history of his own time; as with Eadmer's work, this supplies a mass of special information for which the *Chronicle* had no place.

[1] Ed. Jean Marx, Paris and Rouen, 1914.

[2] See *supra*, xix–xx.

[3] Ed. W. Stubbs, *Willelmi Malmesbiriensis Monachi de Gestis Regum Anglorum libri quinque: Historiæ Novellæ libri tres*, 2 vols., R.S., 1887–9.

[4] *Gest. Reg.* ii, p. cxiv, also p. cxxxiii; compare R. R. Darlington, *Anglo-Norman Historians*, 1947, 5–9, and, for a kinder estimate, V. H. Galbraith, *Historical Research in Medieval England*, 1951, 15 et seq. Marie Schütt, 'The Literary Form of William of Malmesbury's "Gesta Regum" ', *EHR* xlvi (1931), 255–60, argues that Malmesbury's accounts of the first three Norman kings owe their often-criticized form to being intended as a set of Suetonian 'Lives'. See also Dom Hugh Farmer, 'William of Malmesbury's Life and Works', *Journal of Ecclesiastical History*, xiii (1962), 39–54.

[5] *Gest. Reg.* ii. 313.

[6] Ed. N. Hamilton, *Willelmi Malmesbiriensis Monachi de Gestis Pontificum Anglorum libri quinque*, R.S., 1870.

Less impressive in form than William of Malmesbury's work but no less valuable to the historian is the *Chronicon ex Chronicis* usually going by the name of 'Florence of Worcester' (although its compilation may more plausibly be attributed to one John);[1] but unsettled problems about its date, authorship, and debt to other works make precise evaluation of it impossible. Although unlikely even in its earliest form to go back beyond the early twelfth century, 'Florence' does, however, seem to have drawn upon a lost version of the *Anglo-Saxon Chronicle* and to be to that extent an independent witness;[2] not being as closely related to E as Henry of Huntingdon's work is, it can be used as a partial check on it.

Largely dependent on 'Florence' up to 1119, the *Historia Regum* of Symeon of Durham (and his various continuators) has only a limited value and is much inferior to the same author's *Historia Ecclesiæ Dunhelmensis*.[3] But it is not negligible: Symeon alone among the national chroniclers of the time lived far enough north to have direct knowledge of Border and Scottish affairs, so that here his testimony is original.[4]

Apart from its status as a source for Latin historians, the *Chronicle* is also valuable as an English record of the early Norman period, that is to say, one written by men who, although one of them may have lived at the Conqueror's court, have none of the Norman blood or sympathy which lends an ambivalence to most of the Anglo-Latinists.[5]

[1] Ed. B. Thorpe, 2 vols., 1848–9; also a partial edition by J. R. H. Weaver, *The Chronicle of John of Worcester, 1118–1140*, Oxford, 1908. See also R. R. Darlington, ed., *The Vita Wulfstani of William of Malmesbury*, Camden Society, 1928, xv–xvi, also idem, *Anglo-Norman Historians*, 13–15 ('it is far more valuable material for the modern historian than Malmesbury's *Gesta Regum*'), and Galbraith, op. cit. 19–20. For the authorship, see Ordericus, ii. 159–61.

[2] See Whitelock, *Translation*, xx.

[3] Ed. T. Arnold, *Symeonis Monachi Opera Omnia*, 2 vols., R.S., 1882–5 (vol. i contains *Historia Ecclesiæ Dunhelmensis*; vol. ii, *Historia Regum*); see also Peter Hunter Blair, 'Symeon's History of the Kings', *Archaeologia Aeliana*, 4th ser. xvi (1939), 87–100.

[4] See, for instance, 1071/4 n., 1072/4 n., 1093/22 n., 26 n.

[5] Thus, Henry of Huntingdon's father was a priest called Nicholas, presumably of Norman origin (Hen. Hunt. 237–8); compare William of Malmesbury's 'utriusque gentis sanguinem traho' (*Gest. Reg.* ii. 283).

Furthermore, with no aristocratic patron to flatter, it ought not to have been subject to deliberate distortion.

Here and there a certain English patriotism may colour the narrative. Thus, in 1086 the annalist prays that Edgar the Atheling, who has left the Conqueror's court because slighted there, may be granted more honour in the future; and elsewhere Edgar sometimes seems to be given more attention than his role warrants.[1] Taxation and tyranny meet with resentment, in all their many guises—the Domesday Survey, the extortions of Norman sheriffs, the 'Frenchmen' murdering the Glastonbury monks, the retinues of Rufus and of Henry I laying waste all the country they pass through, Rufus himself and his malpractices.[2] Yet, equally, taxes may be quietly deplored, along with storms and plagues, as just one of the necessary afflictions of this world: 'Đis wæs swiðe gedyrfsum gear her on lande, þurh wæstma forwordenessa 7 þurh þa mænigfealde gyld . . .'[3]

How far resentment of tyranny and taxation included ill-will towards the Normans *quâ* Normans is hard to say. Already in 1070 Turold and his French knights are more welcome to the monks of Peterborough than their own countrymen under Hereward (a slight counterbalance to the Glastonbury affair). In 1073 Englishmen were laying Maine waste on the Conqueror's behalf; in 1075 the 'landfolc' of Norfolk were helping the castellans to put down the 'Breton' rebellion; by 1087 the Conqueror is accepted as ruler of England by divine permission, 'swa him God uðe'; and by the 1090s Rufus is recognized as 'our king', to whom Englishmen remain loyal when Normans turn traitor.[4] Indeed, by the twelfth century the early opposition between 'English' and 'French' seems to be abandoned. Nor are the English shown as identifying themselves with Scottish or Welsh resistance against the Normans. In 1091 the Norman barons who repel Malcolm Canmore are 'þa gode mæn þe þis land bewiston', and in 1093 Malcolm invading England to

[1] For instance, 1091 *passim*.

[2] 1085/23 ff., 1087/19 ff., 1083 *passim*, 1097/28 ff., 1104/22 ff., 1100/11 ff.

[3] 1105/12 ff., compare 1097/30 ff., 1098/11 ff., 1103/12 ff., 1110/23 ff.

[4] 1091/37, 1093/16, 34; 1088/40, 44, 51, 62, compare 1101/5 n.

avenge insults offered by Rufus (recorded in the same annal) is somewhat partially said to be acting 'mid maran unræde . . . þone him abehofode'. Even for this native English chronicle, Anglo-Norman unity is not long in becoming established.

The Peterborough Continuations

In both Peterborough Continuations, local and personal colouring gives the *Chronicle* its main value. For after 1121 it ceases to be the main source for other histories and even to be particularly remarkable as a national record.

Yet, although not pre-eminent among histories of its time, the First Continuation does offer, like the preceding section, an independent contemporary record. One of its best passages is the account of the 1123 archiepiscopal election, with all the manœuvrings of the ecclesiastical politicians; William of Malmesbury's verdict may be maturer, but the *Chronicle*, rivalled in this only by Hugh the Chantor, more freshly conveys the movements of the intrigue.[1] In the same entry the account of Robert Bloet's death, although similar to those in parallel records (including that by Henry of Huntingdon, one of Bloet's archdeacons), is alone in offering, in a piece of *oratio recta* unusual for the *Chronicle*, what purport to be the dying bishop's *ipsissima verba*: 'Laferd kyng, ic swelte.'[2]

With this *oratio recta*, and in other ways, the First Continuation is, like the annals for Æthelred's reign, tempering the annalistic tradition with some of the licence allowed to the full-dress historian. It offers not only events, but also the chronicler's view of them, from his cynicism about the Papal Curia ('Ac þet ofercom Rome þet ofercumeð eall weoruld . . .')[3] to his satisfaction at the punishment of the false moneyers ('þet wæs eall mid micel rihte, forði þet hi hafden fordon eall þet land mid here micele fals').[4]

[1] See references at 1123/19.

[2] Compare Hen. Hunt. 300 (*Epistola de Contemptu Mundi*): 'Vivus tamen, sed elinguis, in hospitium suum deportatus.' In any event, Bloet would not have spoken in English.

[3] 1123/61.

[4] 1125/10.

Soon, however, the personal strain comes to dominate these annals. From 1127 to 1131 concern with the intrusion into Peterborough of the pluralist Henry of Angély leads the annalist to treat this local crisis as on a par with national events, or even as more momentous. As literature this is highly successful,[1] but as chronicling rather improper. Historically its value lies in giving a minor abuse a human context and showing how men reacted in such crises; as a picture of the monkish temper these annals stand beside the work of Jocelin of Brakelond.

In the Final Continuation the personal note gains further importance. This section, as we have seen, is not contemporary with most of the events it relates, and, compared with parallel records, it offers an account of the Civil War that is not merely bald but at times unreliable.[2] As a political and military record it is put completely in the shade by *Gesta Stephani*,[3] by William of Malmesbury's *Historia Novella*[4] and Richard of Hexham's *Historia de Gestis Regis Stephani*,[5] and by the final sections of Henry of Huntingdon's *Historia Anglorum* and of Ordericus Vitalis's *Historia Ecclesiastica*.

Its most celebrated contribution to history is the description of the Anarchy entered under 1137. Even that has been impugned as true only in a local sense, with Round arguing that it was specifically based on Geoffrey de Mandeville's depredations in the Fens, of which Peterborough's neighbour Ramsey had been a chief victim.[6] Corbett agreed that such monastic accounts of atrocity were certainly exaggerated, as

[1] See *Essays in Criticism*, xviii (1968), 376–81.

[2] Compare *supra*, xxvi. For chronicle sources for this period, see R. H. C. Davis, *King Stephen*, 1967, 146–51.

[3] Ed. and trans. K. R. Potter, 1955.

[4] Ed. and trans. K. R. Potter, 1955; also in *Gest. Reg.* ii. 523–96. For its bias in favour of Robert of Gloucester, see R. B. Patterson, *American Historical Review*, lxx (1965), 983–97, and *Speculum*, xliii (1968), 487–92; compare Davis, op. cit. 146.

[5] Ed. R. Howlett, *Historia Ricardi, Prioris Ecclesiæ Haugustaldensis, de Gestis Regis Stephani*, in *Chronicles of the Reigns of Stephen, Henry II, and Richard I*, 4 vols., R.S., 1884–9, iii. 139–78.

[6] *Geoffrey de Mandeville: A Study of the Anarchy*, 1892, 220; compare *Chronicon Abbatiæ Rameseiensis*, ed. W. D. Macray, R.S., 1886, 333–5.

'a considerable number of the magnates from Stephen downwards were remarkable for their works of piety'.[1] Poole further suggested that it was just because such outrages as those of Geoffrey de Mandeville were exceptional that they so impressed the chroniclers.[2] H. W. C. Davis, on the other hand, pointed out that Mandeville was by no means the only brutal and rapacious castellan of the time, others being Robert FitzHubert at Devizes and Philip Gay at Bristol—we may add also the William Cumin whose atrocities in the North Symeon's continuator described in language so similar to that of the *Chronicle*;[3] Davis pointed also to the high proportions of waste recorded for nearly all the southern and midland counties in the earliest extant Pipe-Roll of Henry II.[4] His view is partly supported by his son, R. H. C. Davis, who, while denying that governmental machinery ever broke down during the Anarchy, does allow that this was a time of widespread misery.[5] At all events, what cannot be questioned is the truth of this passage to the writer's own experience; it most eloquently expresses a contemporary civilian's feelings when faced with the brutality of robber barons. And, whatever historians may believe about the state of England in Stephen's reign, this experience and these feelings were not peculiar to our chronicler: repeated coincidences between this entry and passages in independent records from widely-scattered areas—*Liber Eliensis*,[6] *Historia Ecclesiæ Dunhelmensis*,[7] William of Malmesbury's *Historia Novella*,[8] and *Gesta Stephani*, recently localized at Bath[9]—

[1] *CMH* v. 552–3.

[2] *From Domesday Book to Magna Carta*, 150–4.

[3] *Hist. Eccl. Dun.* 152–4.

[4] 'The Anarchy of Stephen's Reign', *EHR* xviii (1903), 630–41.

[5] *King Stephen*, 86–9, compare 83–4. Charter evidence also reveals widespread disorder and misery, see F. M. Stenton, *The First Century of English Feudalism, 1066–1166*, 2nd edn., Oxford, 1961, 244–8. See also M. Bell, ed., *Wulfric of Haselbury*, Somerset Record Society, 1933, 68 et seq.

[6] Ed. E. O. Blake, Camden Third Series, xcii, 1962, 328. For parallels, see 1137/17 n., 40 n., 41 n., 54 n.

[7] See 1137/23 n., 26 n., 54 n.

[8] 1137/17 n., 46 n.

[9] See 1137/17 n., 40 n., 41 n., 46 n., 50 n. For the Bath localization, see R. H. C. Davis, 'The Authorship of the *Gesta Stephani*', *EHR* lxxvi (1962), 209–32.

emphasize how far such sufferings were from being merely local or personal.

LANGUAGE

Background

This text of the *Anglo-Saxon Chronicle* was written, at intervals between 1121 and 1155, at Peterborough; and the annals from 1122 onwards were not merely written but also composed there. And, as Peterborough monks, its writers were probably natives of the district; for in the late twelfth century and in the thirteenth, established abbeys recruited their monks locally, and this was probably the practice in the earlier twelfth century also.[1] So, because it is so precisely dated and localized, the *Peterborough Chronicle* is important as a linguistic record, since, apart from the *Ayenbite of Inwyt*, there is hardly another Middle-English text of which it can be said both that it is an original, not a garbled copy, and also that its date and provenance are firmly established.

Peterborough, or, to give it its Old-English name, Medeshamstede, lay 'in regione Gyruiorum',[2] the *Gyrwe* being a tribe which the twelfth-century *Liber Eliensis* describes as 'omnes Australes Angli in magna palude habitantes in qua est insula de Ely'.[3] This does not tell us much about the dialect affinities of the region; but these can be guessed at from other evidence. Hugo Candidus describes the abbey as 'per terram accessibilis preter ad orientalem plagam, per quam non nisi nauigio uenitur', adding that by means of the river Nene flowing south of the town 'liberum habet ire quo quis uult continuo'.[4] Communications were, therefore, fair for the period; but to the east

[1] D. Knowles, *The Monastic Order in England*, Cambridge, 1941, 424.

[2] C. Plummer, ed., *Venerabilis Baedae Historia Ecclesiastica Gentis Anglorum*, 2 vols., Oxford, 1896, i. 218; see also Hugo, 4–5.

[3] Ed. Blake, 3; compare Hugo, 4: 'Gyruii uocantur hii, qui iuxta paludem uel infra paludem habitant. Nam gyr anglice latine profunda palus dicitur.' See also J. E. B. Gover, A. Mawer, and F. M. Stenton, *The Place-Names of Northamptonshire*, EPNS x, 1933, xiii–xvii, and E. Miller, *The Abbey and Bishopric of Ely*, Cambridge, 1951, 11–12.

[4] Hugo, 5.

they would certainly have been limited by the Fen district, which in the Old-English period formed a desolate frontier between Mercia and East Anglia, peopled only by monks and outlaws.[1] The sparse Domesday population of the peat fen on whose western fringes Peterborough stands[2] suggests that communication and recruitment alike would most often have come from the north and west, and possibly also from the south.[3] Dealings would no doubt have been mainly with the abbey's own estates, which mostly lay north and west of Peterborough, and also with the other Fenland abbeys, Ramsey, Crowland, Thorney, and Ely, all lying south or west of the main Fen region.

A priori, then, the Peterborough dialect might be expected to resemble that of the Middle Angles rather than that of the East Angles. This is itself, however, the earliest document (apart from charters written more or less under West-Saxon influence) which can be located in this district.[4] Among Old-English texts, the nearest in language seems to be the tenth-century *Rushworth Gloss to the Gospel of St. Matthew*,[5] of which the colophon says that it was made by Farman priest *æt harawuda*,[6] a place usually identified with Harewood by Leeds, a good hundred miles north of Peterborough; but the language of this text is by no means self-consistent, and its

[1] H. C. Darby, 'The Fenland Frontier in Anglo-Saxon England', *Antiquity*, viii (1934), 185–201. Note the place-name March<*mearc* 'boundary' (P. E. Reaney, *The Place-Names of Cambridgeshire and the Isle of Ely*, EPNS xix, 1943, 253).

[2] Darby, *The Medieval Fenland*, Cambridge, 1940, map on p. 15 (compare geological map on p. 5).

[3] In the early Old-English period at least communication directly to the south must have been hindered by the dense woodland stretching from the valley of the Nene to the edge of the peat fen, see [O. G. S. Crawford,] *Map of Britain in the Dark Ages: South Sheet*, Ordnance Survey, 1939.

[4] The paucity of early East-Midland texts has been attributed to currency of an early West-Mercian *Schriftsprache*: thus, the prose *Guthlac*, on a theme connected with Crowland, appears to have been originally composed in West Mercian (see R. Vleeskruyer, *The Life of St. Chad*, Amsterdam, 1953, 49).

[5] Ed. W. W. Skeat, *The Holy Gospels in Anglo-Saxon, Northumbrian, and Old-Mercian Versions, etc.*, 4 vols. reissued as 1, Cambridge, 1871–87. See also E. M. Brown, *The Language of the Rushworth Gloss to the Gospel of St. Matthew and the Mercian Dialect*, Göttingen, 1892.

[6] Skeat, op. cit., *St. Matthew*, 245, and *St. John*, 188.

true place in the history of English is still subject to dispute.[1] The chief other Old-English texts usually localized in the Midlands, the *Vespasian Psalter Gloss*[2] and the *Life of St. Chad*,[3] represent dialects different from that of the *Peterborough Chronicle*, both being evidently West Mercian, and so are of only limited relevance to it. But the tenth-century *Lindisfarne Gloss* to the *Gospels*,[4] in spite of being Northumbrian, does provide some enlightening parallels with our text, especially in morphological development.

At first sight, excellent opportunities for comparison seem offered by the English documents in the twelfth-century part of the Black Book of Peterborough, entered there in a hand resembling the last one of the Laud manuscript.[5] But, linguistically, these are disappointing. The post-Conquest *Northamptonshire Geld-Roll*,[6] for instance, offers only a limited number of stereotyped phrases, in a spelling obviously influenced by the West-Saxon *Schriftsprache* (as with the common *healf* beside rarer *alf*); and in copies of earlier charters no consistency of language is to be expected, although occasionally they offer interesting forms.[7]

[1] See R. J. Menner, 'Farman Vindicatus', *Anglia*, lviii (1934), 1–27, and S. M. Kuhn, '*E* and *Æ* in Farman's Mercian Glosses', *PMLA* lx (1945), 631–69.

[2] Ed. Sherman M. Kuhn, *The Vespasian Psalter*, Ann Arbor, 1965; also ed. H. Sweet, *The Oldest English Texts*, EETS 83, 1885, 183–420.

[3] Ed. Vleeskruyer.

[4] Ed. Skeat, op. cit. See also A. S. C. Ross, *Studies in the Accidence of the Lindisfarne Gospels*, Leeds School of English Language Texts and Monographs II, Kendal, 1937.

[5] See *supra*, xviii.

[6] Printed in A. J. Robertson, *Anglo-Saxon Charters*, Cambridge, 1939, 230–6; for the date, see J. H. Round, 'The Northamptonshire Geld-Roll', in *Feudal England*, reissued 1964, 124–30, and Stenton, 636, n. 3.

[7] The charters are: Robertson, op. cit. VII, XXX, XXXVII, XXXIX, XL. In particular, compare with the Interpolation, *s.a.* 852 (*infra*, 122) the Black Book copy of the charter on which it is based (Robertson, VII; Black Book, ff. 46^{r-v}):

Ceolred abb*ot* 7 ða higan on Medesha*m*stede sellað Wulfrede ðet land æt Sempingaha*m* in ðas gerednisse, ðet he hit hębbe 7 bruce sua lange sua he life, 7 anu*m* ærfeuuarde æfter him, 7 elce gere sextig foðra wuda to ðęm ham on Hornan ðæm wuda, 7 tuelf foðer græfan, 7 sex foður gerda. End for ðon we him ðis land sellað, ðet he ðes landes fulne friodom bigete in ece

For the Middle-English period material is more plentiful—although with some texts East-Midland localization may rest chiefly on resemblance to the *Peterborough Chronicle*. Certainly from the same district are the early-fourteenth-century works of Robert Mannyng of Bourne, a Lincolnshire town some sixteen miles north of Peterborough.[1] But, as none of these is preserved in a linguistically homogeneous text, the original forms can be established only by rhyme-evidence.[2] In any event, rapid linguistic change in this area means that much of Mannyng's language, particularly his accidence, bears little resemblance to that of the *Chronicle*. The text most relevant to the *Chronicle* is the *Ormulum*, tentatively localized in North Lincolnshire and showing a language in many ways like a systematization of the usage of the Final Continuation.[3] The manuscript of this work, apparently at least partly autograph,[4] is usually dated about 1200, but, as the hand might well be that of an old man, the language need not be two whole generations later than that of the Final Continuation. Other works

ærfeweardnisse æt Sempingaha*m* 7 æt Slioforda, 7 bruce þere cirican lafard on Medeshamstede ðes landes æt Slioforda, 7 Wulfred ðes on Sempingaha*m*. 7 He geselle eghwelce gere to Medeshamstede tua tunnan fulle luhtres aloð, 7 tua slegne'a't, 7 sex hund lafes, 7 ten mittan wę'l's'ces aloð, 7 þere cirican laforde geselle eghwelce gere hors 7 ðrittig scillinga, 7 hine ane niht gefeormige, fiftene mitta luhtres aloð, v mitta welsces aloð, fiftene sestras liðes. 7 Hi sion symle in allu*m* here life eadmode 7 hearsume 7 underþeodde. 7 Ofer here tuega dęg, þonne agefe hio þet land into þere cirican to Medeshamstede mid freodome. 7 We him þis sellað mid felda 7 mid wuda 7 mid fenne sua þerto belimpeð. Sið heora tuuege dæg agan sie, þonne agefe mon tuuenti hida higuum to biodland 7 þere cirican lafe'a'rde xii hida land æt Forde 7 æt Cegle, 7 he wes feorm'i'ed tuuege hida landes æt Lęhcotu*m* his erfeweorda sweolcu*m* swelce him ðonne gesibbast were, 7 þat were [W]ulfredes cynne gefre, swa sua þet oðer into þere cirican.

[1] *Handlyng Synne*, ed. F. J. Furnivall, EETS 119 and 123, 1901 and 1903; *Chronicle*, ed. F. J. Furnivall, R.S., 2 vols., 1887. See also R. Crosby, 'Robert Mannyng of Brunne: A New Biography', *PMLA* lvii (1942), 15–28.

[2] See O. Boerner, *Die Sprache Roberd Mannyngs*, Studien zur englischen Philologie xii, Halle, 1904.

[3] Ed. R. Holt and R. M. White, Oxford, 1878; see also S. Holm, *Corrections and Additions in the Ormulum Manuscript*, Diss. Uppsala, 1922, and R. W. Burchfield, 'The Language and Orthography of the Ormulum MS.', *Transactions of the Philological Society*, 1956, 56–87.

[4] See J. E. Turville-Petre, 'Studies on the *Ormulum* MS.', *JEGP* xlvi (1947), esp. 26–7.

sometimes showing similar linguistic developments are *Genesis and Exodus*,[1] the *Bestiary*[2], and the thirteenth-century Grimsby romance of *Havelok the Dane*;[3] but none of these is preserved in a good text.

Nevertheless, there is evidence enough to establish East-Midland usage, which can be contrasted both with that of West-Midland texts such as the *Katherine Group*[4] and the Corpus Christi *Ancrene Wisse*,[5] or Laȝamon's *Brut*,[6] and with that of more southerly eastern texts such as *Vices and Virtues*.[7]

Context of time presents even more difficulty than that of place. Although early twelfth-century English manuscripts are far from rare, most of them, such as MS. Bodley 343[8] and Cottonian MS. Vespasian D xiv,[9] contain material too uncertain in origin to be considered representative of any current language. Moreover, lack of material from the same dialect area partially invalidates chronological comparisons with other texts. This, and especially the predominance among extant material of literary West-Saxon, may be what makes the morphology of the Final Continuation look so advanced.

The Copied Annals

Before studying the language of any medieval text, we must first estimate the degree of scribal adulteration involved. With

[1] Ed. R. Morris, EETS 7, 186; also ed. O. Arngart, Lund, 1968.

[2] Ed. J. Hall, *Selections from Early Middle English, 1130–1250*, 2 vols., Oxford, 1920, i. 176–96 and ii. 579–626.

[3] Ed. W. W. Skeat, EETS E.S. 4, 1868.

[4] i.e. the homilies preserved in MS. Bodley 34. For the best account of their language, see S. T. R. O. d'Ardenne, ed., *Þe Liflade ant te Passiun of Seinte Iuliene*, EETS 248, 1961 (originally: Liège, 1936).

[5] Ed. J. R. R. Tolkien, *Ancrene Wisse*, EETS 249, 1962. See also A. Zettersten, *Studies in the Dialect and Vocabulary of the Ancrene Riwle*, Lund Studies in English xxxiv, 1965.

[6] Ed. G. L. Brook and R. F. Leslie, vol. i, EETS 250, 1963 (in progress); also ed. F. Madden, 3 vols., 1847.

[7] Ed. F. Holthausen, EETS 89 and 159, 1888 and 1920.

[8] Ed. A. O. Belfour, EETS 137, 1909; see Pope, EETS 259, 1967, 14–18.

[9] Ed. R. D.-N. Warner, EETS 152, 1915. The study by K. Glaeser, *Lautlehre der Ælfricschen Homilien in der Handschrift Cotton Vespasianus D xiv*, Diss. Leipzig, Weida i. Thür., 1916, shows a hotchpotch of inconsistent forms which he labels as 'Saxon patois'; see Pope, op. cit. 24–6.

the *Peterborough Chronicle* this applies mainly to the copied annals; for, whereas the annals from 1122 to the end, being evidently both composed at Peterborough and set down there, may, in spite of a few copyist's errors, be regarded as original documents, those from 1070 to 1121 were copied from an archetype of unknown origin. In general, they seem to represent that archetype fairly accurately, for regular differences, affecting all aspects of language, are maintained between the copied matter and the Peterborough Interpolations written concurrently in the same hand.

To suppose the archetype accurately reproduced, however, only takes the problem back one stage further. Textually, as we have already seen, the archetype can be only vaguely localized as 'southern',[1] with little indication of how many recopyings may lie between the original and the Laud text. Can linguistic analysis help here?

No late-Old-English text is easy to localize by language alone. From the late tenth century at least the 'classical' West-Saxon orthography had been adopted for nearly all Old-English writing of whatsoever provenance, and it was maintained, with only slight modifications, for nearly a century and a half.[2] This is the tradition which the copied annals represent. From time to time, however, irregular forms appear. These are possibly due to discrepancies between the *Schriftsprache* and the scribe's spoken language, discrepancies of dialect, of chronological development, or of both; but they are rarely easy to interpret. Take *forðfyrde* 1077/5, *dryfdon* 1118/6 (=*drēfdon* 'tormented'), and *gedyrfsum* 1105/12. At first sight, *forðfyrde* and *dryfdon* look like 'Kentish' inverted spellings (when [y(:)]>[e(:)], *y* may be used for any [e(:)]); and they were so taken by Bachmann.[3] They may, however, not be Kenticisms,

[1] See *supra*, xxi–xxii.

[2] For 'West-Saxon' documents written in areas where other dialects were spoken, see K. Sisam, *Studies in the History of Old English Literature*, Oxford, 1953, 153, and also A. Campbell, *Old English Grammar*, Oxford, 1959, 6 and n. 1.

[3] W. Bachmann, *Lautlehre des älteren Teiles der Chronik von Peterborough*, Diss. Leipzig, Weida i. Thür., 1927, 85.

but simply 'non-West Saxonisms'. The reflex of *ĕa* in *i*-mutation conditions was spelt *y* in late West Saxon, but *e* in other dialects; in so far as this *ĕ* merged with other *e*-sounds, non-West-Saxon scribes might then have used *y* as an ultra-correct spelling for any [e(:)] in their own speech. This would explain not only *forðfyrde* and *dryfdon* but also the common *wyrre* for the loan-word *werre*. For *gedyrfsum* an analogous explanation might be put forward, assuming a scribe who already pronounced the reflex of broken *eo* as unrounded [e]; but another explanation on the same lines may serve equally well: as broken *io* in *i*-mutation conditions gives *y* in West Saxon but *eo* in most other dialects, several words show *y* and *eo* interchanging according to dialect, thus, *yrre/eorre*, *hyrde/heorde*, etc., so that for a non-West-Saxon scribe *y* could have been an ultra-correct spelling for any [eo], especially before supported *r*.

Given these uncertainties, there is no support for Bachmann's contention that the language of the copied annals is Kentish.[1] Representation of OE *y̆*, for instance, is typically late-West-Saxon, with regular *y*, except in a few examples where palatal unrounding is probable, such as *cing*, *kinehelm*, *gescrid*. Bachmann himself seems to have found hardly any examples of 'Kentish' *e* for short *y* and none at all for long.[2] Occasional confusion between *æ* and *e* (about a fifth of the examples of short [e] of all origins are spelt *æ* or *ea*; and in a much smaller proportion of instances *e* appears for [æ][3]) might seem better evidence of Kentish provenance; but such spellings occur also in the Interpolations and in the Continuations, where no Kentish influence is likely. As such spellings are common in late-Old-English documents,[4] they may have no dialectal

[1] Bachmann, op. cit. 140–1, and *passim*. [2] Ibid. 71, also 72, 88.

[3] In weak-stressed words such as *þet*, *wes*, *e* may represent [ə] rather than [e]. With certain other forms such as *herfest* (for *hærfest*), a genuine variant may be involved (thus, *Ormulum*, *herrfessttid* and *Bestiary*, *heruest*).

[4] See, for instance, W. Schlemilch, *Beiträge zur Sprache und Orthographie spätaltengl. Sprachdenkmäler der Übergangszeit (1000–1150)*, Studien zur englischen Philologie xxxiv, Halle, 1914, 6; and, for inverted spellings with *ea* for [e], ibid. 8; see also A. Flohrschütz, *Die Sprache der Handschrift D der angelsächsischen Annalen*, Diss. Jena, 1909, 9, 10.

significance but merely reflect Latin and French influence.[1] Bachmann also cites as Kentish the rare examples of *e* for West-Saxon *æ* of both origins.[2] But, quite apart from possible confusion of *e* and *æ* for long vowels as well as for short, these forms admit of other explanations. Most of the instances of *e* for the reflex of WG *ā* (not, in any event, necessarily a Kenticism) could be due to various combinative changes, initial palatal influence (as in *agefon*), or palatal umlaut (as in *neh*, etc.). Moreover, *e* never occurs in forms such as *gesawon*, *lagon*, which regularly show 'Saxon' retraction. The instances of *e* for the *i*-umlaut of WG *ai*, at first sight more significant of dialect, mostly occur before point consonants, a position where raising to [e:] was fairly common, especially in Anglian.[3] Thus, the representation here of the sounds corresponding to the [æ:] sounds of West Saxon hardly supports Kentish provenance,[4] although it does suggest influence, at some stage of the textual history, from non-West-Saxon (Anglian) dialect—and we already know that the text was copied at Peterborough.

In the main, the language of the copied annals is 'Standard Late West Saxon', demonstrating the persistence of the *Schriftsprache* rather than telling us anything about current speech. In particular, West-Saxon *unfestes y* occurs regularly: for original *e* after a palatal, alternating with *i* in about equal

[1] O. v. Feilitzen, *Pre-Conquest Personal Names of Domesday*, Uppsala, 1937, 46–7, points out that in Domesday, which shows strong French influence on spelling, representation of OE [æ] wavers between *e* and *a*; see also Schlemilch, op. cit. 3–4, and P. Gradon, *RES* N.S. xi (1960), 64.

[2] Bachmann, *Lautlehre*, 73–4, 75–6, 91.

[3] See K. Luick, *Historische Grammatik der englischen Sprache*, Leipzig, 1921, § 361 Anm. 2, and R. Jordan, *Handbuch der mittelenglischen Grammatik*, rev. H. Ch. Matthes, Heidelberg, 1934, § 48 Anm. 2.

[4] The few examples of *æ*-spellings for original [e:], which might be interpreted as inverted spellings based on correspondence between WS *æ*-spelling and a local [e:], must be treated with caution. Some represent shortenings, and so illustrate the *e/æ* confusion common for the short vowels, thus, *awæston*, *fæddon*, *færde* (cf. *Ormulum*, *ferrde*), *gespædde*, *spæddon*; shortening may also have taken place when [e:] coalesced into a diphthong with following [j], thus, *bægen*, *twægen*. This leaves *cwæne*, *forlæt*, *hæt*, *ræðe*, which might be inverted spellings due to the special raising before point consonants, and also *benæmde*, 1102, 1104, for which see Campbell, *Grammar*, 77, n. 4.

proportions, by contrast with the *e*-spellings normal in the Peterborough sections; for the *i*-umlaut of broken *ĕa*, and for the corresponding long sound, with only three exceptions; and in *sylf*, etc., beside the Peterborough *selue*, etc.

Morphology is equally inconclusive. Forms which might be due to the Peterborough scribe carry little weight, and other dialect indications are rare. Such as they are, these indications suggest southern influence. Thus, although masculine *u*-stems sometimes follow the *ă*-stem pattern, as in the Peterborough language, sometimes they follow the weak declension, thus, n./a. pl. *sunan* 1087/55, 1088/72, 1120/7, as in southern and West-Midland dialects.[1] Strong feminines likewise occasionally show weak forms such as later became common for these nouns in southern and western dialects, thus, post-prep. sing. *trywðan* 1095/21, n. pl. *sciran* 1097/33, etc.; usually, however, they keep the Old-English inflexions, with a high proportion of non-Anglian *a*-endings in n./a. pl.

Vocabulary also emphasizes the adherence of the copied annals to the *Schriftsprache.* No words here can be identified beyond doubt as non-West-Saxon, nor, in spite of some rarities, are there many neologisms. In keeping with its general conservatism, this text is notable for the number of obsolescent words it contains.[2]

The Peterborough Continuations: Dialect

Unlike the inscrutably conventional copied annals, the Peterborough Continuations are, in spite of influence from the *Schriftsprache* both on spelling and on grammar, strongly marked by the East-Midland dialect of the district where they were written. This is no less true of the First Continuation than of the Final one, whose East-Midland character seems never to have been questioned.

Anglian affiliations are clear from the phonology of the First Continuation, and especially from the treatment of the sounds

[1] See d'Ardenne, *Iuliene*, § 70.

[2] See 'Studies in the Vocabulary of the *Peterborough Chronicle*, 1070–1154', *EGS* v (1952–3), 67–89, esp. 68–9, 73–5.

corresponding to the characteristic *unfestes y* of West-Saxon. Here, as in other Anglian texts, the *i*-umlaut of Old-English *ēa* (WG *au*) is regularly represented by *e*, not by the late-West-Saxon *y* normal in the copied annals, thus, *aflemde* 1124, *begemen* 1129, *gemelest* 1070, *hersumnesse* 1131, *stepel* 1070[1] and 1122; compare from the Final Continuation *flemden*, *herde* (but once *atywede*). Broken and mutated *i* is rendered by *eo*, *e* (or *æ*), rather than by West-Saxon *ie*, *y*, thus, *ieornden* 1123, *iærnde* 1127. So too *i*-umlaut of WG *ă* before *r*-groups is represented not by late-West-Saxon *y* but, as in Anglian, by *e* (or *æ*), thus, *dærne* 1114, *erue* 1125; compare from the Final Continuation *ferd*, *færd*, *feord*. And *e* after an initial palatal is rendered not by late-West-Saxon *y* but by *e* or an equivalent, thus, *begeton* (infin.) 1131, *beieten* (past p.) 1127, *geoldes* 1124; compare from the Final Continuation *bigæton* (infin.), *gestes*.[2] All these spellings are characteristically Anglian.

Two isolative developments also are typically North-Eastern. Original [y(:)] (< *ŭ*/*i*) is commonly spelt *i*, as in *dide* passim, *behid* 1070, *hiue* 1127, *fir* 1122, etc. For *ĕo*, *e*-spellings are common beside traditional *eo*, and for the long sound they predominate, thus, *mildhertnesse* 1070, *beneðan* 1125, *clepunge* 1129, and for the long sound, *ben*, *cesen*, *þefas*, *þre*, etc.; the Final Continuation has *erthe*, *sterres*, *clepeden*, *dær*, *frend*, *gæde* (*geeode*), *thre*, *undep*, etc. In both cases traditional spellings still occur, but inverted spellings (*tyma* 1123, *tyde* 1122; *feonlandes* 1070, *geseogen* (past p.) 1122, *leong* 1123, etc.) suggest that there is no longer any phonetic distinction between old spellings and new.

A more complex problem arises over representation of WG *ă*. In the First Continuation *æ*-spellings predominate, but *e* occurs in about a tenth of the examples and *a* occasionally

[1] Forms from the Interpolations are listed with those of the First Continuation, because in general they show similar developments.

[2] The only exception is *give*, which, both in the infin. and in the past p., regularly has *i* or *y*; but, as such forms occur in the North and East in Old as well as in Middle English, they are, therefore, not specifically West-Saxon (see Luick, *Grammatik*, § 172 Anm. 2 and § 173 Anm. 3, and E. Sievers, *Altenglische Grammatik*, rev. K. Brunner, Halle, 1942, § 91 Anm. 5).

(*acer*, *hakeles*, *was*, *hafden*). In the Final Continuation, by contrast, *a*-spellings predominate, with *æ* in only two-fifths of the examples and *e* only in *dei*, *æuez* (*æfæst*), *efter*, *hefden* (beside *hæfden*, *hadden*). Interpreting these distributions is not easy. The paucity of *e*-spellings certainly distinguishes this dialect from that of the West Midlands; the few *e*'s that do occur are perhaps mainly due to orthographic confusion of *æ*, *ę*, *e*. The increasing proportion of *a*-spellings may show lowering of [æ]>[a]. But there is also the possibility of continental influence on spelling: in French (presumably also in Latin as spoken by Frenchmen) *a* seems to have represented a somewhat fronted sound,[1] so that if replacement of *æ* by *a* were due to French influence, the new spellings need not indicate retraction.

Morphology shows the East-Midland basis of this language even more clearly than phonology does. Thus, in the present indicative the third person singular normally shows the absence of mutation and syncopation characteristic of non-West-Saxon dialects, as in *beræfoð* 1124, *ritteð*, *dæleth* 1130, *ofercumeð* 1123, *singað*, *dragað* 1127, and, similarly, contracted verbs show *h*-less forms, as in *seoð*, *seð*, *ofslæð* 1124. The few syncopated forms nearly all come from verbs with stems ending in a dental, thus, *frett* 1127 and *læt* < *lædan* 1124, for which syncopated forms are common throughout the Midland dialects.[2] In *doð* 675, 1127, and *gað* 656, both 3 sing., the original mutation has been abandoned, a change occurring earliest in Northern and Eastern dialects. As far as paucity of examples allows us to judge, the present indicative already shows the opposition of pl. -(*e*)*n* to sing. -(*e*)*ð*, which by the turn of the century characterizes all East-Midland dialects,[3] thus, pl. *liggen*, *liggan* 656, *lin* 963, *dragen*, *seggen* 1127 (although sometimes the Interpolations

[1] See A. Ewert, *The French Language*, 1933, 51, and M. K. Pope, *From Latin to Modern French*, Manchester, 1952, § 182.

[2] See W. Öfverberg, *The Verbal Inflections of the East Midland Dialects in Early Middle English*, Lund, 1924, 57–8, and also d'Ardenne, *Iuliene*, § 108.

[3] For the genesis of pres. pl. -*en*, see W. F. Bryan, 'The Midland Present Plural Indicative Ending -*e*(*n*)', *Modern Philology*, xviii (1921), 457–73.

have pl. forms in -*ð*); compare from the Final Continuation *willen*, *lien*. It is, of course, this system (modified, as in Robert Mannyng's usage, by substitution of Northern -*s* for sing. -*ð*) that lies behind that of Modern English, and it adds to the importance of our text to be the earliest one extant to show it.[1]

Weak verbs of the second class also show Eastern and Northern forms, losing medial -*i*(*g*)- and so falling together with those of the first class. Such forms, common in the Interpolations, are almost regular in the First Continuation: thus, simple infinitive *ðolen*, *beweddan* 1127, etc., beside much rarer examples with -*ian*, -*ien*, as *wunien* 1128; inflected infinitive *to locen* 1129; first person sing. present indicative *loue*, *lufe*, *tyðe* 656 beside forms in -*ie* (this person does not occur in either of the Continuations); present subjunctive singular *geare* 1128, *scawe* 1127, beside *adylege* 1130. Compare the Final Continuation, which regularly has infinitives such as *axen*, *enden*, *rixan*, *þolen*, but *uuerrien*. Such forms are distinctively Anglian; for, as Anglian normally formed the inflected infinitive and the past participle of -*ōjan* verbs without medial -*i*(*g*)-, already in Old English it kept WI and WII conjugations less distinct than in West Saxon and, when obscuration of unstressed vowels caused other parts of the paradigm to fall together, was readier to assimilate WII forms completely to those of WI. Southern texts, by contrast, and also those from the West Midlands and from the South-East (e.g. *Vices and Virtues*), not only preserve the distinction between WI and WII well into the Middle-English period but also show WII phonetically bifurcated into two vigorous and independent conjugations.[2]

Nouns also show typically East-Midland forms. Whereas in Western and Southern dialects weak pl. -*n* not only survives

[1] Brown, *Language of the Rushworth Gloss*, §§ 26, 28, claimed to find some examples of pres. ind. pl. -*en* in *Rushworth St. Matthew*, but these may be due to confusion with the subjunctive.

[2] See J. R. R. Tolkien, '*Ancrene Wisse* and *Hali Meiðhad*', *Essays and Studies*, xiv (1929), 117–26.

into Middle English but also spreads to some nouns originally strong, here it is rapidly yielding place to the *-s* pl. generalized from the masculine *ă*-stems, thus, *bucces*, *huntes* 1127, etc., but *ægon* (post-prep.) 1124, until in the Final Continuation the process is almost complete, with *bryniges*, *neues*, *snakes*, *steorres*, *swikes*, *þumbes*, beside *halechen*. The few survivals of the *-n* pl. can be paralleled from later East-Midland texts, thus, *Ormulum*, *hallȝhenn* (post-prep.) and *eȝhne*, *Bestiary*, *egen*.[1] Old strong feminines also take *-s* pl. rather than *-n*, thus, *gife* 1125 but *brigges*, *lagas* 1125; compare *dædes*, *sinnes*, *treothes*, etc., from the Final Continuation. With all originally strong nouns *-n* pl. is exceptional, thus, *beniman ealla þa minetere* . . . *heora liman—þet wæs here elces riht hand 7 heora stanen* 1125 (but the intended case is uncertain here).

On the other hand, both Continuations show, as well as East-Midland forms, certain features apparently 'Saxon' rather than 'Anglian'. The most important of these is the representation of the two long vowels both written *æ* in West-Saxon. For $æ_1$ (WG *ā*) the First Continuation has only five spellings with 'Anglian' *e* (*red* 1129, *sed* 1124 3×, and *sprece* 1114) beside a large majority with *æ* (or the 'inverted' equivalent *ea*). For $æ_2$ (WG *ai*/*i*) a somewhat higher proportion of *e*-spellings occurs beside the usual *æ* spellings, thus, *elces* 1125, *flesc* 1131, *hese* 1123, *heðene* 1128, *neframa* 1129, *totwemde*, *sibreden* 1127. Usage in the Final Continuation is similar: beside some seven spellings of $æ_1$ as *e*, over thirty occur with *æ*, whereas for $æ_2$ we find *del*, *todeld*, *todeled*, *fle*[*s*]*c*, *hethen*, *lered*, *manred*, *neure*, beside *æure*, *æuer*, *æfre*, *næure*, *todælde*, and *sæ*. Such distribution, with *e* used more often for $æ_1$ than for $æ_2$, seems to correspond to no recognized English dialect. Most *e*-spellings of $æ_2$, however, occur before dentals, where $æ_2$ often appears as Middle-English [e:], especially in the East Midlands; once these are discounted,

[1] Weak *-n* is almost always dropped in the oblique singular. The First Continuation keeps it only in the set phrase *for --es luuen* and in *mæssan* 1122. In the Final Continuation *circewican* and *horderwycan* probably show incorporation of *-n* into the stem, as in Orm's nom. sing. *wikenn*. In *Sunendæi*, *Monendæg*, the *-n* would no longer have been treated as inflexional.

the remaining spellings for *æ*$_2$ are no more varied than might be expected at a time of orthographic confusion, when *æ* was a recessive symbol. But the spellings for *æ*$_1$ show a distribution just the reverse of that expected from a Middle-Anglian, East-Mercian dialect. Some anomalous *æ*-spellings may be due to influence from the *Schriftsprache*, which other evidence suggests the scribe of the First Continuation was trying to imitate. But other texts assigned to this area show similar distributions: *Rushworth St. Matthew* has *æ*-spellings for about a third of the instances of *æ*$_1$;[1] Orm offers a number of *æ*-spellings, although when the vowel is shortened he invariably represents it by *e*;[2] Robert Mannyng, although distinguishing in rhyme between the close sound developed from *æ*$_1$ and the open one from *æ*$_2$, shows shortened *æ*$_1$ varying between *e* and *a*.[3] Northamptonshire place-names, moreover, notwithstanding the strong Anglian element in this county, usually show the reflex of shortened *æ*$_1$ as *a*.[4] Taken together, this evidence suggests that, as well as the [e:] attested by such spellings as *breokan* (pret. pl.) 1102, an open pronunciation of *æ*$_1$, such as is usually called 'Saxon', was also current in this district. The linguistic evidence seems to be confirmed by grave-finds from Middle Anglia, which also suggest a mixed-race settlement there.[5]

A similar problem arises over representation of WG *ă* before *l*-groups. For this the First Continuation shows spellings varying between *ea* (or the equivalent *æ*) and *a*, thus, *cwealm* 1125, *eall* passim, *eald* 1127, *healfe* 1122, *wealden* 1123, *sælde* 1124, *ælmæst* 1130, beside *alle* 1128, *alre* 1124, *alswa* 1129, *derfald* 1123 and 1127, *half* 4×, *orfcwalm* 1131. In the Final

[1] For discussion of these, see Menner, *Anglia*, lviii. 15–18, and Kuhn, *PMLA* lx. 653–7.

[2] See P. F. Lambertz, *Die Sprache des Orrmulums*, Diss. Marburg, 1904, 64–7; E. E. Hale, 'Open and Close *ê* in the "Ormulum"', *MLN* viii (1893), 37–46; and H. M. Flasdieck, 'Die sprachliche Einheitlichkeit des Orrmulums', *Anglia*, xlvii (1923), 314.

[3] Boerner, *Die Sprache Roberd Mannyngs*, 210, 58, 65–6.

[4] *EPNS Northants.*, p. xxxi.

[5] See R. G. Collingwood and J. N. L. Myres, *Roman Britain and the English Settlements*, Oxford, 1936, 348–9.

Continuation *a*-spellings predominate: *al* passim, *als*(*e*) 5×, *alsuic*, *ald*, *halden* 3×, *half*, *hals*, beside *ælle*, *mænifældlice*, *stæl*. Spelling-distribution in the First Continuation is again the opposite of what might have been expected in Northamptonshire, which is usually classed among districts where WG *ă* before supported *l* was retracted, not broken,[1] as in *Rushworth St. Matthew*, where *a* greatly predominates over *ea*.[2] The easiest explanation, as traditional *ea* so greatly predominates over monophthongized *æ*, would be imitation of the *Schriftsprache*. But, as Peterborough lay near the apparently mixed-dialect areas of Huntingdonshire and Cambridgeshire,[3] its dialect may not have been homogeneous in this any more than in treatment of $æ_1$. And currency of *eal*-forms here is at least not contradicted by the spellings found where lengthening is likely, thus, beside *ald*, *derfald*, *halden* (compare Orm's *āld*, *hāldenn*), we find *sælde* (Orm *sāldenn*, pl.) and *mænifældlice* (Orm *anfāld*, etc.), forms all the likelier to be phonetic for being untraditional. A further slight confirmation is that inverted *ea*-spellings are common for [æ] but not for [a].

Another sound-change usually considered 'Saxon' which appears in our text is loss of [j] between a front vowel and *d*, *ð*, or *n*. This appears occasionally in the First Continuation, thus, *sæde* etc. three times, beside *sæide*, *seide*, in the majority of instances; and rather oftener in the Final Continuation. Such forms, however, are not confined to the South but are also found in such South-East-Midland texts as *Vices and Virtues*, *Trinity College Homilies*, *King Horn*, and, admittedly a century and a half later, in the works of Robert Mannyng of Bourne.

[1] See E. Ekwall, 'Contributions to the History of Old English Dialects', *Lunds Universitets Årsskrift*, N.F. Avd. 1, Bd. 12, Nr. 6 (1916), 33; M. S. Serjeantson, 'The Dialectal Distribution of certain Phonological Features in Middle English', *ES* iv (1922), 105, 107; and *EPNS Northants.*, p. xxxi.

[2] Menner, *Anglia*, lviii. 15.

[3] See Ekwall, loc. cit.; Serjeantson, op. cit. 102–3; *EPNS Cambs.*, p. xxxix; but A. Mawer and F. M. Stenton, *The Place-Names of Bedfordshire and Huntingdonshire*, EPNS iii, 1926, p. xxiii, give ME *old* for the reflex of lengthened *ald*/*eald* in these counties.

The First Continuation: Early Middle English

The language of both Continuations appears, then, to be basically Anglian, although somewhat influenced by the *Schriftsprache*. The Final Continuation is also incontrovertibly Middle English; but what of the First? Is it to be classed as Old or as Middle English?[1]

The classic test of Middle English is obscuration of vowels in unstressed syllables. In the First Continuation this obscuration is well advanced. In over two-thirds of the examples the plural ending of masculine *ă*-stems is *-es*. Regular *-es* when this ending is extended to other nouns (e.g. former strong neuters, *geoldes*, *huses*, *limes*, *wifes*; strong feminines, *brigges*, *mæssahakeles*; weak nouns, *bucces*, *huntes*) suggests that occasional *-as* with *ă*-stems is merely traditional. The genitive-plural inflexion, as far as still used, is reduced to *-e*, thus, *cnihte* 1124, *manne* 1124 and 1131, *munece* 4×, and other instances in the Interpolations. So too with the dative plural, thus, *fram his agene manne* 1127, *on ealle westme* 1124 and 1125. Verbal inflexions also show unstressed vowels obscured: over half the instances of the preterite plural and nearly five-sixths of those of the infinitive have *-en*.

Morphology shows even more clearly than unstressed vowels do the stage of evolution that has been reached. Noun-declension is already far advanced towards Modern English. With *-s* for nominative and accusative plural extended to all classes of nouns, only a few vestiges remain of other inflexions for these cases. The Old-English genitive plural, although still in use, thus, *ealre biscope curs* 675, *þære munece* 1070, *oðre godre*

[1] The text usually classed as the earliest ME one is the *Sermo in Festis Sancte Marie Virginis* in MS. Vespasian D xiv (ed. Warner, EETS 152, 134–9), which Förster dated 1108–22, or possibly 1108–14 ('Abt Raoul d'Escures und der spätae. "Sermo in festis S. Mariae"', *Archiv für das Studium der neueren Sprachen*, lxii (1932), 43–8); this is much less advanced morphologically than the First Continuation. See K. Malone, 'When did Middle English begin?', *Curme Volume of Linguistic Studies: Language Monographs*, vii (1930), 110–17, and F. P. Magoun, 'Colloquial Old and Middle English', *Harvard Studies and Notes in Philology and Literature*, xiv (1937), 167–73.

cnihte, manne 1124 (compare *al his gewiten ræd* 656), is sporadically replaced by the *-s* form which became general in Middle English, thus, *earcedæcnes, preostes* 1129; compare *preostes* in the Final Continuation.[1]

The dative not only suffers reduction of inflexion but is almost abandoned as a case, a usage which, although foreshadowed in the *Lindisfarne Gospels*[2] and in *Rushworth St. Matthew*,[3] is certainly Middle rather than Old English. The indirect object is now regularly expressed by the accusative or by an uninflected form: *se cyng heafde gifen þet abbotrice an frencisce abbot* 1070, *geaf . . . þone abbotrice an munec* 1114, *betæhte þa eall Engleland . . . þone biscop Roger* 1123, etc., and compare from the Final Continuation, *Pais he makede men 7 dær, alle þe pines ðat hi diden wrecce men*, etc.; but, however, *beniman ealla þa minetere . . . heora liman—þet wæs here elces riht hand 7 heora stanen* 1125.[4] Uninflected forms also appear as complement to adjectives, thus, *leaf eall folc* 1066, and to express point of time (here replacing either dative or genitive), thus, *þe Tywesdæi* 1122, *Đis gear* 1131; compare from the Final Continuation *ælc gær, þat ilc gær*. Loss of distinctive dative forms, whatever its ultimate cause,[5] must have been hastened by the fact that already in Old English accusative and dative singular were identical in many declensions (weak masculine and feminine, *ō*-stems, short *i*-stems, long *jă*-stems, and, after final vowels had been obscured, *u*-stems also); then, with reduction of unstressed syllables, the dative plural fell together with the uninflected plural everywhere except in the *ă*-declension. In abandoning their distinct dative forms

[1] D'Ardenne, *Iuliene*, § 65, takes ME g. pl. *-s* as an extension of g.s. *-s*, not of nom./acc. pl. *-s*; compare Orm's use of g. pl. *-es* with anomalous nouns, thus, nom./acc. pl. *shep, menn*, g. pl. *shepess, menness*, and see also M. Lehnert, *Sprachform und Sprachfunktion im 'Orrmulum'*, Berlin, 1953, 153–9.

[2] See A. S. C. Ross, *Studies*, 121, and L. Blakeley, 'Accusative-Dative Syncretism in the Lindisfarne Gospels', *EGS* i (1947–8), 6–31.

[3] Brown, *Language of the Rushworth Gloss*, 71, 73.

[4] Usage with *beniman* varied between acc. of person with gen. of thing and dat. of person with either acc. (e.g. 1094/11) or gen. (e.g. 1093/39) of thing; compare a few lines later, *benam ælc ðone riht hand 7 þa stanes*.

[5] See *infra*, lxx, lxxiv.

ă-stems presumably went by analogy with the other declensions; but it is strange that such analogy works earliest and most thoroughly in the very dialects, Northern and Midland, which earliest suppressed those other declensions, whereas the more southerly dialects which preserved those longest, also preserved dative inflexion longest.

After prepositions rather more vestiges of dative inflexion survive. In the plural examples are: *æfter alle his þægne, toforen ealle his ðægna, to þa munecan* 656, *mid ealle deofle* 675, *in þa ealde wealle* 963, *undernæðen his fote* 1070, *on ealle westme* 1124 and 1125, *fram his agene manne* 1127 (*of here ægon* 1124 may represent weak nom./acc. pl.); compare *on fote* 1140. But more often the nom./acc. form is used, thus, *wið his agene men* 1124, *on swarte hors 7 on swarte bucces* 1127, etc.; compare from the Final Continuation *efter þe muneces, on her fet*, etc. Inflected forms are commoner in the singular, but the principle behind their use seems changed: whereas in Old English the preposition determined the case, here the form seems partly determined by the noun, with post-prepositional inflexions almost confined to certain words and phrases.[1] Set phrases include: *to wife* passim (compare *Ormulum, to wife*, and *Genesis and Exodus, to wife* beside *wið wif*), *mid wrange* 1124, *to biworde* 1130; compare *in tune* 1137. In general, monosyllables most often show dative inflexion, thus, *to his inne* 1123, *on corne* 1124, *in his mycele codde* 1131, but also *on þes abbotes settle* 1131; compare *in quarterne* 1137. Some common monosyllables (e.g. *gear, cyng, land*) show inflected and uninflected forms interchanging after prepositions, and so also in the Final Continuation, but with a lower proportion of inflected forms; compare Orm's variations with *land*(*e*), *king*(*e*), etc. Post-prepositional use resembles Orm's, being much more advanced than that of the West Midlands, where post-prepositional *-e* was normally kept in early Middle English.[2]

[1] With *mynstre, seolure*, the original dative form seems to have been generalized to all singular cases, thus, *Ðus wæs se mynstre* 1070, *þet is gold 7 seolure* 1123, etc.; compare Orm's *minnstre* (acc.).

[2] Compare d'Ardenne, *Iuliene*, § 60.

Loss of case-distinctions affects the old feminine nouns in various ways. For long-stemmed feminines to become indeclinable in the singular, either the nominative or the oblique form had to be generalized, and here the nominative was usually chosen. After prepositions, forms with *-e* still occur fairly often, thus, *on þa litle hwile* 1124, *on hiue* 1127, but uninflected forms also appear, thus *þurh his agen cwen* 654, *þurh heora gemelest* 1070, *on an half* 1123, *for sibreden* 1127 2×; compare from the Final Continuation *mid ormete færd, mid micel ferd, abuton nontid dæies*. In other oblique functions also usage varies, thus, *ofercumeð eall weoruld* 1123, *eall þet lententid* 1127, beside *eall Eastrentyde* 1123; compare from the Final Continuation *toc his feord, macod he his gadering, bare his byrthen*, beside *scæ hedde litel blisse, nan helpe ne hæfden*. The First Continuation offers no nominative form, but compare from the Final Continuation, *þa com þe kinges cuen, sib 7 sæhte sculde ben* . . . Since the *-e* ending of the *ō*-stem accusative singular had spread to *i*-stems in Old English, and especially in Mercian,[1] these *-e*-less forms can hardly represent the old *i*-stem accusative singular, and distribution of the forms here bears this out. In Middle English, including East-Midland texts such as the *Ormulum* and *Genesis and Exodus*, the *-e*-form was usually generalized to all singular functions, but, although rarer, generalization of the uninflected forms, as here, is not unparalleled: it appears in the *Lindisfarne Gospels*,[2] and occasionally in the *Ormulum* (thus, nom. sing. *tid, weorelld, cwen, ferd, wen*, and post-prep. *on hallf, forr ned, affterr mahht*) and in other East-Midland texts.[3]

Declension is being simplified in pronouns as well as in nouns. Already in the First Continuation the accusative function of animate pronouns is being taken over by the dative form (the reverse of the process operating in the nouns), and by the Final Continuation this change is complete. Analysis of the forms is enlightening. After prepositions, dative forms are

[1] Campbell, *Grammar*, § 604. [2] Ross, *Studies*, 119–21.
[3] Öfverberg, *Inflections*, 21; also Lehnert, *Sprachform*, 22–3, 139–47.

regular, logically enough, since in Old English the dative was the commonest post-prepositional case. Other functions show more variation. As direct object, both *hine* and *him*, *hi* and *he(o)m* occur, but only *hire*; but, whereas *he(o)m* is commoner than *hi*, *hine* remains commoner than *him*. Likewise, for the indirect object, the inverted *hine* for *him* (*ealle hine iæfen micele gife* 1125, *iæf hine þone eorldom* 1127) is far commoner than *hi* for *he(o)m* (*ic gife hi min curs* 675). Such distributions suggest that generalization took place first in the feminine singular, where it is already complete, and then in the plural—doubtless because the triple ambiguity of *hi*, which in late Old English was not only nominative and accusative plural but also accusative (and in some dialects nominative too) feminine,[1] encouraged use of the more distinctive dative forms. As *hine* was involved in no such ambiguity, its eventual yielding to *him*, the last of these changes, must have been solely due to analogy with the rest of the system. The neuter *hit*, however, remains; note also *nama hit gauen Medeshamstede* 654. So, the First Continuation gives evidence, although it is not alone in so doing,[2] of the way the Modern system of pronouns evolved from the Old-English one. At this date such usage is advanced, and typical of the Midlands as against the South, where, especially in Kentish texts such as the *Ayenbite*, old accusative forms remain in use into the fourteenth century.

Adjectival development is also advanced. With the general obsolescence of the dative, its special inflexions, both singular and plural, are almost lost. The dative plural inflexion survives only to the same limited extent and in the same reduced form as that of nouns, thus, *mid ealle deofle* 675, *on ealle westme* 1124 and 1125, *fram his agene manne* 1127; the singular inflexion may appear in *in his mycele codde*, *þurh his mycele sotscipe* 1131,

[1] This may thus be added to the homonymic conflicts among English pronouns discussed by R. J. Menner, 'The Conflict of Homonyms in English', *Language*, xii (1936), 236–8.

[2] *The History of the Holy Rood-Tree* (ed. A. Napier, EETS 103, 1894), for instance, shows dative forms replacing accusative in fem. sing. and in pl., but *hine* and *him* still clearly distinguished.

but here confusion with the weak form is possible, and compare *þon hæge ælmihti God* 656. Accusative singular inflexions appear, but in only a few of the possible instances, thus, masc., *ænne peni, at anne market* 1125 (beside *at an market* 1124), *fram anne swein* 1128, and fem. *on ane circe* 1127. Normally a strong adjective qualifying any singular noun is uninflected both for accusative and, as far as these survive, for dative functions, thus, *þurh his agen cwen* 654, *ofer eal Sumersetescire* 1122, *eall Eastrentyde, on an Wodnesdei, ofer eal Englalande* 1123, *eall digelnesse* 1124, *eall þone wintre* 1125, *mid micel wurðscipe* passim, etc.[1] With a genitive-singular noun also, a strong adjective may be uninflected, thus, *eall þes geares* 1123, *eall Cristenes folces* 1131, *al Cristene folces* 656;[2] but, as these last examples show, uninflected forms were not yet universal. Although the *-e* of the strong nom./acc. plural usually survives, several endingless forms appear, thus, *of eall þa feonlandes* 1070, *ealle frencisc 7 englisc* (apparently dative plural in function) 1127; compare from the Final Continuation *al landes, nan martyrs, lered men, hethen men, cnotted strenges*. At all events, nom./acc. pl. *-e* was vigorous enough to generate, by analogy with the possessive adjectives *min–mine*, etc., a new adjectival plural *hise*, thus, *hise biscopes 7 hise abbotes 7 hise þeignes* 1123, etc.; this form, although common in the First Continuation and to become regular in all Middle-English dialects, is, however, found only once in the Final Continuation beside several instances of *his* with a plural noun. The weak nom./acc. plural has fallen together with the strong form, partly at least because of phonetic weakening, thus, *þa ilce lagas* 1125, *þa micele unrihte 7 þa micele unsibbe* 1127, *betwenen ða Cristene 7 þa heðene* 1128, *of þa ricceste men* 1129, *for þa wrecce muneces* 1131, but also, exceptionally, *ða*

[1] The Final Continuation shows strong adjectives inflected in the singular only in *onne* (referring back to fem. *rachentege*), *be gode rihte* (probably a set phrase), and *untellendlice pining, alle þe ilce pining* (possibly, however, pl.)

[2] Perhaps loss of inflection began in adjectives thus separated from their nouns, compare from the copied annals, in general so conservative, *eall þone here, sum þone here* 1085, *eall Beorclea Hyrnesse* 1088, *to eall swilcre gehyrsumnisse* 1091, *wið sum þæra dæle* 1094, *mid eall his fyrde* 1101 (if these forms are not due to the Peterborough scribe).

forsprecon biscopes 1130 (compare from the Final Continuation, *te other æuez men*). For the genitive plural only strong inflexions seem to survive, and then not consistently, thus, *ealre halgane curs* 656, *of Godes half . . . 7 ealra halgan 7 ealre hadode heafde* 675 (cf. also 963), *ealre biscope curs . . . 7 here ealre þe her be gewitnesse* 675, *on Ælre Halgan mæsseniht* 1066, *secræman*[*ne*] *in* 1070, *fela oðre godre cnihte* 1124, but *ealle gewitene mot* 675, *ealle þa muneke red* 777. In the singular the weak declension usually remains distinct from the strong, with weak forms taking *-e* (*-æ*, *-a*) regardless of case, thus, *se forensprecene abbot* 1128, *se firste fare* 1128, *þet ærme folc* 1124, *þeos ilce geares* 1122, *þes feorðe dæges* 1130, *for þet micele unsibbe*, *on þone seolue minstre* 1127, *on þa litle hwile* 1124, *æt þe forme slæp* 1131. Sometimes, however, perhaps because of the falling-together in the plural, strong forms replace weak in the singular also, thus, *se eadig biscop* 1124, *ðone riht hand*, *ðone heh messe* 1125,[1] *þet yfel dæde* 1070, *ðes ilces geares* passim (in this phrase, *ilces* is now far commoner than the historical *ilce*<*ilcan*); compare from the Final Continuation *þat ilc gær*, *þe micel eie*, *þe cosan abbot*. Such simplified adjectival declension, although already seen in the *Lindisfarne Gospels*,[2] is at this date still advanced and so typical of Northern and Midland dialects as against Southern ones; southerly texts such as *Owl and Nightingale* and *Laȝamon A* maintain accusative-singular-masculine *-ne* and dative-singular-feminine *-re* until the early thirteenth century at least.

In one respect, however, the First Continuation appears at first sight less advanced than might be expected. Whereas the Final Continuation has indeclinable *þe* as its normal definite article, the First shows a variety of forms, with *se* still predominating for nominative singular masculine, the only instances of *þe* in this function being: *þa kyning* 656, *þe scyrbiscop* 675, *þe arcebiscop* 963, *þe landfolc*, *þe cyng* 1066, *þa densce biscop* 1070, *þa drane* 1127, *ða flescmete* 1131, and, with an

[1] But *riht hand* and *heh messe* may have been felt as compounds; on the other hand, *heh* stands at the end of a line (f. 84ᵛ, line 5), with no hyphen to join it to *messe* in the next line.

[2] Ross, *Studies*, 104–8.

original feminine, *þa cyrce* 1070. This apparent conservatism requires investigation.

It does not correspond to survival of grammatical gender.[1] Exactly how far loss of gender has gone in the First Continuation presents some problems. The copied annals had preserved the Old-English system, with only rare lapses; the Final Continuation abandons it altogether: does the First Continuation occupy an intermediate position, or does it resemble the Final one? In the use of personal pronouns it shows, unlike the copied annals, no signs of gender-feeling. Admittedly, pronouns referring to inanimate nouns are rare here, but, whereas the copied annals can use masculine or feminine pronouns, as historically appropriate, for referring to nouns such as *castel*, *cynehelm*, *steorra*, *wind*, *pallium*, *mona*, *Lundenburh*, *hid*, the First Continuation has: *wæs se heouene* (f.) . . . *eall swilc* hit *wære bærnende fir* 1131, and, Hit *is litel*, *þeos gife*, *ac ic wille þet hi* hit *hælden* 656. And with adjectives, as we have seen, gender-distinctive endings hardly survive, owing to the weakening of case-distinction. The article alone shows a fair range of case/gender forms; but their distribution no longer corresponds to historical genders, nor even, on occasion, to sex: thus, apart from the common, probably phonetic, confusion between *se*/*seo* seen in *seo kyning* Interpolations passim and *se cwen* 1126, note especially *þes cwenes canceler* 1123. The evidence indicates almost complete effacement of the Old-English gender-system.

To explain the survival of inflected forms of the article in this text (and others), it has been suggested that the original gender/case indicators have been redeployed to indicate case alone, with a certain preference for the originally masculine forms.[2]

[1] I no longer agree with all my former conclusions in 'Gender in "The Peterborough Chronicle" 1070–1154', *ES* xxxviii (1957), 109–15; in particular, I would now prefer to say that gender had been lost, with some originally masculine forms temporarily generalized before all gender-forms were superseded by indeclinable *þe*.

[2] C. Jones, 'The Functional Motivation of Linguistic Change: a study of the development of the grammatical category of gender in the late Old English period', and 'The Grammatical Category of Gender in Early Middle English', *ES* xlviii (1967), 97–111 and 289–305.

But, if this were so, then usage ought to be accurate and consistent, at least with regard to case; and it is not. Even if we leave aside all dubious examples—unhistorical uses of *þet*;[1] use of *þone* for dative function (probably linked with merging of the accusative and dative cases elsewhere); *þa* or *þe* corresponding to older *þam*—the number of false case-forms remains formidable, and, as they are a matter of some controversy, a list may not be out of place:

se/seo for direct object: *seo mynstre* 2×, *swa æl se feon* (=Hugo, 10, *totam paludem*) 656, *seo wurðfulle Æþelred . . . 7 se ærcebiscop . . . 7 seo Myrcene biscop* 675, *geaf . . . him þet abbotrice on Byrtune, 7 se . . . 7 se . . . 7 se* 1066, *se oðer abbot* 1131.

se/seo used post-prepositionally: *buton seo abbot, to seo forensprecone Norðburh, to seo Papa Uitalianus, buton . . . se ærcebiscop* 656, *at se kyning* 777, *to se cyng, æt se king, buton se abbot* 2× 963, *mid se cyng* 1114, *butan se captelhus 7 se slæpperne* 1116, *ðurh se biscop* 2×, *toforen se kyng, fram se biscop . . . 7 se biscop . . . 7* (5× in all) 1123, *for se miccle unfrið, wið se king, wið se eorl* 1124, *þurh se Scotte kyng* 1126, *of se eorl* 1127.

se/seo for genitive singular: *be se ærcebiscopes ræd* 656, *seo kyninges Æðelredes geornunge* 675.

se for nominative plural: *se munecas* 1123.

se for post-prepositional plural: *buton . . . se muneces* 656.

þone for nominative singular: *swa þone abbot wile* 675, *þone hæcce* 1070, *þone abbotrice* 1127.

þone for genitive singular: *þone eorles sunu* 1127.[2]

þone for post-prepositional plural: *of þone muneca* 675.

Statistically, false case-forms may be few; but their occurrence is none the less significant. Nominative and oblique cases have not in general fallen together in this text: in the pronouns they are regularly distinguished (as indeed they are

[1] For *þet* as an independent emphatic demonstrative, see *infra*, lxi–lxii.

[2] Jones, op. cit. 295, would construe *þone* with *sunu*, not with *eorles*; this seems contrary to all normal usage here.

to the present day). If, then, confusion occurs with the demonstrative, the weakness must lie in the demonstrative, not in the case-system. Now, since in the Final Continuation the article is invariable, it would be odd if it had not already been well on the way to invariability when the Interpolations and First Continuation were written, basically in the same dialect, thirty years (and less) earlier. The forms here can indeed be explained on the assumption that this was so. For the orthography of the First Continuation suggests that the scribe, aware that by the standards of the *Schriftsprache* his own usage was both provincial and newfangled, was trying to palliate his own provincialism and modernity. If in his speech stressed [þe:], unstressed [þə], corresponded to West-Saxon *se*, then he might have substituted *se* for his own form; and the evidence is compatible with his having done so. This supposition explains the frequency of nominative-singular-masculine *se*, and also its unhistorical uses: for, if Peterborough [þə] corresponded not only to *se*/*seo*, but also to plural *þa* and dative (singular and plural) *þam*, mechanical substitution would give forms such as *of se eorl*, *se munecas*. The unhistorical uses of *þone* are to be explained by an analogous substitution, on the assumption that in Peterborough speech [þə] occurred for accusative masculine and neuter as well as for cases where it had evolved phonetically (this is consistent also with the ultra-correct use of *se* for the direct object) and so gave rise to a further equation [þə]= West-Saxon *þone*. So, the apparent conservatism of the First Continuation proves to be false archaism and evidence of advanced spoken usage, probably with indeclinable *þe*.

Beside these usages evidently attributable to false archaism, a new development is observable: the shift of *þet* from nom./acc. neuter article to independent emphatic demonstrative. This is not yet complete, for not until the *Ormulum* is *þat* recorded with animate as well as inanimate nouns. Both the Interpolations and the First Continuation, however, show *þet* used with singular inanimates of any original gender, in contexts where an emphatic form is appropriate and especially with the antecedent of a defining relative clause, thus, *þet ilce forgiuenesse . . . þet he scolde hauen* 675, *þet hæcce þe þær wæs behid* 1070, *þet dugeð þet wæs . . .* 1114, *þet micele unsibbe þet wæs on þet land* 1127, etc.

Some of these last examples show another development of *þet*: its increased use as a relative pronoun.[1] With abandonment of grammatical gender and reclassification of nouns as animate and inanimate, this extension of relative *þet* is to be expected; but in fact relative *þet* is here used in a much wider range of contexts than is the corresponding demonstrative, including both animate feminine, thus, *his dohter þet . . .* 1126, and animate plural, thus, *ealle þa þet . . . hæfdon* 1129. Such uses are, however, exceptional here. Normal distribution is: for inanimate singular, *þet* predominating, with *þe/þa* occurring in about a third of the examples in the Interpolations, but in less than a fifth of those in the First Continuation; for inanimate plural, *þa/þe* (in the First Continuation only *þa*), with occasional *þet*; for animate singular, *se* and *þe/þa* as alternatives, with the latter becoming commoner in the First Continuation, and *þet* once; for animate plural, *þe/þa*, with two examples of *þet* in the First Continuation. The extension of *þet* is notable. An explanation recently put forward for the general usurpation in early Middle English of the former roles of the indeclinable relative *þe* by relative *þat* invokes a clash between the former and the weak-stressed indeclinable article *þe*;[2] if this were acceptable, then the spread here of relative *þet* could be taken as further evidence of the currency of the indeclinable article.

In vocabulary as well as in phonology and grammar the First Continuation shows Middle-English trends.[3] It contains fewer obsolescent terms than the copied annals do, and, on the other hand, offers early, often first, records of several neologisms: Latin loans, such as *cardinal*, *concilie*, *legat*, and French ones,

[1] See A. McIntosh, 'The Relative Pronouns *þe* and *þat* in Early Middle English', *EGS* i (1947–8), 73–90.

[2] See R. D. Stevick, 'Historical Selection of Relative *þat* in Early Middle English', *ES* xlvi (1965), 29–36.

[3] See further Clark, 'Vocabulary'.

such as *duc*, *Pasches*, *sotscipe*;[1] Norse loans, such as *band*, *rot(fest)*, *swein*, *tacan*, *utlaga*, *wrang*, and, most important, the grammar-words *oc* and *fra(ward)*; and also native terms not previously recorded but destined to spread, such as the conjunctions *for* (replacing *for þæm þe*, *for þy þe*) and *oðer/ouðer* (replacing *oððe*).

The Final Continuation: Further Developments

In general, as has been noted, the Final Continuation represents a fulfilment of tendencies shown in the First. Even here, some influence from the *Schriftsprache* survives, as in the use of *æ* and in isolated archaisms such as *se king* 1135. By now, however, this influence is sufficiently weakened for this part of the text to give a fair picture of contemporary Peterborough usage.

The superficially different appearance of the language is mainly due to orthographical changes, stemming from French and Latin influences, too often accepted uncritically. Native ȝ is replaced, regardless of phonetic value, by Caroline *g* (so also in the similar hand in the Black Book), thus, *godæs*, *king*, *gear*, *gyuen*, *undergæton*, *flugæn*, even *heglice*. The scribe does make some unsystematic attempt to distinguish some of the sounds in this range. Occasionally he uses *i* for [j], thus, *iaf*, *iunge*, *winiærd*, *iiuen* beside *gyuen* (compare from the First Continuation *beiet*, *ieden*, *iæfen*, etc.); he also uses *i* for [dʒ] in *iustise*. For the back spirant [γ] various spellings occur beside *g*, thus, *sloghen*, *halechede*, *halechen*, *folecheden*. These *ch*-spellings (compare, for instance, *halechen* in the interpolation at 890 A) resemble *halhin*, *folhin*, in MS. Bodley 34[2] and may result from a similar equation: if *h/ch*=[χ] finally, as in *Burh/Burch*, then medially it may denote the voiced equivalent [γ]. In *rachenteges*, *ch* seems to denote [k].[3] Similar lack of system affects the rendering of the dental spirants [þ] and [ð]. These sounds,

[1] For the loan-word *sot*, recorded from Ælfric as well as from *Byrhtferth's Manual* (ed. S. J. Crawford, EETS 177 (1929), 96), see H. M. Flasdieck, *Anglia*, lxx (1951), 255–6.

[2] See d'Ardenne, *Iuliene*, § 2.

[3] See NED, s.v. *Rackan*.

although lacking special symbols in Franco-Latin orthography, did occur in twelfth-century Norman and were represented there either by the etymological *t*, or by *d*, or else by the digraph *th*.[1] Scribes trained on Latin and French often used these spellings for English, even when, like our Continuator, they were English-speaking and knew the native symbols *þ* and *ð*.[2] Here *t* or *d* occurs finally, spirantal pronunciation being commonest there in Norman, thus, *maket*, *wart*, *wærd*, *ward*, *uuard* (all=*warð*), *haued*, *fordfeorde*, *wyd*, but also *Torn*' for Thorney; initially and medially, *th*-spellings alternate with *þ*, *ð*, thus, *the*, *tharof*, *throte*, *hethen*, *nouther*, *uurythen*, etc., also *warth*.[3] Franco-Latin influence is most unfortunate with the labial spirants. In Old English, [f], which occurred only initially and finally, and [v], which occurred only medially, formed a single phoneme and were adequately represented by the one letter *f*. In French and Latin, by contrast, [f] and [v] were separate phonemes needing separate symbols. Already in Old English, Latin influence sometimes led scribes to replace medial *f* by *u*, and after the Conquest French influence increased this tendency, so that the First Continuation shows forms such as *iuele*, *neue*, *seolure*, and in the Final Continuation these have become the rule and *f*-spellings the exceptions. This change was trebly unfortunate: it added to the stock of ambiguous minim-letters; it made distinction between [v] and [u] difficult;[4] and it led to a clash with another un-needed borrowing

[1] Pope, *From Latin to Modern French*, §§ 1210, 694b, 1215.

[2] French influence on representation of these sounds apparently began in the reign of Ethelred II, when coins first show *Ægel-* for *Æþel-* (compare *Ægelric* 1070, *Egelric* 1072, *Egelwine* 1071, *Ægelwig* 1077); the ME forms *Ailred*, *Ailwin*, etc., imply that the change was more than merely orthographic (compare inverted spellings, such as *Wiðreceastrescire* 1088 and *Leþecæstrescire* 1124, with *ð*, *þ*, for ȝ). Von Feilitzen, *Personal Names*, § 111, connected this with French effacement of intervocalic [ð]; but this hardly explains how such forms became so widespread.

[3] Also *Norhtwic*, *Norhthamtune* 1122; such spellings can be paralleled in Anglo-Norman texts, thus, *Guhtlande*, *Suhtwales*, *Suhthamptune*, in a thirteenth-century manuscript of Marie de France's *Lais* (ed. A. Ewert, Oxford, 1947, 102, 123, 110); compare *Burhc* 1127, *þurhc* 1140.

[4] In French also: see F. Whitehead, ed., *La Chanson de Roland*, Oxford, 1947, xv–xvi, on expedients for distinguishing [vr] from [ur].

from Romance orthography, *uu*, *u*, for [w], which already in our text is beginning to replace the less ambiguous *ƿ*.

The most important phonological change shown here is that of [a:]>[ɔ:] seen in two examples of *mor*(*e*) and one of *onne*.[1] Since *o*-spellings, although common in early South-Midland texts such as *Vices and Virtues* and the *Worcester Fragments*, are not found at all in more northerly ones such as the *Ormulum* or the *Katherine Group*, the restricted scope of the change here seems dialectally appropriate. On the other hand, retention of the *a*-spelling need not mean unchanged pronunciation: as the old spelling distinguished this vowel well enough and was not yet needed for any new [a:], there would, whatever the pronunciation, have been little need to change the spelling until the adoption of French words containing [a:].

Among minor sound-changes shown here (occasionally also in the similar hand of the Black Book) is assimilation of initial [þ] of the definite article to a preceding dental stop, thus, *ðat te*, *7* (= *and*) *te*, *æt te*, *mid te*, etc. Although seen sporadically in Old English,[2] such spellings are rare until the early-Middle-English period, when they become regular in texts such as the *Ormulum* and the *Katherine Group*.

Another minor change sometimes shown here is elision of unstressed *-e* of the weak preterite singular before another vowel or *h*, thus, *todeld it*, *macod he*, *henged up*, *smoked heom*, *behoued 7*, *goded it* (compare the preterite subjunctive singular *wær it* 1128), and sometimes in other positions also, thus, *mint to*, *henged bi*, *scatered sotlice*. Preterite-plural *-n* sometimes falls before another dental, thus, *wurðe sæhte*, *sahtlede sua*, *makede ðat* (compare *wære þær* 1129); and before a vowel or *h*, *-en* may be lost altogether, thus, plural *pined heom*, *bebyried him*, *læd him*, but *cursede æure*.[3] Compare the loss of inflexional *-e* from plural adjectives of similar phonetic structure, thus, *cnotted strenges*, etc.

[1] The two examples of *to* for the pl. demons. *þā* are probably scribal errors.

[2] e.g. *þæt tæt* in 755 A.

[3] For similar forms in other East-Midland texts, see Öfverberg, *Inflections*, 69, 71.

Grammatical innovation in the Final Continuation follows on from that already shown in the First. Resolution of pronominal ambiguities, begun by use of *hire* and *he(o)m* respectively for accusative feminine and accusative plural, is continued by substitution of *scæ* for the historical nominative-singular-feminine pronoun (probably *he*<*heo*, possibly *hi*<*hie*,[1] and in either case involved in homonymic conflict with other members of the paradigm). This substitution cannot be dated, as the First Continuation happens not to contain any nominative feminine pronoun. Nor is the origin of the new form, and of the related *scho*, settled, the only certainty being that both first arose in the North-East, to which they remain confined until the fourteenth century. No theory so far put forward seems wholly satisfactory, mainly because all postulate an unusual shift of stress, either *síe* > [sjè], or *híe* > [hjè]. Most favoured recently has been derivation from *heo/hie*, through a chain of development [hi] > [hj] > [ç] > [ʃ]. The decisive change [ç] > [ʃ] has been variously explained, either as an example of a Norse sound-change found elsewhere only in a few place-names (the so-called 'Shetland theory'),[2] or as substitution of a common initial phoneme for a rare one, linked with the need to maintain the distinction both from masculine *he* and from second-person plural *ȝe*.[3] Geographical distribution of *h*- and *sch*-forms during the Middle-English period is said to support derivation from stress-shifted [hjè] or [hjò].[4] There

[1] The only extant text regularly using *hie* is the *Vespasian Psalter Gloss*, but see B. Gericke, *Das Personalpronomen der 3. Person in spätags. Texten*, Palaestra, cxciii, 1934, 5, 7, and compare *Beowulf*, 2019. If our dialect had nom. *sie* (see opposite), then it may well have had nom. sing. fem. *hie* as well.

[2] G. Sarrazin, 'Der Ursprung von NE. "She" ', *Englische Studien*, xx (1895–6), 330–1; G. T. Flom, 'The Origin of the Pronoun "She" ', *JEGP* vii (1908), 115–25; A. H. Smith, 'Some Place-Names and the Etymology of "She" ', *RES* ii (1925), 437–40; E. Dieth, '*Hips*: A Geographical Contribution to the "She" Puzzle', *ES* xxxvi (1955), 209–17.

[3] See the different explanations on these lines put forward by J. Vachek, 'On Peripheral Phonemes of Modern English', *Brno Studies in English*, iv (1964), 21–9, and R. D. Stevick, 'The Morphemic Evolution of Middle English *She*', *ES* xlv (1964), 381–8.

[4] M. L. Samuels, 'The Role of Functional Selection in the History of English', *Transactions of the Philological Society*, 1965, 21–3.

still seems, however, something to be said for the older theory put forward in *NED*: that *scæ* developed from *síe*, through [sjè]. Certainly the demonstrative *seo* was used as an emphatic pronoun, as, for instance, in *Sermo in Festis S. Marie*;[1] and, although the variant nom. sing. *sie* is regularly used only in the *Vespasian Psalter Gloss* (once in *Rushworth St. Matthew*),[2] such forms as *sy ea* in the E Preface (beside DF *seo*) and *si læfdi* in the *Northamptonshire Geld-Roll*[3] suggest that it may have been current in Peterborough usage as well. This theory explains better than that of derivation from stress-shifted *heo/hie* the coexistence of *sch-* and *h*-forms in the same text, as in *Sir Gawain* (*scho* and *ho*) and *William of Palerne* (*sche* and *he*). Its weakness lies in failing to explain why the [ʃ], regular in the pronoun, never occurs in the demonstrative, and why *s*-, or the more current *þ*-, never appears in the pronoun. Thus it implies that, even though not recorded until now, *scæ* must have been established as a pronoun before *þ*- was generalized to nominative masculine and feminine of the demonstrative. A third theory is now generally disregarded; this was that initial [ʃ] was generated in sandhi when [hj] or [ç] in the stress-shifted pronoun was preceded by a dental or alveolar, i.e. in such collocations as *wæs hjò/hjè*, *þæt hjò/hjè*.[4] Some proponents of derivation from *heo/hie* do, however, allow that influence from such contexts may have encouraged substitution of [ʃ] for [ç].[5]

The Final Continuation also continues the two developments of *þæt* (now usually spelt *ðat*) foreshadowed in the First: as emphatic demonstrative and as relative. The emphatic singular *ðat*, thus, *ðat mynstre* (i.e. Peterborough, mentioned in the preceding line) 1132/3, *þat ilc gær* 1135, *al ðat iren* 1137, *to ðat forewarde ðat . . .*, *ðat sahte ðat . . .* 1140, now has a

[1] e.g. EETS 152, 134/11, etc.

[2] Campbell, *Grammar*, 290–1.

[3] Robertson, *Charters*, 232.

[4] M. B. Ruud, 'A Conjecture concerning the Origin of Modern English *She*', *MLN* xxv (1920), 222–5, and '"She" once more', *RES* ii (1926), 201–4; H. Lindkvist, 'On the Origin and History of the English Pronoun *she*', *Anglia*, xlv (1921), 1–50.

[5] e.g. Vachek, loc. cit.

corresponding emphatic plural *þa*, thus, *þa xix wintre wile Stephne was king* 1137; but *þa*, unlike *ðat* in this text, can also be used with animate nouns, thus, *þa rice men þe . . ., þa oþre* 1135, *þa men þe hi wenden ðat . . .* 1137: a development natural enough, as it was only in stress that [þa:] was not reduced to [þə]. The relative use of *ðat* is now more systematic than in the First Continuation, with *ðat* used with any inanimate antecedent, without regard to number, thus, *al þe god ðat þarinne was, alle þe wunder ne alle þe pines ðat hi diden* 1137, etc., and *þe* similarly with an animate, thus, *Willelm Malduit, þe heold . . .* 1137, *þa rice men þe wæron swikes* 1135, etc., the only exception being one inanimate plural *þe*, *þe landes þe lien to þe circewican* 1137.

The indefinite article as we know it is not yet developed, thus, *micel þing* 1135, *plantede winiærd, wæs god munec 7 god man, was hali martyr* 1137, *mid ormete færd* 1138, *God wimman scæ wæs* 1140, *held þære micel curt, cusen oþer, god clerc 7 god man, mid micel processiun* 1154, etc. But *an* is being more freely used than in earlier texts, and in such ways as to show how, by first replacing singular *sum* (common in the copied annals, this survives here only in the set phrase *sum wile*) in such phrases as *iaf ðat abbotrice an prior* 1132 (compare *an frencisce abbot, an cyrceweard* 1070, etc.), and then spreading to other contexts, thus, *in an cęste, diden an scærp iren* 1137, and, especially, *was an yuel man* 1140 (compare *at an market* 1124, *at anne market* 1125, *wæs an hæfod* 1127, and *com an mycel storm* 1070), it was already placed for evolving into the indefinite article.[1]

In vocabulary also the Final Continuation continues the development away from Old-English usage already seen in the First.[2] It shows few archaisms or obsolescent terms, but increasing use of Romance borrowings, which are adopted not only to express new concepts but also to replace native terms: *hired* is replaced by *curt*, *frið* by *pais*, *gersume* (itself a Norse loan) by *tresor*, *rihtwisnesse* by *iustise*.

[1] See P. Christophersen, *The Articles: A Study of their Theory and Use in English*, Copenhagen and Oxford, 1939, 98–107.

[2] See further Clark, 'Vocabulary'.

Norse influence is also becoming more evident, not surprisingly, as Peterborough lay in the Danelaw, only a few miles from Stamford, one of the Five Boroughs. The grammar-words *oc* and *fra*(*ward*) had already occurred in the First Continuation; they are now joined by *þoh*, *um*, *til*. Use of *til* as a conjunction, in *dide ælle in prisun til hi iafen up here castles* 1137, may be elliptical for *til þat*, from Norse *til þess*, possibly with some influence from native *to þam þæt*. Likewise, verbal constructions with adverbs/prepositions, such as *feren mid*, *gyfen up*, *leten ut*, *tacen to*, and perhaps *æten bi* and *begeten in*, are influenced by Norse usage. So, although few, the Norse loans here do show intimate penetration of English by Norse grammar, and in this they contrast with the Romance loans, which are limited here, as we have seen, to words associated with government or with the ruling classes.[1]

Syntax

Such drastic simplifications in accidence as are taking place here must be accompanied by some syntactic change; the functions which inflexions can no longer fulfil must be carried out by other means. Many indeed believe that changes in syntactic procedure preceded loss of inflexion and so caused, or allowed, the latter to take place.[2]

Declension, as we have seen, has been greatly simplified both in pronouns and, even more, in nouns: in pronouns

[1] Norse influence is sometimes alleged behind certain preterite plurals of strong classes IV and V: *drapen*, *forbaren*, *iafen*, *aiauen*, *stal*[*en*], *waren*, etc., and the pret. subj. *bare*, *ware*, beside *bræcon*, *undergæton*, *wæron* (the commoner form). Likelihood of this is, however, reduced by absence of such forms from the *Ormulum*, where Norse influence is usually stronger. No purely phonological explanation will fit, as the forms are confined to this morphological group. Most probably they are early examples of influence on the pret. pl. from the pret. s., later common in the East Midlands (see Öfverberg, *Inflections*, 13, and Menner, *Language*, xii. 239–40).

[2] For this view, see, for instance, E. Classen, 'A Theory of the Development of Language: II', *MLR* xiv (1919), esp. 308–10, B. Trnka, 'Analysis and Synthesis in English', *ES* x (1928), esp. 142 et seq., and M. Lehnert, 'The Interrelation between Form and Function in the Development of the English Language', *Zeitschrift für Anglistik und Amerikanistik*, iv (1957), 43–56; also T. F. Mustanoja, *A Middle English Syntax*, Part I, Helsinki, 1960, 67–8.

accusative and dative are merged; in nouns syncretism has gone so much further that by the Final Continuation the genitive is the only case consistently distinguished in form. How are these losses related to sentence-construction?

The indirect-object function of the dative is now expressed by the common-case form of nouns, or any current acc./dat. form of pronouns, normally without any preposition: thus, *heafde gifen þet abbotrice an frencisce abbot* 1070, *geaf . . . þone abbotrice an munec* 1114, *geaf . . . ðone biscoprice . . . þes cwenes canceler* 1123, *ealle hine iæfen micele gife, beteahte hine siððon þone ærcebiscop* 1125, *his dohter þet he æror hafde giuen þone Kasere, betahte hine his sune* 1126, *lett hire beweddan þes eorles sunu* 1127, *ealle hersumnesse swa swa hi scolden don here abbot* 1131, *iaf ðat abbotrice an prior* 1132, *Pais he makede men 7 dær* 1135, *him bræcon alle þe limes, alle þe pines ðat he diden wrecce men, fand þe munekes 7 te gestes al . . .* 1137, *iiuen heom up Wincestre, alle diden him manred* 1140. In most such sentences it is mainly sense which distinguishes between direct and indirect objects. Prepositional constructions do occur in a few instances, thus, *seide to þam kyng* 1123, *sei to him* 1135, beside *sægde him* 1070, *cuðe oþer secgen* 1123, *sæde heom* 1140, also *underþeden ðat mynstre to Clunie* 1132, but it could hardly be said that the lost inflexions are fully replaced in these functions, either by prepositions or by fixed word-order.

Likewise, adverbial phrases originally using dative (or instrumental) forms can still be used in plain common-case form, even in the Final Continuation, thus, *Ðat oþer dei, þat ilc gær, þat ilce dæi*; but prepositional constructions also occur fairly often, thus, *on Sancte Petres mæssedei*, and, especially, *On þis gære* 1135, *On þis gær* 1138, 1140, 1154, beside *Ðis gære* 1137 and *Dis gear* 1132.

With the genitive case, in spite of its retaining a distinctive form, loss of case-feeling is shown by elimination of the less usual uses. Whereas Old English, and this includes the copied annals, uses the genitive after verbs such as *wealdan, giernan*, etc., and after adjectives such as *eald, full, litel, micel, wær*, etc., the Peterborough Continuations normally use other constructions, thus, *wealde eall Engleland* 1123 (compare *þes landes weold* 1092, *þises landes weoldan* 1107), *iærnde . . . þone abbotrice* 1127 (compare *þære forewarde gyrnde* 1093), *thre niht ald* 1135, *ful of castles* 1137 (compare *full goldes* 1087), *wart it war* 1140 (compare *his gewær wurdon* 1095), *Micel hadde Henri king gadered gold 7 syluer* 1137, *suithe micel of his genge* 1138 (compare *hu mycel landes* 1085). With partitives, however, even though prepositional or appositional phrases were sometimes substituted for genitives already in Old English (thus, from the copied annals, *sume of ðam cnihtan, sume þa munecas* 1083), some inflected forms still occur here, thus, *litles hwat* 1070, *her nouþer* 1140, as well as the intensive *alre fyrst* 1135 (to survive until Chaucer's time and after in such set phrases as *alderbest*). In general, there now seems some reluctance to use genitive inflexions with inanimate nouns, so that, whereas the copied annals offer phrases such as *maniges landes hlaford* 1087, *þises landes earmða* 1104, the Peterborough Continuations have constructions such as *þa muneces of þe mynstre, underþeodnysse of ealle ða þing* 1123, *þe uurecce men of þe land, an of alle þe landes of þabbotrice* 1137. Adverbial genitives survive in *sume here þankes 7 sume here unþankes* 1140 (another phrase current at least until Chaucer's time), but in *on nihtes* 1127, *be nihtes 7 be dæies* 1137, are reinforced by prepositions (compare *on niht* 1140).

On the larger scale, sentence structure might *a priori* be expected to become less flexible: for, with subject-noun, object-noun, and indirect-object-noun (and, on occasion, adverbial noun as well) formally indistinguishable, they may have to take up, as they do in Modern English, set positions with relation to the verb.

This is beginning to be so. To a great extent, word-orders carrying a risk of bringing two or more nouns into ambiguous relation with the verb—and risks of ambiguity were increased by growing vagueness of number-indication in the verbal preterite—are avoided. In particular, inverted order, noun-object–verb–subject, is now rare, even though in some instances meaning can be clear in spite of inflexional inadequacies, thus, *þis, 7 te othre foruuardes þet hi makeden, suoren to halden þe king 7 te eorl* 1140. Indeed, subject–verb order may be preferred even when pronominal inflexion adequately indicates the relationship between the words, thus, not only *Pais he makede* 1135, *Mani þusen hi drapen* 1137, where **Pais makede . . .* or **Mani þusen drapen . . .* might have been felt to be ambiguous as sentence-openings, but also *God man he wes* 1135, *God wimman scæ wæs* 1140 (compare *Ful heui gær wæs hit* 1124).

One consequence of these limitations on word-order is that final placing of verbs in subordinate clauses, typical of Old English although by no means invariable there, is becoming rarer.[1] In the copied annals, subordinate clauses, and those introduced by *and* or *ac*, fairly often had verbs finally placed, thus, *þe æror þær þes landes weold* 1092, *And se cyng syððan þone castel æt Bures gewann* 1094, *forþi þe he . . . his had æt þam Papan underfeng* 1119, etc. In the Final Continuation such placing can still occur, thus, *for æuric rice man his castles makede, ðat ani god hefden* 1137, but, with loss of inflexion, it is ceasing to be viable, carrying too great a risk of ambiguity. How important subject–verb contact was becoming appears from *þe þe king adde beteht Euorwic* 1138: **þe þe king Euorwic adde betaht* (or, *betaht adde*) would have been ambiguous, and **þe adde betaht þe king Euorwic* (or, *Euorwic þe king*) would have meant the opposite; contrast the freedom of the copied annals to use word-order such as *And þone eorl Rotbert het se cyng to Windlesoran lædan* 1095. The place immediately before the verb now belongs to its subject and can be taken by another noun only when the meaning is unmistakable, either because of pronominal or verbal inflexions or because of the sense, thus, *7 na iustise ne dide* 1137, *þat he alle his castles sculde iiuen up, 7 hi nan helpe ne hæfden of þe king* 1140.

[1] For statistics, see B. Mitchell, 'Syntax and Word-Order in *The Peterborough Chronicle* 1122–1154', *Neuphilologische Mitteilungen*, lxv (1964), 135–7.

Nor is it only for nouns, with which it could often have been ambiguous, that pre-verbal placing of objects is now avoided. Pronoun-objects too, in spite of their distinctive inflexional forms, show a similar tendency to follow the verb rather than to precede it as they normally did in Old English, thus, *7 man ferode hine . . . 7 bebyrigde hine . . . 7 hine bebyrigde se biscop* 1123, *7 se king hine underfeng . . . beteahte hine siððon* 1125, *7 pineden him . . . 7 on Lang Fridæi him on rode hengen . . . 7 sythen byrieden him, . . . 7 te munekes him namen 7 bebyried him* 1137, *7 brohten hire into Oxenford 7 iauen hire þe burch* 1140, etc. Why this shift took place is not clear: analogy with the word-order now necessary with nouns may have been responsible, but, on the other hand, a fixed subject–verb–object word-order with noun-objects is not (as Modern French shows) incompatible with pre-verbal placing of pronoun-objects. At all events, this shift of pronoun-objects from pre-verbal to post-verbal position is one early-Middle-English change which cannot be attributed to French influence, for Old French, although allowing such placing of pronouns, did so only in exceptional instances.[1]

In all the matters so far discussed, syntax is at a transitional stage: direction of change is clear, but change is not yet complete. And in one respect word-order remains purely traditional. For, in main clauses introduced by an adverbial headword, the verb–subject inversion characteristic of Old English is maintained, even being more regular here than in some of Ælfric's writing.[2] Nor was there any reason why this should not be so: this order, unlike those being eliminated, carried no risk of bringing several nouns into ambiguous relationship with the verb.

The syntax of the Peterborough Continuations is, then, at a very revealing stage: before our eyes English is beginning to change from a synthetic language to an analytic one. And what can be perceived of the chronological relationships between the

[1] See L. Foulet, *Petite syntaxe de l'ancien français*, CFMA, 3rd edn., Paris, 1965, 131–4.

[2] See Mitchell, op. cit. 124–31.

various changes is significant. Contrary to the view that it was the previous existence of analytic machinery which brought about loss of inflexion, inflexional loss here seems to be more advanced than the procedures needed to replace it. Noun-inflexions are virtually reduced to the Modern-English level, whereas the analytic procedures destined to supply their place—fixed word-order, prepositional constructions—are only partially developed. It would be rash to deduce too much: this is only one text among many, and its evidence is not clear-cut. Such as it is, however, the evidence suggests that loss of the dative case, for instance, takes place rather in spite of a lack of substitute procedures than because its functions had already been usurped by them.

STYLE

As well as being an historical source and a philological hunting-ground, the *Peterborough Chronicle* is also the latest surviving example of non-homiletic English prose written before the fourteenth-century revival.

Basically, the style of these annals is still, in spite of the various influences now perceptible from other genres, that characteristic of the *Anglo-Saxon Chronicle* since its inception: simple in syntax, relying largely on co-ordination, and rarely using subordinate clauses other than temporal and relative ones, and those only sparingly; sparing too with comment and emotive expression. The impersonal manner and stereotyped language can be illustrated more or less at random, as, for instance, by the entry for 1099, only a degree less laconic than the lapidary entries from the early ninth century:

Her wæs se cyng Willelm to Midewintra on Normandig; 7 to Eastron hider to lande com, 7 to Pentecosten forman siðe his hired innan his niwan gebyttlan æt Westmynstre heold. 7 þær Rannulfe his capellane þet biscoprice on Dunholme geaf, þe æror ealle his gemot ofer eall Engleland draf 7 bewiste. 7 Sona þæræfter ofer sæ for 7 þone eorl Elias of þære Manige adraf, 7 hy syððan on his geweald gesætte; 7 swa to Sancte Michaeles mæssan eft hider to lande com.

Note the impersonal presentation of Rannulf Flambard here, in contrast with the frank condemnation of him by most contemporary annalists.[1] And an impersonal simplicity to some extent persists even in the Final Continuation, in spite of the generally very different presentation there, thus, in 1140, '7 Hi wurthen war widuten 7 folecheden heom, 7 namen Rodbert eorl of Gloucestre 7 ledden him to Rouecestre 7 diden him þare in prisun'.

The Copied Annals

The impersonal manner, already often abandoned at earlier periods, is, however, far from universal here. In the copied annals some passages indeed rise to the grand style, displaying both rhetorical skill and emotional power, the most striking of these being the account of the Conqueror's death by one who had 'looked on him and once dwelt at his court'.[2] Such passages, far removed though they are from the classic impersonality which accorded Alfred the Great's death only a terse factual notice, are not, of course, unprecedented in the *Chronicle*: previous entries included rhetorical set pieces such as those in praise of Edgar at 959 DE and 975 D (both usually attributed to Archbishop Wulfstan)[3] and that lamenting Edward's murder at 979 DE; and the whole record of Æthelred's reign is personal and outspoken.

In this entry for 1087 the dominant tone becomes homiletic, so much so that, had some of the passages survived only as

[1] See 1099/4 n.; compare, for instance, Florence, ii. 46, *s.a.* 1100: 'Rannulfus *contra jus ecclesiasticum, et sui gradus ordinem*, presbyter enim erat, ad censum primitus abbatias, dehinc episcopatus . . . accepit a rege, et inde singulis annis, summam pecuniam non modicam persolvit illi . . . . Pauperiores autem *gravi injustoque tributo* incessanter oppressit . . . etc.'

[2] The theme inspired more than one writer of the time: for some parallel passages from Latin chroniclers, see 1087/50 n. and 144 n.

[3] See K. Jost, 'Wulfstan und die angelsächsische Chronik', *Anglia*, xlvii (1923), 105–25; also D. Whitelock, ed., *Sermo Lupi ad Anglos*, 1939, 14, and D. Bethurum, *The Homilies of Wulfstan*, Oxford, 1957, 47.

fragments, they would scarcely have been identifiable as parts of the *Chronicle.* At once, before any mention of the Conqueror, the pulpit affinities are manifest:

> Eala, hu earmlice 7 hu reowlic tid wæs ða, ða ða wreccæ men lægen fordrifene fullneah to deaðe 7 syððan com se scearpa hungor 7 adyde hi mid ealle! Hwam ne mæg earmian swylcere tide? Oððe hwa is swa heardheort þet ne mæg wepan swylces ungelimpes? . . . Eala, reowlic 7 wependlic tid wæs þæs geares, þe swa manig ungelimp wæs forðbringende!

That style, with exclamations and rhetorical questions implying appeal to a listening audience, is far from annalistic. Nor is the emotive vocabulary—*earmlice*, *reowlic*, *wreccæ*, *scearpa*, *earmian*, *heardheort*, *wepan*, *wependlic*, and especially the repeated *Eala!*[1]—typical of the *Chronicle*, and certainly not in such concentration as here. Such appeal to emotion belongs not to chronicling but to the preacher's art.[2]

Even more than the style, the moral tone implies the pulpit:

> Ac swylce þing gewurðaþ for folces synna, þet hi nellað lufian God 7 rihtwisnesse. Swa swa hit wæs þa on ðam dagum þet litel rihtwisnesse wæs on þisum lande mid ænige menn . . .

The theme is familiar from such pieces as Wulfstan's *Sermo ad Anglos*, with its insistence that misfortune is punishment for sin (compare the more worldly view of 1011 CDE that 'Ealle þas ungesælða us gelumpon þuruh unrædas, þæt man nolde him a timan gafol beodon'). With the mention of the Conqueror's death, this theme of retribution is further developed and modulated into the mutability of all earthly success:

[1] Found nowhere else in the *Chronicle*; but compare *wala þet hi* . . . 999 CE (D, *wala wa* . . .).

[2] For the role of emotion in medieval preaching, see C. S. Baldwin, *Medieval Rhetoric and Poetic*, Gloucester (Mass.), repr. 1959, 70, 230–1, and E. Auerbach, *Literary Language and its Public in Late Latin Antiquity and in the Middle Ages*, 1965, 27 et seq., 53. In *De Doctrina Christiana* Book IV Augustine says that what distinguishes the high style, whose function is to 'move' the audience, is not ornament but vehemence; and in the passages he quotes to illustrate it rhetorical questions are frequent (trans. D. W. Robertson, New York, 1958, 150–2; compare *Rhetorica ad Herennium*, ed. and trans. H. Caplan, Loeb, 1954, 254–6).

Reowlic þing he dyde, 7 reowlicor him gelamp. Hu reowlicor? Him geyfelade 7 þet him stranglice eglade. Hwæt mæg ic teollan? Se scearpa deað þe ne forlet ne rice menn ne heane, seo hine genam. . . . Eala, hu leas 7 hu unwrest is þysses middaneardes wela! Se þe wæs ærur rice cyng 7 maniges landes hlaford, he næfde þa ealles landes buton seofon fotmæl; 7 se þe wæs hwilon gescrid mid golde 7 mid gimmum, he læg þa oferwrogen mid moldan.

Both in vocabulary—*reowlic*, *stranglice*, *se scearpa deað*, *Eala!*—and in use of exclamations and rhetorical questions this echoes the earlier passage. And here other figures of speech, *repetitio*, *adnominatio*, *similiter cadens*, also come into play, and antitheses especially (note the opposite turn from those of 979 DE on the murdered Edward, 'Ða þe nolden ær to his libbendum lichaman onbugan, þa nu eadmodlice on cneowum abugað to his dædum banum'). In the summing-up the moral intent is emphasized:

Ðas þing we habbað be him gewritene, ægðer ge gode ge yfele, þet þa godan men niman æfter þeora godnesse 7 forfleon mid ealle yfelnesse 7 gan on ðone weg þe us lett to heofonan rice.

Such an injunction, although not unknown in Christian historiography—compare, for instance, the Praefatio to Bede's *History*:

Siue enim historia de bonis bona referat, ad imitandum bonum auditor sollicitus instigatur; seu mala commemoret de prauis, nihilominus religiosus ac pius audito siue lector deuitando quod noxium est ac peruersum, ipse sollertius ad exsequenda ea, quae bona ac Deo digna esse cognouerit, accenditur[1]—

particularly recalls the perorations of many Anglo-Saxon homilies, as, for instance, that of Ælfric's sermon on the Nativity of St. Paul:

Is nu forði munuchades mannum mid micelre gecnyrdnysse to forbugenne ðas yfelan gebysnunga, and geefenlæcan þam apostolum, þæt hi, mid him and mid Gode, þæt ece lif habban moton;[2]

[1] Ed. Plummer, i. 5; compare also Hen. Hunt. 2, and Ordericus, i. 1.

[2] B. Thorpe, ed., *The Homilies of the Anglo-Saxon Church: The First Part Containing the Sermones Catholici or Homilies of Ælfric*, 2 vols., 1844–6, i. 400; compare i. 28, ii. 282, 332, 380.

and, from Wulfstan:

> On Godes naman ic bidde þæt cristenra manna gehwylc hine sylfne georne beþence 7 geornlice to Gode gebuge 7 from ælcum hæþenscipe 7 synnum gecyrre 7 geearnige þæt he gemanan habban mote on heofona rice mid þam þe leofað 7 rixað a butan ende.[1]

Nowhere else in the *Chronicle* is there a homiletic note as powerful or as sustained as in 1087; but neighbouring annals seem to offer faint echoes of it. Thus, in 1083 the Glastonbury scandal is presented in similar emotive language, with antitheses ('dyde heom yfele 7 beheot heom wyrs'; 'to Gode . . . æt mannum') and a rhetorical question:

> Ac reowlic þing þær gelamp on dæg, . . . 7 þa wreccan munecas lagon onbuton þam weofode—7 sume crupon under—7 gyrne cleopedon to Gode, his miltse biddende ða þa hi ne mihton nane miltse æt mannum begytan. Hwæt magon we secgean? . . .

Less impassioned yet also somewhat outside the classic *Chronicle* tradition of impersonality are the comment in 1085 on the Domesday Survey, 'hit is sceame to tellanne, ac hit ne þuhte him nan sceame to donne', and in 1086 the prayers for Edgar the Atheling, 'ac se ælmihtiga God him gife wurðscipe on þam toweardan!' and for the whole country, 'Gebete hit God elmihtiga þonne his willa sy!' The long entry for 1088, although mainly factual, offers a Biblical allusion, '7 he þohte to donne be him eallswa Iudas Scarioth dyde be ure Drihtene'; and in 1089 the obituary of Lanfranc, brief as it is, catches something of the 1087 tone: 'se arwurða muneca feder 7 frouer, Landfranc arcebiscop, gewat of þissum life, ac we hopiað þet he ferde to þet heofanlice rice.' But these are only faint touches and how far the work of the 1087 annalist can be traced must remain uncertain. In 1090 the phrase 'eallswa wæ ær abufan sædan' seems to imply that the author is still that of 1088; but the faint ironies here, 'þurh his geapscipe oððe þurh gærsuma' and 'for his lufan oððe for his mycele gersuma'[2] suggest a more detached

[1] *Homilies of Wulfstan*, 133, also 156, 206, 210, 220.

[2] Note how William of Malmesbury differs here, see Commentary *ad loc.*

observer than in 1083 or 1087. Nor does the homiletic tone reappear, except for the brief moral drawn from Rufus's death:

And, þeah þe ic hit læng ylde,[1] eall þet þe Gode wæs lað 7 rihtfulle mannan, eall þet wæs gewunelic on þisan lande on his tyman; 7 forþi he wæs forneah ealre his leode lað 7 Gode andsæte, swa swa his ænde ætywde, forþan þe he on middewardan his unrihte buten behreowsunge 7 ælcere dædbote gewat;

but here, in spite of the opportunity offered, the obituary notice never approaches the power or eloquence of that of the Conqueror.

The First Continuation

With the First Peterborough Continuation we come to work by one of the early masters of English prose, who deserves to be ranked at least as high as the chronicler of Æthelred's reign, neither of them being any the less individual for being an anonymous annalist.

This continuator's great gift is for story-telling. His account of the 1123 archiepiscopal election admirably conveys the movements of the dispute between Roger of Salisbury and his colleagues on the one hand and the monks of Canterbury on the other, with the Legate, Henry of Angély, intervening on the monastic side. His masterpiece is the later account of this Henry's unjust preferment to Peterborough itself.[2] Superficially simple and repetitive, relying on the conjunctions *and* and *oc*, this narrative proves on closer reading to be constructed with some subtlety:

He wæs on his clærchade biscop on Scesscuns; *siððan warð he* munec on Clunni, *7 siððon* prior on þone seolue minstre; *7 siððon he wærð* prior on Sauenni. Þaræftor . . . þa geaf se eorl him þone abbotrice of Sancte Iohannis minstre of Angeli. *Siððon*, þurh his micele wrences, *ða beiæt he* þone ærcebiscoprice of Besencun, 7 hæfde hit þa on hande þre dagas; þa forlæs he þet mid rihte, forþi þet he hit hæfde æror beieten mid unrihte. *Siððon þa beiet he* þone

[1] Compare 1085/31, 'þeah ic hit lengre telle'.

[2] See *Essays in Criticism*, xviii (1968), 376–81.

biscoprice of Seintes, þet wæs fif mile fram his abbotrice; þet he hæfde fulneah seoueniht on hande . . .

If the diction is monotonous, so was Henry's pursuit of preferment: the recurrent *siððan* (also *siððan warð he*, *siððon þa beiet he*) shows most apt use of *repetitio*. And the variation between '7 hæfde hit þa on hande þre dagas' and 'þet he hæfde fulneah seoueniht on hande', with the ironical *fulneah* and the emphatic word-order of the second version, makes an economical comment. Monotony is, moreover, relieved by the antithetic interposition, 'þa forlæs he þet mid rihte, forþi þet he hit hæfde æror beieten mid unrihte'.

How well this writer grasped the need for appropriate variation is made clear by his use of a different sort of accumulation, asyndeton, for expressing the swift and joyful action by which the monks of Angély at last expelled their abbot:

7 Ðes oðer dæies æfter Sancte Iohannis messedæi, cusen þa muneces abbot of hemself and brohten him into cyrce mid processionem; sungen 'Te Deum Laudamus', ringden þa belle, setten him on þes abbotes settle, diden him ealle hersumnesse swa swa hi scolden don here abbot.

This is capped by the comment: 'Hi scolden nedes: on fif 7 twenti wintre ne biden hi næfre an god dæi.'

The cumulative syntax typical of the *Chronicle* is further exploited in the indirect speeches given to Abbot Henry. He first appears piling up specious arguments in his own favour, the accumulation being pointed by the repeated *7 ðurh*:

Oc se ilce Heanri dide þone king to understandene þet he hæfde læten his abbotrice for þet micele unsibbe þet wæs on þet land, 7 þet he dide *ðurh* þes Papes ræd 7 leue of Rome *7 ðurh* þes abbotes of Clunni *7 þurh* þæt he wæs legat of ðone Romescott.

Later, after crisp summing-up of his hidden motives, 'þa beþohte he him þet gif he mihte ben rotfest on Engleland þet he mihte habben eal his wille', similar syntax shows him slyly piling on the self-pity and then slipping in his demand:

Besohte þa ðone kyng 7 sæide him þet he wæs eald man 7 forbroken man, 7 þet he ne mihte ðolen þa micele unrihte 7 þa micele unsibbe ða wæron on here land, 7 iærnde þa þurh him 7 ðurh ealle his freond namcuðlice þone abbotrice of Burhc.

Again, there is variation: not all the *oratio obliqua* has this structure. Indeed, even with indirect speech, the annalist at times almost creates a sense of dialogue. Thus, in the interchange between Henry and the abbot of Cluny—

Sæide se abbot of Clunni þet hi heafdon forloron Sancte Iohannis mynstre þurh him 7 þurh his mycele sotscipe. Þa ne cuþe he him na betre bote bute behet hem 7 aðes swor on halidom þet, gif he moste Engleland secen, þet he scolde begeton hem ðone mynstre of Burch, swa þet he scolde setten þær prior of Clunni 7 circeweard 7 hordere 7 reilþein, 7 ealle þa ðing þa wæron wiðinne mynstre 7 wiðuten, eall he scolde hem betæcen—

the reply in a complex syntax broken by conditional and final clauses and ending with an emphatic inversion contrasts with the preceding forthright charge; it suggests the flustered protestation of a cornered man. And in 1123 this writer offers something unusual in the *Chronicle*,[1] a scrap of *oratio recta*:

Þa aseh dune se biscop of Lincolne 7 seide to þam kyng, 'Laferd kyng, ic swelte.'

Sometimes, too, this annalist allows himself a novelist's insight into mind and motives, most strikingly in the metaphor of Abbot Henry's 'bag of shabby tricks':

Her him trucode ealle his mycele cræftes: nu him behofed þet he crape in his mycele codde in ælc hyrne, gif þær wære hure an unwreste wrenc þet he mihte get beswicen anes Crist 7 eall Cristene folc.

Likewise, although less forcefully, the entry for 1123 first comments on the king's motives—'ac se kyng hit nolde undon, for þes biscopes luuen of Særesbyrig'—and then analyses with traditional cynicism those of the Roman curia:

Þet wæs forþan þet hit wæs don ðone Pape to understanden þet he hæfde underfangen ðone ærcebiscoprice togeanes þa muneces of þe mynstre 7 togeanes rihte. Ac þet ofercom Rome þet ofercumeð eall weoruld—þet is gold 7 seolure; 7 se Pape sweðolode . . .

[1] See, however, Preface DE, 656 E, 755 A and 995 F.

Sometimes judgement is more outspoken, and, when it is, is often accompanied by exclamatory prayers for deliverance from oppression. Thus, the indignation against the pluralist Henry of Angély is sometimes expressed with a prayer, 'God ælmihtig haue his milce ofer þet wrecce stede!', sometimes with a bitter pun, '7 na god þær ne dide ne na god ðær ne læuede'. But the chronicler's indignation and compassion extend beyond his own abbey, embracing the sufferers from the 1131 famine, those deluded by the false Crusade preached in 1128, and all victims of rapacity, as in 1124:

> Ure Laford God ælmihtig, þa eall digelnesse seð 7 wat—he seoð þet man læt þet ærme folc mid ealle unrihte: ærost man hem beræfoð her eahte and siþðon man hem ofslæð. Ful heui gær wæs hit: se man þe æni god heafde—him me hit beræfode mid strange geoldes 7 mid strange motes; þe nan ne heafde stærf of hungor.[1]

Championing the victims, he therefore approves the mutilation of the counterfeiters: '7 þet wæs eall mid micel rihte, forði þet hi hafden fordon eall þet land mid here micele fals þet hi ealle abohton.' Neither moralizing nor prayer, however, ever comes to dominate these annals; the homiletic touches remain touches, never ousting narrative but simply putting events into their medieval Christian setting.

How much apart from the First Continuation this writer may have contributed to the *Chronicle* we cannot say. Some of the Interpolations seem to reflect his manner, especially that at 1070, with its lively account of Hereward's raid on Peterborough. Technique here resembles that of the First Continuation. To express swift, swarming movement the writer uses asyndeton:

> . . . geodon into þe mynstre; clumben upp to þe halge rode, namen þa þe kynehelm of ure Drihtnes heafod, eall of smeate golde, namen þa þet fotspure . . ., þet wæs eall of read golde; clumben upp to þe stepel, brohton dune þet hæcce þe þær wæs behid, hit wæs eall of gold 7 of seolfre.

[1] See also Commentary *ad loc.*

The interwoven *repetitio* 'clumben . . . namen . . . namen . . . clumben' is partially echoed in the following lines by the *repetitio* 'Hi namen . . . 7 hi namen . . . Hi namen'; and the *conversio* and *traductio* 'golde . . . golde . . . of gold 7 of seolfre' is both carried on there and varied by *adnominatio*, 'gildene . . . seolferne', the stress on these words emphasizing the magnitude of the robbery:

Hi namen þære twa gildene scrines 7 ix seolferne, 7 hi namen fiftene mycele roden, ge of golde ge of seolfre. Hi namen þære swa mycele gold 7 seolfre, 7 swa manega gersumas . . . swa nan man ne mæi oðer tællen.[1]

Then comes a terse, ironical comment, 'sægdon þet hi hit dyden for ðes mynstres holdscipe'. What else in the Interpolations may be due to the same hand can only be guesswork: the earlier ones are mostly too closely related to (spurious) charters to allow many personal turns of phrase. Even so, the entries for 656 and, to a lesser extent, 675, show some imagination in the way charters and Bulls are combined to make the semblance of a dramatic scene with *oratio recta*: 'Ða cwæð sco kyning: "Hit is litel, þeos gife; ac ic wille þet hi hit hælden . . ." '[2] The Interpolation at 963 offers the descriptive phrase 'calde weallas 7 wilde wuda' and that at 1013 the minor *repetitio*, 'ærm stede, ærm abbot, 7 ærme muneces';[3] 1066 has the antithesis, 'þa wearð Gildene Burh to wrecce Burh'.[4] In 1066 and 1070, however, the exclamations, 'Syððon comen ealle dræuednysse 7 ealle ifele to þone mynstre—God hit gemyltse!' and 'Ðus wæs se mynstre of Burch forbærnd 7 forhærgod, ælmihtig God hit gemiltse þurh his mycele mildhertnesse!', although very like the Continuator's prayers, hardly seem appropriate for work composed fifty years after the event.

[1] The corresponding passage in Hugo, 78, although not otherwise closely similar in sentence structure, also uses *repetitio* based on *Acceperunt*.

[2] The corresponding passages in Hugo, 9 et seq., although they do show some *oratio recta*, keep in general more closely to the documents.

[3] Neither phrase is paralleled in Hugo.

[4] This time compare Hugo, 80 (in a slightly different context): 'Tunc illa que uocabatur ciuitas aurea facta est pauperima.'

The Final Continuation

The Final Continuation too shows a fair command of language: the fame of the entry for 1137 is not due solely to its subject-matter. Style is emphatic. Inversion is often used to underline a point: 'God man he wes'; 'Pais he makede'; 'Alle he wæron forsworen'; 'Mani þusen hi drapen'; 'God wimman scæ wæs'; and, with antithesis also, '*Micel* hadde Henri king gadered gold 7 syluer, *na god* ne dide me for his saule tharof'. *Repetitio* is also used:

Me henged up bi the fet 7 smoked heom mid ful smoke. Me henged bi the þumbes other bi the hefed 7 hengen bryniges on her fet. Me dide cnotted strenges abuton here hæued 7 uurythen it ðat it gæde to þe hærnes.

The near-parallel structure of the sentences, with the last slightly varied and then weighted by an adverbial clause in place of the earlier short phrases, shows conscious control; and the repetitive syntax and rhythm, reinforced by slight alliteration (*h. f. sm. f. sm. h. h. h. f. h. h.*), aptly represents the relentlessness of the oppressors. Other figures of repetition, such as *traductio* and *adnominatio*, are also used to drive points home:

. . . for æuric rice man his *castles* makede 7 agænes him heolden; 7 *fylden* þe land ful of *castles*. Hi suencten suyðe þe uurecce men of þe land mid *castel*weorces; þa þe *castles* uuaren maked, þa *fylden* hi . . .

. . . 7 *pined* heom efter gold 7 syluer untellendlice *pining*; for ne uuæren næure nan martyrs swa *pined* alse hi wæron.

. . . *ne forbaren hi* nouther *circe* ne *cyrce*iærd, oc namen al þe god ðat þarinne was 7 brenden sythen þe *cyrce* 7 al tegædere. *Ne hi ne forbaren* biscopes land . . .

. . . 7 *pineden* him alle þe ilce *pining* ðat ure Drihten was *pined*.

And, on a larger scale, the phrase *wrecce men* occurs four times in less than thirty lines.[1] All these repetitions hammer home the cruelty and oppression and represent its inexorable continuance. Similar emphasis is achieved by comparisons, each

[1] 1137/15, 35, 38, 42.

time with extreme cases—'ne uuæren næure nan martyrs swa pined alse hi wæron'; 'ne næure hethen men werse ne diden þan hi diden'—and by *occultatio*—'I ne can ne I ne mai tellen alle þe wunder . . .', 'Suilc, 7 mare þanne we cunnen sæin . . .'

This writer's most striking figure comes in 1135. First, he memorably (even though quite inaccurately) makes the eclipse attending Henry I's final departure from England into a portent of his immediate death:

> Wurþen men suiðe ofuundred 7 ofdred, 7 sæden ðat micel þing sculde cumen herefter: sua dide, for þat ilc gær warth þe king ded . . .

Then, with a picturesque metaphor, he links this with the succeeding horrors of the Anarchy:

> þa þestrede þe dæi ouer al landes . . . þa þestreden sona þas landes, for æuric man sone ræuede oþer þe mihte.[1]

Although valid only imaginatively, the image is poetic and forceful.

Even minor rhetorical devices have their role. Word-patterns, especially doublets and triplets, often near-synonyms, are used for extra weight and emphasis, thus, '*of*uundred 7 *of*dred', 'todeld it 7 scatered', 'manred maked 7 athes suoren', 'he wæron *for*sw*oren* 7 here treothes *for*l*oren*', 'deoules 7 yuele men', 'þa mannes throte 7 his hals', '*alle þe* wunder ne *alle þe* pines', 'man in tune sittende ne land tiled', 'mun*ekes* 7 cler*ekes*', 'biscopes 7 lered men', '*god m*unec 7 *god m*an', 'wunder*lice* 7 *m*anifæld*lice m*iracles', 'þe sunne 7 te dæi', 'in prisun 7 in feteres', 'ath*es* suor*en* 7 treuth*es* f*æ*st*on*', 'suor on halidom 7 gysles fand', 'lauerd 7 king', '*s*ib 7 *s*æhte', '*god* clerc 7 *god* man'; 'al unfrið 7 yfel 7 ræflac', 'milde man was 7 softe 7 god', 'nadr*es* 7 snak*es* 7 pad*es*', 'scort 7 nareu 7 undep', 'ne sitt*en* ne li*en* ne slep*en*', 'flesc 7 cæse 7 butere', 'biscop*es* land ne abbot*es* ne preost*es*', '*for*cursæd 7 *for*suo*ren* 7 *for*lo*ren*' (note the frequent grouping of words with the same inflectional

[1] See Commentary *ad loc.* This is the only figurative use of the verb *þestren* that I know. Hugo, 104, also has 'celi contenebrati sunt. . . . Tunc contenebrata est terra . . .'.

ending, with full rhyme, with alliteration, or with the same prefix).

Emphatic constructions and word-patterns are, however, markedly less common after the entry for 1137. To some extent this is offset by the greater use in 1140 of balance and antithesis, figures less common in the earlier entries. Here these figures grow naturally out of the material itself, the seesaw movement of the wars between Stephen and Matilda and between Stephen and the barons, thus: 'oc æfre þe mare he iaf heom, þe wærse hi wæron him', 'leten ut þe king of prisun for þe eorl 7 te eorl for þe king', 'sume he iaf up, 7 sume ne iaf he noht', 'sume helden mid te king, 7 sume mid þemperice', 'þa þe king was in prisun . . . þa þe king was ute', 'sume here þankes 7 sume here unþankes', 'he helde him for fader 7 he him for sune'; and, with the embellishment of alliteration, 'For þe king him sithen nam in Hamtun *þurhc wicci ræd* . . . 7 efsones he let him ut *þurhc wærse ræd*'. Use of word-patterns is deliberate and apt.

Yet, in spite of these evidences of continuing stylistic control, the entries from 1138 on fall below the literary level of the earlier ones: the imperfect grasp of the material evident throughout the entry for 1140 seems accompanied by loss of stylistic skill. Indeed, by contrast with the highly-wrought account of the Anarchy the plainer prose of the entries for 1138, 1140, and 1154 seems at first sight almost to suggest different authorship.

On closer scrutiny, however, the whole Final Continuation seems not only to be the work of one author but also to have been consciously composed as a unit. Thus, the two Peterborough passages here offer a neat distinction between Abbot Martin, who 'wæs god *munec* 7 god man, 7 forþi him luueden *God* 7 gode men', and Abbot William, who was 'god *clerc* 7 god man 7 wæl luued *of þe king* 7 of alle gode men'. Similarly, the characterization of Henry II is linked with those of his grandfather Henry I and of his immediate predecessor Stephen. The future Henry II, it is said, was received at Winchester, and then

hit ward sone suythe god *pais* sua ðat neure was herere . . . 7 Te eorl ferde ouer sæ; 7 al folc him luuede, for he *dide god iustise 7 makede pais*. . . . þa was þe eorl beionde sæ; 7 *ne durste nan man don oþer bute god* for *þe micel eie* of him.

It cannot be coincidental that this is woven from phrases already used about the other two kings and only about them. Henry II is contrasted with Stephen, who 'milde man was 7 softe 7 god, *7 na iustise ne dide*', and likened to Henry I, of whom the annalist had said:

God man he wes 7 *micel æie* wes of him: *durste nan man* mis*don* wið oðer on his time. *Pais he makede* men 7 dær. Wua sua bare his byrthen gold 7 sylure, *durste nan man* sei to him naht *bute god*.

The strong verbal echoes embody the hope that the second Henry will bring back the good times known under the first; indeed, the last passage loses all force unless it is read as an allusion to the previous two. So, for all his chronological ineptitude, the Final Continuator shows some architectonic sense; and perhaps it would be fairer to regard all his work, not as a set of incompetent annals, but as an essay in panegyric by implication and contrast.

NOTE ON THE TEXT

THE aim has been to produce a reliable text in a readable form. Modern punctuation has been used throughout and all contractions, except the note for *and*, have been expanded, with the usual italicization of the letters supplied. When a new sentence begins with 7, the initial of the following word has been capitalized; this seemed defensible since it is occasionally done in the manuscript itself. Emendations have been made wherever this seemed advisable, and these and conjectural fillings of lacunae are enclosed in square brackets. Words and letters which in the manuscript are inserted above the line or in the margin are enclosed between raised vertical strokes (ˡ. . .ˡ); to avoid confusion only double inverted commas are used as quotation marks. Erasures etc. are not normally noted, unless they seem to have some bearing on the reading.

THE PETERBOROUGH CHRONICLE

1070–1154

f. 58ᵛ Mill*esi*mo lxx. Her se eorl Walþeof griðede wið þone cyng. 7 **Þ**æs on lengten se cyng let hergian ealle þa mynstra þe on Englalande wæron. **Þ**a on þa*m* ilcan geare com Swegn cyng of Denmarcan into Humbran; 7 þ*et* landfolc comen him ongean
5 7 griðedon wið hine, wændon þ*et* he sceolde þet land ofergan. **Þ**a comen into Elig Cristien þa densce b*iscop* 7 Osbearn eorl 7 þa densca huscarles mid heo*m*; 7 þet englisce folc of eall þa feonlandes comen to heo*m*, wendon þ*et* hi sceoldon winnon eall þ*et* land. **Þ**a herdon þa munecas of Burh sægen þ*et* heora
10 agene menn wolden hergon þone mynstre, þ*et* wæs Hereward 7 his genge. **Þ***et* wæs forðan þet hi herdon sæcgen þet se cyng
f. 59ʳ heafde gifen þ*et* abbotrice an frencisce / abbot, Turolde wæs gehaten, 7 þ*et* he wæs swiðe styrne man 7 wæs cumen þa into Stanforde mid ealle hise frencisce menn. **Þ**a wæs þære an cyrce-
15 weard, Yware wæs gehaten; na*m* þa be nihte eall þet he mihte— þet wæron Cr*ist*es bec 7 mæssahakeles 7 cantelcapas 7 reafes 7 swilce litles hwat, swa hwat swa he mihte—7 ferde sona ær dæg to þon*e* abbot Turolde, 7 sægde hi*m* þ*et* he sohte his griðe, 7 cydde hi*m* hu þa utlages sceolden cumen to Burh. **Þ***et* he
20 dyde eall be þære mu˥n˥ece ræde. **Þ**a sona on morgen comen ealle þa utlaga mid fela scipe 7 woldon into þ*am* mynstre; 7 þa munecas wiðstoden þ*et* hi na mihton in cumen. **Þ**a lægdon hi fyr on 7 forbærndon ealle þa munece huses 7 eall þa tun buton ane huse. **Þ**a comen hi þurh fyre in æt Bolhiðe geate,
25 7 þa munecas comen heo*m* togeanes, beaden heo*m* grið. Ac hi na rohten na þing—geodon into þe mynstre; clumben upp to þe halge rode, namen þa þe kynehelm of ure Drih˥t˥nes heafod eall of smeate golde, namen þa þet fotspure þe wæs under-næðen his fote, þ*et* wæs eall of read golde; clumben upp to þe
30 stepel, brohton dune þ*et* hæcce þe þær wæs behid, hit wæs

4 *MS.* onf, *with* n *blurred out.* 6 *MS.* xpistien

eall of ˡgoldˡ 7 of seolfre. Hi namen þære twa gildene scrines 7 ix seolferne, 7 hi namen fiftene mycele roden, ge of golde ge of seolfre. Hi namen þære swa mycele gold 7 seolfre, 7 swa manega gersumas on sceat 7 on scrud 7 on bokes swa nan man ne mæi oðer tællen—sægdon þ*et* hi hit dyden for ðes mynstres 35 holdscipe. Syððon geden heo*m* to scipe, ferden heom to Elig; betæhtan þær þa ealla þa gærsume þa denescæ menn—wændon þ*et* hi sceoldon ofercumen þa frencisca men. Þa todrefodon ealle þa munekes. Beleaf þær nan butan an munec, he wæs gehaten Leofwine lange, he læi seoc in þa secræman[ne] / in. f. 59ᵛ Ða co*m* Turold abbot 7 æhte siþe twenti frencisce men mid 41 hi*m* 7 ealle full wepnode. Þa he þider co*m*, þa fand he forbærnd wiðinnan 7 wiðutan eall butan þa cyrece ane. Þa wæron þa utlagas ealle on flote, wistan þ*et* he scolde þider cumen. Þis wæs don þæs dæges iiii° No*narum* Iunii. Þa twegen kyngas, 45 Will*el*m 7 Swægn, wurðon sæhtlod. Þa ferdon þa dænesca menn ut of Elig mid ealle þa forenspræcena gærsume 7 læddon mid heo*m*. Þa hi comen on middewarde þe sæ, þa co*m* an mycel storm 7 todræfede ealle þa scipe þær þa gersumes wæron inne: sume ferdon to Norwæge, sume to Yrlande, sume 50 to Dænmarce—7 eall þ*et* þider co*m*, þ*et* wæs þone hæcce 7 sume scrine 7 sume roden 7 fela of þa oðre gærsume. 7 Brohten hit to an cynges tun, hatte, 7 dyden ˡhitˡ eall þa in þone cyrce. Ða syððon, þurh heora gemelest 7 þurh heora druˡnˡcenhed, on an niht forbærnde þa cyrce 7 eall þet þærinnæ 55 wæs. Ðus wæs se mynstre of Burch forbærnd 7 forhærgod—ælmihtig God hit gemiltse þurh his mycele mildhertnesse! And þus se abbot Turolde ˡco*m*ˡ to Burh. 7 Þa munecas comen þa ongean 7 dydan Cr*ist*es þeudom in þære cyrce, þ*et* ær hæfde standen fulle seofeniht forutan ælces cynnes riht. Ða herde 60 Ægelric biscop þet gesecgon, þa amansumede he ealle þa men þa þ*et* yfel dæde hæfden don. Ða wæs mycel hunger þæs geares. 7 Þa þæs sumeres co*m* þet lið norðan of Humbran into Tæmese, 7 lagon þær twa niht, 7 heoldan syððon to

36–39 *For the MS. punctuation, see Notes.* 40 *MS.* secræman / in.
53 *After* tun, *an apparent erasure* (*¾ in. long, enough for about 10 letters*).

65 Dænmercan. And Baldewine eorl forðferde, 7 his sunu Arnulf feng to rice; 7 Will*el*m eorl sceolde ben his geheald 7 Franca cyng eac. 7 Co*m* þa Rodbriht eorl 7 ofsloh his mæg Arnulf 7 þone eorl, 7 þone cyng aflymda and his menn ofsloh fela
69 þusenda.

f. 60r Mill*esi*mo lxxi. Her Ædwine eorl 7 Morkere eorl / ut hlupon 7 mislice ferdon on wudu 7 on felda. Þa gewende Morkere eorl to Elig on scipe. And Eadwine eorl wearð ofslagen arhlice fra*m* his agenu*m* mannu*m*. 7 Co*m* se b*iscop* Egelwine, 7
5 Siward Bearn, 7 fela hund manna mid heo*m* into Elig. 7 Þa þe se cyng Will*el*m þ*et* geaxode, þa bead he ut scipfyrde 7 landfyrde 7 þet land abutan sæt 7 brycge gewrohte 7 inn for, 7 seo scipfyrde on þa sæhealfe. 7 Þa utlagan þa ealle on hand eodan: þ*et* wæs Egelwine b*iscop* 7 Morkere eorl 7 ealle þa þe
10 mid heo*m* wæron, buton Herewarde ane 7 ealle þa þe mid hi*m* woldon, 7 he hi ahtlice ut lædde. 7 Se cyng gena*m* scipa 7 wæpna 7 sceattas manega; 7 þa men he ateah swa swa he wolde. 7 Þone b*iscop* Egelwine he sende to Abbandune; 7 he
14 þær forðferde sona þæs wintres.

Mill*esi*mo lxxii. Her Willelm cyng lædde scipfyrde 7 landfyrde to Scotlande, 7 þ*et* land on þa sæhealfe mid scipu*m* ymbelæg 7 his landfyrde æt þa*m* Gewæde inn lædde. 7 He þær naht ne funde þæs þe him þe bet wære. 7 Se cyng Melcolm co*m* 7
5 griðede wið þone cyng Willelm 7 gislas sealde 7 his man wæs. 7 Se cing ha*m* gewende mid ealre his fyrde. 7 Se b*iscop* Egelric forðferde. He wæs to biscop hadod to Eoferwic, ac hit wæs mid unrihte him of genumon, 7 man geaf him þ*et* b*iscop*rice on Dunholme; 7 he heafde hit þa hwile þe he wolde, 7 forlet hit
10 syððan 7 ferde to Burch to S*anct*e Petres mynstre, 7 þær drohtnode xii gear. Þa æft*er* þa*m* þe Willelm cyng gewan Englalande, þa na*m* he hine of Burch 7 sende ˡhineˡ to Westmynstre. 7 He forðferde on Id*us* Octob*ris*, 7 he is bebyrged
14 þær innan þa*m* mynstre innon S*ancte*s Nicholaus portice.

Mill*esi*mo lxxiii. On þisum geare Willelm cyng lædde engliscne here 7 frencisce ofer sæ, 7 gewan þ*et* land Mans. 7 Hit englisce men swyðe amyrdon: wingeardas hi fordydon 7 burga forbærndon 7 swiðe þet land / amyrdon; 7 hit eall abegdon Willelme to handa. 7 Hi syððon ham gewendon to Englalande. f. 60v 5

Millesimo lxxiiii. On þisum geare for Willelm cyng ofer sæ to Normandig. 7 Eadgar cild com of Scotland to Normandige, 7 se cyng hine geinlagode 7 ealle his men; 7 he wæs on þes cynges hyrede 7 nam swilce gerihta swa se cyng him geuðe. 4

Millesimo lxxv. On þisum geare Willelm cyng geaf Raulfe eorle Willelmes dohtor Osbearnes sunu. 7 Se ylca Raulf wæs bryttisc on his moder healfe, 7 his fæder wæs englisc, Raulf hatte, 7 wæs geboren on Norðfolce. Þa geaf se cyng his sunu þone eorldom on Norðfolc 7 Suðfolc. Þa lædde he þet wif to Norðwic, 5

þær wes þet brydeala
mannum to beala.

Ðær wæs Roger eorl 7 Walþeof eorl 7 biscopas 7 abbotes, 7 ræddon þær swa þet hi woldon þone cyng gesettan ut of Englelandes cynedome—7 hit wearð sona gecydd þam cynge to Normandige hu hit wæs geræd. Þet wæs Roger eorl 7 Raulf eorl þe wæron yldast to ðam unreode. 7 Hi speonan þa Bryttas heom to, 7 sendon east to Denmearcan æfter sciphere heom to fultume. 7 Roger ferde west to his eorldome 7 gegaderode his folc to þæs cynges unþearfe; ac he wearð gelet. 7 Raulf eac on his eorldome wolde forðgan mid his folce; ac þa castelmen þe wæron on Englalande, 7 eac þet landfolc, him togeanes comen 7 gemacodon þet he naht ne dyde, ac for to scipe æt Norðwic. 7 His wif wæs innan þam castele, 7 hine heold swa lange þet man hire grið sealde; 7 heo ut ferde þa of Englalande, 7 ealle hire menn þe hire mid woldon. 7 Se cing syððan com to Englalande, 7 genam Roger eorl his mæg 7 gefestnode hine; 7 Walþeof eorl he genam eac. / 7 Sona æfter þam comon eastan of Denmearcan cc scipa, 7 þæron wæron twægen heafodmenn, Cnut Swægnes sunu 7 Hacun eorl; 7 hi ne dorstan nan gefeoht healdan wið Willelm cynge, ac heoldon ofer sæ to Flandran. 7 Eadgið seo hlæfdig forðferde on Winceastre vii 10 15 20 f. 61r 25

nihton ær Cr*ist*esmæssan; 7 se cyng hi let bryngan to West-
30 mynstre mid mycclan wurðscipe 7 lægde hi wið Eadward kyng
hire hlaforde. 7 Se [cyng] wæs on Westmynstre þone Mide-
winter. 7 Man fordyde þær ealle þa Bryttas þe wæron æt þam
brydealoð æt Norðwic:

sume hy wurdon ablænde, 7 sume of lande adrifene;
35 swa wurdon Will*el*mes swican geniðrade.

Mill*esi*mo lxxvi. On þisu*m* geare forðferde Swægn cyng on
Dænmercan, 7 Harold his sunu feng to ˈþeˈ kynerice. 7 Se
cyng geaf Westmynster Vithele abbode se wæs ær abb*ot* on
Bærnege. 7 Walþeof eorl ˈwesˈ beheafdod on Winceastre, 7
5 his lic wearð gelead to Crulande. 7 Se cyng for ofer sæ 7
lædde his fyrde to Brytlande 7 beset þone castel Dol; 7 þa
Bryttas hine heoldon þ*et* se cyng co*m* of Francland; 7 Willelm
þanon for 7 þær forleas ægðer ge men ge hors 7 feola his
9 gersuma.

Mill*esi*mo lxxvii. Her on þisu*m* geare wurdon sæhte Francˈaˈ
cyng 7 Willelm Englalandes cyng: ac hit heold litle hwile. 7
Ðes geares forbarn Lundenburh anre nihte ær Assu*m*ptio
S*an*c*t*e Marię swa swyðe swa heo næfre ær næs syðþan heo
5 gesta[þ]eled wæs. And on þisu*m* geare forðfyrde Ægelwig
abb*ot* on Euesha*m* on þa*m* dæge xiiii K*alendarum* M*artii*. And
Hereman b*iscop* eac forðferde on þa*m* dæge x K*alendarum*
8 M*artii*.

Mill*esi*mo lxxviii.

Mill*esi*mo lxxviiii. On þisu*m* geare co*m* Melcolm cyng of Scotlande into Englelande betwyx þa*m* twa*m* Mariam mæssan mid
f. 61ᵛ mycclu*m* fyrde, 7 gehergode Norðhymbraland / oð hit com to
Tine, 7 ofsloh feala hund manna, 7 ham lædde manige sceattas
5 7 gersuma 7 menn ˈon hˈeftninge. And þi ilcan geare se cyng
Willelm gefeaht togeanes his sunu Rotbearde wiðutan Normandige be anu*m* castele, Gerborneð hatte. 7 Se cyng Will*el*m
wearð þær gewundod 7 his hors ofslagen þe he on sæt, 7 eac his
9 sunu Willelm wearð þær gewundod 7 fela manna ofslagene.

1075/31 *MS.* 7 se wæs 1077/5 *MS.* gestabeled

Mill*esi*mo lxxx. On þisum geare wæs se b*iscop* Walchere ofslagen on Dunholme æt anu*m* gemote, 7 an hund manna mid him, frencisce 7 flemisce—7 he sylf wæs on Hloðeringa geboren. Ðis dydon Norðhymbran on Maies monðe. 4

Mill*esi*mo lxxxi. On þisu*m* geare se cyng lædde fyrde into Wealan 7 þær gefreode fela hund manna. 2

Mill*esi*mo lxxxii. Her nam se cyng Odan b*iscop*. 7 Her wæs mycel hungor. 2

Mill*esi*mo lxxxiii. On þisu*m* geare aras seo unge[þ]wærnes on Glæstingabyrig betwyx þa*m* abbode Þurstane 7 his munecan. Ærest hit co*m* of þæs abbotes unwisdome, þ*et* he misbead his munecan on fela þingan. 7 Ða munecas hit mændon lufelice to hi*m* 7 beadon hine þ*et* he sceolde healdan hi rihtlice 7 lufian 5 hi, 7 hi woldon hi*m* beon holde 7 gehyrsume. Ac se abbot nolde þæs naht, ac dyde heo*m* yfele 7 beheot heom wyrs. Anes dæges þe abbot eode into capitulan 7 spræc uppon þa munecas, 7 wolde hi mistukian, 7 sende æf*ter* læwede mannu*m*. 7 Hi comon into capitulan on uppon þa munecas full gewepnede. 10 7 Þa wæron þa munecas swiðe afcrede of heo*m*, nyston hwet heo*m* to donne wære. Ac toscuton—sume urnon into cyrcean 7 belucan þa duran into heo*m*. 7 Hi ferdon æft*er* heo*m* into þa*m* mynstre, 7 woldon hig ut dragan, þa ða hig ne dorsten na ut gan. Ac reowlic þing / þær gelamp on dæg, þ*et* þa fren- f. 62r cisce men bræcen þone chor 7 torfedon towærd þa*m* weofode 16 [þ]ær ða munecas wæron. 7 Sume of ðam cnihtan ferdon uppon þone uppflore 7 scotedon adunweard mid arewan toweard þa*m* haligdome swa þ*et* on þære rode þe stod bufon þa*m* weofode sticodon on mænige arewan. 7 Þa wreccan munecas lagon 20 onbuton þa*m* weofode—7 sume crupon under—7 gyrne cleopedon to Gode, his miltse biddende ða þa hi ne mihton nane miltse æt mannu*m* begytan. Hwæt magon we secgean?—buton þ*et* hi scotedon swiðe, 7 þa oðre ða dura bræcon þær adune 7 eodon inn, 7 ofslogon sume þa munecas to deaðe 7 mænige 25 gewundedon þærinne, swa þ*et* ðet blod co*m* of ða*m* weofode

1083/1 *MS.* ungehwærnes 1083/17 *MS.* Þær

uppon þ*am* gradan 7 of ðam gradan on þa flore. þreo þær wæron ofslagene to deaðe 7 eahteteone g*e*wundade. 7 On þæs ilcan geares forðferde Mahtild, Will*el*mes cynges cwen, on þone dæg
30 æft*er* Ealra Halgena mæssedæg. And on þes ylcan geares æft*er* Midewint*er* se cyng let beodan mycel gyld 7 hefelic ofer eal Englaland, þ*et* wæs æt ælcere hyde twa 7 hundseofenti peanega,

Mill*esi*mo lxxxiiii. Her on ðisum geare forðferde Wulfuuold
2 abb*ot* on Ceortesege on þ*am* dæge xiii K*alendarum* Mai.

Mill*esi*mo lxxxv. On þisu*m* geare menn cwydodon 7 to soðan sædan þ*et* Cnut cyng of Denmearcan, Swægnes sune cynges, fundade hiderward 7 wolde gewinnan þis land mid Rodbeardes eorles fultume of Flandran, forðan ˡþeˡ Cnut heafde Rodbeardes
5 dohter. Ða Will*el*m Englalandes cyng, þe þa wæs sittende on Normandige forðig he ahte ægðer ge Englaland ge Normandige, þis geaxode, he ferde into Englalande mid swa mycclan here ridendra manna 7 gangendra of Fraˡnˡcrice and of Brytlande swa næfre ær þis land ne gesohte, swa þ*et* menn wundredon hu /
f. 62ᵛ 10 þis land mihte eall þone here afedan; ac se cyng ˡletˡ toscyfton þone here geond eall þis land to his mannon, 7 hi fæddon þone here, ælc be his landefne. 7 Men heafdon mycel geswinc þæs geares. 7 Se cyng lett awestan þ*et* land abutan þa sæ, þet gif his feond comen upp þ*et* hi næfdon na on hwam hi fengon
15 swa rædlice. Ac ˡþaˡ se cyng geaxode to soðan þ*et* his feond gelætte wæron 7 ne mihten na geforðian heora fare, þa lett he sum þone here faren to heora agene lande, 7 sum he heold on þisu*m* lande ofer winter. Ða to þ*am* Midewintre wæs se cyng on Gleaweceastre mid his witan 7 heold þær his hired v dagas.
20 7 Syððan þe arceb*iscop* 7 gehadode men hæfden sinoð þreo dagas. Ðær wæs Maurici*us* gecoren to b*iscope* on Lundene, 7 Will*el*m to Norðfolce, 7 Rodbeard to Ceasterscire: hi wæron ealle þæs cynges clerecas. Æfter þisu*m* hæfde se cyng mycel geþeaht 7 swiðe deˡoˡpe spæce wið his witan ymbe þis land,
25 hu hit wære gesett oððe mid hwylcon mannon. Sende þa ofer eall Englaland into ælcere scire his men 7 lett agan ut hu fela hundred hyda wæron innon þære scire, oððe hwet se cyng

himsylf hæfde landes 7 orfes innan þa*m* lande, oððe hwilce gerihtæ he ahte to habbanne to xii monþum of ðære scire. Eac he lett gewritan hu mycel landes his arceb*iscopa*s hæfdon 7 his 30 leodb*iscopa*s 7 his abb*oda*s 7 his eorlas, 7, þeah ic hit lengre telle, hwæt oððe hu mycel ælc mann hæfde þe landsittende wæs innan Englalande, on lande oððe on orfe, 7 hu mycel feos hit wære wurð. Swa swyðe nearwelice he hit lett ut aspyrian þ*et* næs an ælpig hide ne an gyrde landes, ne furðon—hit is sceame 35 to tellanne, ac hit ne þuhte hi*m* nan sceame to donne—an oxe ne an cu ne an swin næs belyfon þ*et* næs gesæt on his gewrite. 7 Ealle þa gewrita wæron gebroht to him syððan. / 38

Mill*esi*mo lxxxv[i]. Her se cyng bær his corona 7 heold his f. 63r hired on Winceastre to þa*m* Eastran. 7 Swa he ferde þ*et* he wæs to þa*m* Pentecosten æt Wæstmynstre, 7 dubbade his sunu Henric to ridere þær. Syððan he ferde abutan swa þ*et* he com to Lammæssan to Searebyrig. 7 þær hi*m* comon to his witan and 5 ealle þa landsittende men þe ahtes wæron ofer eall Engleland, wæron þæs mannes men þe hi wæron; 7 ealle hi bugon to hi*m* 7 weron his menn 7 hi*m* holdaðas sworon, þ*et* hi woldon ongean ealle oðre men hi*m* holde beon. Đanon he ferde into Wiht, forþig he wolde faran into Normandige, 7 swa dyde syððan. 10 And þeah he dyde ærest æfter his gewunan: begeat swiðe mycelne sceatt of his mannan þær he mihte ænige teale to habban, oððe mid rihte oððe elles. Ferde þa syððan into Normandige. 7 Eadgar æþeling, Ædwardes mæg cynges, beah þa fra*m* hi*m*, forþig he næfde na mycelne wurðscipe of hi*m*—ac 15 se ælmihtiga God hi*m* gife wurðscipe on þam toweardan! 7 Cristina, þæs æðelinges swuster, beah into mynstre to Rumesege 7 underfeng halig reft. 7 þæs ilcan geares wæs swiðe hefelic gear 7 swiðe swincfull 7 sorhfull gear innan Englelande on orfcwealme; 7 corn 7 wæstmas wæron ætstandene; 7 swa mycel 20 ungelimp on wæderunge swa man naht æðelice geþencean ne mæg—swa stor þunring 7 lægt wes swa þ*et* hit acwealde manige men. 7 Aa hit wyrsode mid mannan swiðor 7 swiðor. Gebete hit God elmihtiga þonne his willa sy! 24

108[6]/1 *MS.* lxxxv. 108[6]/6 *MS.* land st sittende, *with* st *subpuncted.*

Mill*esi*mo lxxxvi[i]. Æfter ure Drihtnes Hælendes Cristes gebyrtide an þusend wintra 7 seofan 7 hundeahtatig wintra, on þa*m* an 7 twentigan geare þæs þe Will*el*m weolde 7 stihte Engleland swa hi*m* God uðe, gewearð swiðe hefelic and swiðe
5 wo[l]berendlic gear on þissu*m* lande. Swylc coðe co*m* on /
f. 63v mannum þ*et* fullneah æfre þe oðer man wearð on þa*m* wyrrestan yfele, þet is, on ðam drife, 7 þet swa stranglice þ*et* mænige menn swulton on ðam yfele. Syððan co*m*, þurh þa mycclan ungewiderunge þe comon swa we beforan tealdon, swyðe mycel
10 hungor ofer eall Engleland, þ*et* manig hundred manna earmlice deaðe swulton þurh þone hungor. Eala, hu earmlice 7 hu reowlic tid wæs ða, ða ða wreccæ men lægen fordrifene fullneah to deaðe 7 syððan co*m* se scearpa hungor 7 adyde hi mid ealle! Hwa*m* ne mæg earmian swylcere tide? Oððe hwa is swa heard-
15 heort þ*et* ne mæg wepan swylces ungelimpes? Ac swylce þing gewurðaþ for folces synna, þ*et* hi nellað lufian God 7 ri[ht]wisnesse. Swa swa hit wæs þa on ðam dagu*m* þ*et* litel rihtwisnesse wæs on þisu*m* lande mid ænige menn, buton mid munecan ane þær þær hi wæll ferdon. Se cyng 7 þa heafodmen lufedon
20 swiðe 7 oferswiðe gitsunge on golde 7 on seolfre, 7 ne rohtan hu synlice hit wære begytan buton hit come to heo*m*. Se cyng sealde his land swa deore to male swa heo de|o|rost mihte. Đonne co*m* su*m* oðer 7 bead mare þonn*e* þe oðer ær sealde, 7 se cyng hit lett þa*m* menn þe him mare bead. Đonne co*m* se
25 þridde 7 bead geat mare, 7 se cyng hit let þa*m* men to handa þe hi*m* eallra meast bead, 7 ne rohte na hu swiðe synlice þa gerefan hi begeatan of earme mannon ne hu manige unlaga hi dydon. Ac swa man swyðor spæc embe rihte lage, swa mann dyde mare unlaga. Hy arerdon unrihte tollas, 7 manige oðre
30 unriht hi dydan þe sindon earfeþe to areccenne. Eac on ðam ilcan geare ætforan hærfeste forbarn þ*et* halige mynster S*anct*e Paule, þe b*iscop*stol on Lundene, 7 mænige oðre mynstres, 7 þ*et* mæste dæl 7 þ*et* rotteste eall þære burh. Swylce eac on ðam ilcan timan forbarn fullneah ælc heafodport on eallon Engle-
35 lande. Eala, reowlic 7 wependlic tid wæs þæs geares, þe swa

1 *MS.* lxxxvi. 5 *MS.* woldberendlic 16 *MS.* rithwisnesse

manig ungelimp wæs forðbringende! Eac / on þam ilcan geare, f. 64r
toforan Assu*m*ptio S*anct*e Marie, for Will*el*m cyng of Normandige into France mid fyrde, 7 hergode uppan his agenne hlaford, Philippe þa*m* cynge, 7 sloh of his mannon mycelne dæl, 7 forbearnde þa burh Maðante 7 ealle þa halige mynstres 40
þe wæron innon þære burh; 7 twegen halige menn þe hyrsumedon Gode on ancersettle wuniende þær wæron forbearnde. Ðissu*m* þus gedone, se cyng Willelm cearde ongean to Normandige. Reowlic þing he dyde, 7 reowlicor hi*m* gela*m*p. Hu reowlicor? Him geyfelade 7 þ*et* him stranglice eglade. Hwæt 45
mæg ic teollan? Se scearpa deað þe ne forlet ne rice menn ne heane, seo hine gena*m*. He swealt on Normandige on þone nextan dæg æft*er* Natiuitas S*anct*e Marie, 7 man bebyrgede hine on Caþum æt S*anct*e Stephanes mynstre; ærer he hit arærde 7 syððan mænifealdlice gegodade. Eala, hu leas 7 hu 50
unwrest is þysses middaneardes wela! Se þe wæs ærur rice cyng 7 maniges landes hlaford, he næfde þa ealles landes buton seofon fotmæl; 7 se þe wæs hwilon gescrid mid golde 7 mid gimmu*m*, he læg þa oferwrogen mid moldan. He læfde æfter hi*m* þreo sunan: Rodbeard het se yldesta, se wæs eorl on Nor- 55
mandige æft*er* him; se oðer het Willelm, þe bær æft*er* him on Engleland þone kinehelm; se þridda het Heanric, þa*m* se fæder becwæð gersuman unatealլendlice. Gif hwa gewilnige[ð] to gewitane hu gedon mann he wæs, oððe hwilcne wurðscipe he hæfde, oððe hu fela lande he wære hlaford, ðonne wille we be 60
hi*m* awritan swa swa we hine ageaton ðe hi*m* on locodan 7 oðre hwile on his hirede wunedon. Se cyng Willelm þe we embe specað wæs swiðe wis man, 7 swiðe rice, 7 wurðfulre and strengere þonne ænig his foregenga wære. He wæs milde þa*m* godu*m* mannu*m* þe God lufedon, 7 ofer eall gemett stearc þa*m* 65
mannu*m* þe wiðcwædon his willan. On ða*m* ilcan / steode þe f. 64v
God him geuðe þ*et* he moste Engleland gegan, he arerde mære mynster 7 munecas þær gesætte 7 hit wæll gegodade. On his dagan wæs þ*et* mære mynster on Cantwarbyrig getymbrad, 7 eac swiðe manig oðer ofer eall Englaland. Eac þis land wæs 70

58 *MS.* gewilniged

swiðe afylled mid munecan, 7 þa leofodan heora lif æft*er* S*anct*es
Benedict*us* regule. 7 Se Cr*ist*endom wæs swilc on his dæge *þet*
ælc man hwæt his hade to belumpe folgade se þe wolde. Eac
he wæs swyðe wurðful. Þriwa he bær his cynehelm ælce geare
75 swa oft swa he wæs on Englelande: on Eastron he hine bær
on Winceastre, on Pentecosten on Westmynstre, on Midewintre
on Gleaweceastre; 7 þænne wæron mid hi*m* ealle þa rice men
ofer eall Englaland, arcebiscopas 7 leodb*iscopa*s, abbodas 7
eorlas, þegnas 7 cnihtas. Swilce he wæs eac swyðe stearc man 7
80 ræðe, swa *þet* man ne dorste nan þing ongean his willan don.
He hæfde eorlas on his bendu*m* þe dydan ongean his willan;
biscopas he sætte of heora biscoprice, 7 abbodas of heora
abb*ot*rice, 7 þægnas on cweartern. 7 Æt nextan he ne sparode
his agene broðor, Odo het. He wæs swiðe rice b*iscop* on Nor-
85 mandig*e*—on Baius wæs his b*iscop*stol—7 wæs manna fyrmest
toeacan þa*m* cynge; 7 he hæfde eorldo*m* on Englelande, 7 þonne
se cyng [wæs] on Normandige, þonne wæs he mægest*er* on
þisum lande. 7 Hine he sætte on cweartern. Betwyx oðru*m*
þingu*m*, nis na to forgytane *þet* gode frið þe he macode on
90 þisan lande, swa *þet* an man þe himsylf aht wære mihte faran
ofer his rice, mid his bosum full goldes, ungederad. 7 Nan man
ne dorste slean oðerne man, næfde he næfre swa mycel yfel
gedon wið þone oðerne. 7 Gif hwilc carlman hæmde wið wimman hire unðances, sona he forleas þa limu þe he mid pleagode.
f. 65r He rixade ofer Englæ/land; 7 hit mid his geapscipe swa þurh-
96 smeade *þet* næs an hid landes innan Englælande *þet* he nyste
hwa heo hæfde, oððe hwæs heo wurð wæs, 7 syððan on his
gewrit gesætt. Brytland him wæs on gewealde, 7 he þærinne
casteles gewrohte 7 þet manncynn mid ealle gewealde. Swilce
100 eac Scotland he hi*m* underþædde for his mycele strengþe.
Normandige þet land wæs his gecynde; 7 ofer þone eorldo*m*
þe Mans is g*e*haten he rixade. 7 Gif he moste þa gyt twa gear
libban, he hæfde Yrlande mid his werscipe gewunnon 7
wiðutan ælcon wæpnon. Witodlice on his timan hæfdon men
105 mycel g*e*swinc 7 swiðe manige teonan.

86–7 *MS.* þonne se cyng on

Castelas he let wyrcean,
7 earme men swiðe swencean.
Se cyng wæs swa swiðe stearc,
7 bena*m* of his underþeoddan manig marc
goldes 7 ma hundred punda seolfres. 110
Ðet he na*m* be wihte
7 mid mycelan unrihte
of his landleode,
for litte[l]re neode.
He wæs on gitsunge befeallan, 115
7 grædinæsse he lufode mid ealle
He sætte mycel deorfrið,
7 he lægde laga þærwið
þ*et* swa hwa swa sloge heort oððe hinde,
þ*et* hine man sceolde blendian. 120
He forbead þa heortas,
swylce eac þa baras.
Swa swiðe ˡheˡ lufode þa headeor
swilce he wære heora fæder.
Eac he sætte be þa*m* haran 125
þ*et* hi mosten freo faran.
His rice men hit mændon,
7 þa earme men hit beceorodan;
ac he [wæs] swa stið
þ*et* he ne rohte heora eallra nið. 130
Ac hi moston mid ealle
þes cynges wille folgian,
gif hi woldon libban,
oððe land habban,
land oððe eahta, 135
oððe wel his sehta.
Walawa, þ*et* ænig man
sceolde modigan swa,
hine sylf upp ahebban
7 ofer ealle men tellan. 140

109 *MS.* man manig marc 114 *MS.* littere 129 *MS.* he swa stið

Se ælmihtiga God cyþæ his saule mildheortnisse,
7 do hi*m* ⸢his⸣ synna forgifenesse!

Đas þing we habbað be hi*m* gewritene, ægðer ge gode ge yfele, þ*et* þa godan men niman æft*er* þeora godnesse 7 for[f]leon mid
f.65ᵛ ealle / yfelnesse 7 gan on ðone weg þe us lett to heofonan rice.
146 Fela þinga we magon writan þe on ðam ilcan geare gewordene wæron. Swa hit wæs on Denmearcan þ*et* þa Dænescan, þe wæs ærur geteald eallra folca getreowast, wurdon awende to þære meste untriwðe 7 to þa*m* mæsten swicdome þe æfre mihte
150 gewurðan: hi gecuron 7 abugan to Cnute cynge 7 hi*m* aðas sworon, 7 syððan hine earhlice ofslogon innan anre cyrcean. Eac wearð on Ispanie þ*et* þa hæðenan men foran 7 hergodan uppon þa*m* Cr*ist*enan mannan 7 mycel abegdan to heora anwealde; ac se Cr*ist*ena cyng—Anphos wæs gehaten—he sende
155 ofer eall into ælcan lande 7 gyrnde fultumes; 7 hi*m* co*m* to fultu*m* of ælcen lande þe Cr*ist*en wæs; 7 ferdon 7 ofslogon 7 aweg adrifan eall þet hæðena folc 7 gewunnon heora land ongean, þurh Godes fultum. Eac on þisan ilcan lande on þa*m* ilcan geare forðferdon manega rice men: Stigand b*iscop* of
160 Ciceastre, 7 se abb*ot* of S*anct*e Augustine, 7 se abb*ot* of Baðon, 7 þe of Perscoran; 7 ða heora eallra hlaford, Willelm, Englælandes cyng, þe we ær beforan embe spæcon. Æfter his deaðe, his sune—Will*el*m hæt eallswa þe fæder—feng to þa*m* rice, 7 wearð gebletsod to cynge fra*m* Landfrance arceb*iscope* on
165 Westmynstre þreo*m* dagum ær Mich⸢a⸣eles mæssedæg; 7 ealle þa men on Englalande hi*m* to abugon 7 him aðas sworon. Đisu*m* þus gedone, se cyng ferde to Winceastre 7 sceawode þ*et* madmehus 7 þa gersuman þe his fæder ær gegaderode: þa wæron unasecgendlice ænie men hu mycel þær wæs gegaderod
170 on golde 7 on seolfre 7 on faton 7 on pællan 7 on gimman 7 on manige o[ð]re deorwurðe þingon, þe earfoðe sindon to ateallene. Se cyng dyde þa swa his fæder him bebead ær he dead wære: dælde þa gersuman for his fæder saule to ælcen mynstre þe wes innan Englelande—to suman mynstre x marc goldes, to sum

144 *MS.* forleon, *see Notes.* 171 *MS.* odre 174 *MS.* innan *altered from* on

vi, 7 to ælcen cyrcean / uppeland lx pæn*ega*; 7 into ælcere scire f. 66r
man seonde hundred punda feos to dælanne earme mannan for 176
his saule. 7 Ær he forðferde, he bead þ*et* man sceolde unlesan
ealle þa menn þe on hæftnunge wæron under his anwealde. 7
Se cyng wæs on ðam Midewintre on Lundene. 179

Mill*esi*mo lxxxvii[i]. On þisu*m* geare wæs þis land swiðe
astirad 7 mid mycele swicdome afylled, swa þ*et* þa riceste
frencisce men þe weron innan þisan lande wolden swican heora
hlaforde þa*m* cynge 7 woldon habban his broðer to cynge,
Rodbeard, þe wæs eorl on Normandige. On þisu*m* ræde wæs 5
ærest Oda b*iscop* 7 Gosfrið b*iscop* 7 Will*el*m b*iscop* on Dunholme—swa wæll dyde se cyng be þa*m* b*iscope* þ*et* eall Englaland færde æft*er* his ræde 7 swa swa he wolde, 7 he þohte to
donne be him eallswa Iudas Scarioth dyde be ure Drihtene;
7 Rogere eorl wæs eac æt þa*m* unræde, 7 swiðe mycel folc mid 10
heo*m*, ealle frencisce men. 7 Þæs unræd wærð geræd innan þa*m*
lengtene. Sona swa hit co*m* to þa*m* Eastron, þa ferdon hi 7
hergodon 7 bærndon 7 aweston þæs cynges feorme hames, 7
eallra þæra manna land hi fordydon þe wæron innan þæs
cynges holdscipe. / Heora ælc ferde to his castele, 7 þone 15
mannoden 7 metsoden swa hig betst mihton. Gosfrið b*iscop* 7
Rodbeard a Mundbræg ferdon to Bricgstowe 7 hergodon 7
brohton to þa*m* castele þa hergunge, 7 syððon foron ut of ðam
castele 7 hergodon Baðon 7 eall þ*et* land þærabutan, 7 eall
Beorclea Hyrnesse hi awæston. 7 Ða men þe yldest wæron of 20
Hereforde, 7 eall þeo scir forð mid, 7 þa men of Scrobscyre, mid
mycele folce of Brytlande, comon 7 hergodon 7 bærndon on
Wiðreceastrescire forð þ*et* hi comon to þa*m* porte sylfan, 7 woldon
þa ðæne port bærnen 7 þ*et* mynster reafian 7 þæs cynges castel
gewinnan heo*m* to handa. Ðas þing geseonde, se arwurða 25
b*iscop* Wlstan wearð swiðe gedrefed on his mode, forðig him
wæs betæht þe castel to healdene. Þeahhweðer, / his hiredmen f. 66v
ferdon ut mid feawe mannan of þa*m* castele, 7 þurh Godes
mildheortnisse 7 þurh þæs b*iscope*s geearnunga, ofslogon 7
gelæhton fif hundred manna 7 þa oðre ealle aflymdon. Se 30

108[8]/1 *MS*. lxxxvii.

b*iscop* of Dunholme dyde to hearme þ*et* he mihte ofer eall be norðan. Roger het an of heo*m*, se hleop into þa*m* castele æt Norðwic 7 dyde git eallra wærst ofer eall þ*et* land. Hugo eac [het] an þe hit ne gebette nan þing, ne innan Lægreceastrescire
35 ne innan Norðha*m*tune. Ðe b*iscop* Odo, þe þas [þ]yng of awocan, ferde into Cent to his eorldome 7 fordyde hit swyðe, 7 þæs cynges land 7 þæs arceb*iscope*s mid ealle aweston, 7 brohte eall þ*et* god into his castele on Hrofeceastre. Ða þe cyng undergeat ealle þas þing 7 hwilcne swicdo*m* hi dydon toweard his, þa
40 wearð he on his mode swiðe gedrefed: sende þa æfter englisce mannan 7 heo*m* fore sæde his neode 7 gyrnde heora fultumes, 7 behet heom þa betsta laga þæ æfre ær wæs on þisan lande 7 ælc u[n]riht geold he forbead 7 geatte mannan heora wudas and slætinge; ac hit ne stod nane hwile. Ac englisce men swa
45 þeah fengon to þa*m* cynge heora hlaforde on fultume. Ferdon þa toweard Hrofeceastre 7 woldon þone b*iscop* Odan begytan, þohtan gif hi hæfdon hine þe wæs ærur heafod to ðam unræde þ*et* hi mihton þe bet begytan ealla þa oðre. Hi comon þa to þa*m* castele to Tonebricge. Þa wæron innan þa*m* castele Oda
50 b*iscope*s cnihtas 7 oðre manige þe hine healdon woldan ongean þon*e* cyng. Ac þa englisce men ferdon 7 tobræcon þone castel, 7 þa men þe þærinne wæron griðodon wið þone cyng. Se cyng mid his here ferde toweard Hrofeceastre, 7 wendon þ*et* se b*iscop* wære þærinne; ac hit wearð þam cynge cuð þet se b*iscop*
55 wæs afaren to ðam castele a Pefenesea; 7 se cyng mid his here ferde æft*er* 7 besætt þon*e* castel abutan mid swiðe mycele here
f. 67r fulle six wucan. Betwyx þissu*m*, se eorl of Nor/mandige, Rodbeard þes cynges broðer, gaderode swiðe mycel folc 7 þohte to gewinnane Engleland mid þæra manna fultume þe wæron
60 innan þisan lande ongean þon*e* cyng. 7 He sende of his ma[nn]an to þisu*m* lande, 7 wolde cuman himsylf æft*er*. Ac þa englisce men þe wærˡdˡedon þære sæ gelæhton of þa*m* mannon 7 slogon 7 adrengton ma þonn*e* ænig man wiste to tellanne. Syððan heo*m* ateorede mete wiðinnan þa*m* castele, ða gyr[n]don

33–4 *MS.* Hugo eac an 36 *MS.* þe þas cyng 43 *MS.* uriht
61 *MS.* mannan 64 *MS.* gyrdon

hi griðas 7 agefan hine þa*m* cynge. 7 Se b*iscop* swor þ*et* he wolde 65
ut of Englelande faran 7 na mare cuman on ðisan lande butan
se cyng hi*m* æft*er* sende, 7 þ*et* he wolde agifan þon*e* castel on
Hrofeceastre. Ealswa se b*iscop* ferde 7 sceolde agifan þon*e*
castel 7 se cyng sende his men mid hi*m*, ða arisan þa men þe
wæron innan þa*m* castele 7 namon þone b*iscop* 7 þes cynges men 70
7 dydon hi on hæftnunge. Innan þa*m* castele wæron swiðe gode
cnihtas, Eustati*us* þe iunga 7 Rogeres eorles þreo sunan, 7
ealle þa betstboren men þe wæron innan þisan lande oððe on
Normandige. Ða se cyng undergeat þas þing, þa ferde he
æft*er* mid þa*m* here þe he ðær hæfde; 7 sende ofer eall Engla- 75
lande 7 bead þ*et* ælc man þe wære unniðing sceolde cuman to
hi*m*, frencisce 7 englisce, of porte 7 of uppelande. Hi*m* co*m* þa
mycel folc to; 7 he for [to] Hrofeceastre 7 besætt þone castel
oððet hi griðedon þæ þærinne wæron 7 þone castel ageafon. Se
b*iscop* Odo, mid þa*m* mannu*m* þe innan þa*m* castele wæron, 80
ofer sæ ferdon; 7 se b*iscop* swa forlet þone wurðscipe þe he on
þis lande hæfde. Se cyng syððan sende here to Dunholme 7
let besittan þone castel; 7 se b*iscop* griðode and ageaf þone
castel, 7 forlet his biscoprice 7 ferde to Normandig*e*. Eac manige
frencisce men forleton heora land 7 ferdon ofer sæ; 7 se cyng 85
geaf heora land þa*m* mannu*m* þe him holde wæron. /

Mill*esi*mo lxxxix. On þisum geare se arwurða muneca feder 7 f. 67v
frouer, Landfranc arce*biscop*, gewat of þissu*m* life, ac we hopiað
þet he ferde ˡtoˡ þ*et* heofanlice rice. Swilce eac gewarð ofer eall
Engleland mycel eorðstyrunge on þone dæg iii Id*us* Aug*usti*;
7 wæs swiðe lætsum gear on corne 7 on ælces cynnes wæstmum, 5
swa þ*et* manig men ræpon heora corn onbutan Martines mæssan
7 gyt lator.

M*illesimo* xc. INDICTIONE XIII. Ðissu*m* þus gedon
eallswa wæ ær abufan sædan be þa*m* cynge 7 be his broðer 7
be his mannon, se cyng wæs smægende hu he mihte wrecon
[hine 7] his broðer Rodbeard swiðost swencean 7 Normandige
of him gewinnan. Ðeah, þurh his geapscipe oððe þurh gærsuma, 5

108[8]/78 *MS.* he for hrofeceastre. 1090/3–4 *MS.* wrecon his broðer

he begeat þone castel æt S*anct*e Waleri, 7 þa hæfenan. 7 Swa he begeat þone æt Albemare; 7 þarinne he sette his cnihtas, 7 hi dydon hearmes uppon þa*m* lande on hergunge 7 on bærnete. Æft*er* þisu*m* he begeat ma castelas innan þa*m* lande 7
10 ˡþærˡinne his rideras gelogode. Se eorl of Normandige, R*odbeard*, syððan he undergeat þ*et* his gesworene men him trucedon 7 agefon hera castelas him to hearme, þa sende he to his hlaforde, Philippe Francena cynge. 7 He co*m* to Normandig*e* mid mycelan here. 7 Se cyng 7 se eorl mid ormætre fyrde besæton
15 þon*e* castel abuton þær þæs cynges men of Engleland inne wæron. Se cyng Willelm of Englalande sende to Philippe Francena cynge; 7 he, for his lufan oððe for his mycele gersuma, forlet swa his man, þon*e* eorl Rodbeard, 7 his land, 7 ferde ongean to France 7 let heo*m* swa weorðan. 7 Betwyx
20 þisum þingu*m* þis land wæs swiðe fordon on unlagagelde 7 on oðre manige ungelimpe.

Mill*esi*mo xci. On þisu*m* geare se cyng Will*el*m heold his hired
f. 68ʳ to Cr*ist*esmessan on Wæstmynstre. 7 þæræft*er* to / Candelmæssan he ferde for his broðær unþearfe ut of Englalande into Normandige. Onmang þa*m* þe he þær wæs, heora sehte togæ-
5 dere eode, on þ*et* gerad þ*et* se eorl hi*m* to handan let Uescam 7 þone eorldo*m* æt Ou 7 Kiæresburh; and þærtoeacan þes cynges men sacleas beon moston on þa*m* castelan þe hi ær þes eorles unþances begiten hæfdon; 7 se cyng hi*m* ongean þa Manige behet, þe ær heora fæder gewann 7 þa fra*m* þa*m* eorle gebogen
10 wæs, gebygle to donne 7 eall þ*et* his fæder þærbegeondan hæfde, butan þa*m* þe he þa[m] cynge þa geunnen hæfde; 7 þ*et* ealle þa þe on Englelande for þa*m* eorle æror heora land forluron hit on þisum sehte habban sceoldan, 7 se eorl on Englelande eallswa mycel swa on heora forewarde wæs; and gif se eorl forðferde
15 butan sunu be rihtre æwe, wære se cyng yrfenuma of eallon Normandig; be þisre sylfan forewarde, gif se cyng swulte, wære se eorl yrfenuma ealles Englalandes. Ðas forewarde gesworan xii þa betste of þes cynges healfe and xii of þes eorles,

1090/20 *MS.* on *altered from* an   1091/11 *MS.* þa cynge

þeah hit syððan litle hwile stode. Onmang þisu*m* sæhte wearð
Eadgar æþeling belandod of þa*m* þe se eorl him æror þær to 20
handa gelæten hæfde, 7 ut of Normandig for to þa*m* cynge his
aðume to Scotlande 7 to his swustor. Onmang þa*m* þe se cyng
W*illelm* ut of Englelande wæs, ferde se cyng Melcolm of
Scotlande hider into Englu*m* 7 his mycelne dæl oferhergode,
oðþ*et* þa gode mæn þe þis land bewiston hi*m* fyrde ongean 25
sændon 7 hine gecyrdon. Ða þa se cyng W*illelm* into Normandige
þis gehyrde, þa gearcode he his fare 7 to Englelande co*m*,
7 his broðer se eorl Rodbeard mid hi*m*; 7 sona fyrde het ut
abeodan, ægðær scipfyrde 7 landfyrde—ac seo scipfyrde, ær he to
Scotlande cuman mihte, ælmæst earmlice forfor feowan dagon 30
toforan S*anct*e Michæles mæssan. And se cyng 7 his broðer mid
þære landfyrde ferdon, ac þa ða / se cyng Melcolm gehyrde þ*et* f. 68v
hine man mid fyrde secean wolde, he for mid his fyrde ut of
Scotlande into Loðene on Englaland 7 þær abad. Ða þa se cyng
W*illelm* mid his fyrde genealehte, þa ferdon betwux Rodbeard 35
eorl 7 Eadgar æðeling, 7 þæra cinga sehte swa gemacedon þ*et*
se cyng Melcolm to uran cynge co*m* 7 his man wearð to eall
swilcre gehyrsu*m*nisse swa he ær his fæder dyde 7 þ*et* mid aðe
gefestnode, 7 se cyng W*illelm* him behet on lande 7 on eallon
þinge þæs þe he under his fæder ær hæfde. On þisu*m* sehte wearð 40
eac Eadgar eþeling wið þone cyng gesæhtlad. 7 þa cyngas þa
mid mycclu*m* sehte tohwurfon: ac þ*et* litle hwile stod. And
se eorl Rodbeard her oð Cr*ist*esmæsse forneah mid þa*m* cynge
wunode; 7 litel soðes þæronmang of heora forewarde onfand;
7 twa*m* dagon ær þære tide on Wiht scipode 7 into Normandig 45
for, 7 Eadgar æðeling mid him.

Mill*es*imo xcii. On þisu*m* geare se cyng W*illelm* mid mycelre
fyrde ferde norð to Cardeol, 7 þa burh geæ[d]staþelede 7 þone
castel arerde; 7 Dolfin ut adraf þe æror þær þes landes weold 7
þon*e* castel mid his mannan gesette; 7 syððan hider suð gewænde
7 mycele mænige [c]yrlisces folces mid wifan 7 mid orfe 5
þyder sænde, þær to wunigenne þ*et* land to tilianne.

1092/2 *MS.* ge æðstaþelede 1092/5 *MS.* eyrlisces

Mill*esi*mo xciii. On þisu*m* geare to þa*m* længtene warð se cyng W*illelm* on Gleaweceastre to þa*m* swiðe geseclod þ*et* he wæs ofer eall dead gekyd. 7 On his broke he Gode fela behæsa behet, his agen lif on riht to lædene, 7 Godes cyrcean griðian 7
5 friðian 7 næfre ma eft wið feo gesyllan, 7 ealle rihte lage on his þeode to habbene; and þ*et* arceb*iscop*rice on Cantwarbyrig, þe ær on his agenre hand stod, Anselme betæhte, se wæs ær abb*ot* on Bæc, 7 Rodbeard his cancelere þ*et* biscoprice on Lincolne, 7 to manegan mynstren land geuðe—ac þ*et* he syððan ætbræd,
f. 69r þa hi*m* gebotad wæs, 7 ealle þa gode laga / forlæt þe he us ær
11 behet. Ða æft*er* þisson, sende [se] cyng of Scotlande 7 þære forewarde gyrnde þe hi*m* behaten wæs; and se cing W*illelm* him steofnode to Gloweceastre, 7 hi*m* to Scotlande gislas sende 7 Eadgar æþeling æft*er*, 7 þa men syððan ongean þe hine mid
15 mycclon wurðscipe to þa*m* cynge brohtan. Ac þa ða he to þa*m* cynge co*m*, ne mihte he beon weorðe naðer ne ure cynges spæce ne þæra forewarde þe hi*m* ær behatene wæron; 7 forþi hi þa mid mycclon unsehte tohwurfon, 7 se cyng Melcolm ha*m* to Scotlande gewænde. Ac hraðe þæs þe he ha*m* com, he his
20 fyrde gegaderode 7 into Englelande hergende mid maran unræde ferde þone hi*m* abehofode. 7 Hine þa Rodbeard se eorl of Norðhymbran mid his mannan unwæres besyrede 7 ofsloh: hine sloh Moræl of Bæbbaburh, se wæs þæs eorles stiward 7 Melcolmes cinges godsib. Mid hi*m* wæs eac Eadward his sune
25 ofslagen, se æft*er* hi*m* cyng beon sceolde, gif he hit gelifode. Ða þa seo gode cwen Margarita þis gehyrde, hyre þa leofstan hlaford 7 sunu þus beswikene, heo wearð oð deað on mode geancsumed, 7 mid hire prestan to cyrcean eode 7 hire gerihtan underfeng 7 æt Gode abæd þ*et* heo hire gast ageaf. 7 Ða
30 Scottas þa Dufenal to cynge gecuron, Melcolmes broðer, 7 ealle þa Englisce ut adræfdon þe ær mid þa*m* cynge Melcolme wæron. Ða þa Dunecan, Melcolmes cynges sunu, þis eall gehyrde þus gefaren, se on þæs cynges hyrede W*illelmes* wæs swa swa his fæder hine ures cynges fæder ær to gisle geseald
35 hæfde 7 her swa syððan belaf, he to þa*m* cynge co*m* 7 swilce

11 *MS.* sende cyng

getrywða dyde swa se cyng æt him habban wolde; 7 swa mid his unne to Scotlande for mid þa*m* fultume þe he begytan mihte engliscra 7 frenciscra, and his mæge Dufenal þes rices bena*m* 7 to cynge wearð underfangen. Ac þa Scottas hi eft sume gegaderoden 7 forneah / ealle his mæn[i]u ofslogan, 7 he sylf mid feawu*m* ætbærst. Syððan hi wurdon sehte on þa gerad þ*et* he næfre eft englisce ne frencisce into þam lande ne gelogige. f. 69v 41

Mill*esi*mo xciiii. Her hæfde se cyng W*illelm* to Cristesmæssan his hired æt Gleaweceastre. 7 Him þider fram his broðer Rodbearde of Normandig bodan coman, þa cyddon þ*et* his broðer grið 7 forewarde eall æft*er*cwæð butan se cyng gelæstan wolde eall þet hi on forewarde hæfdon ær gewroht, 7 uppon þ*et* 5 hine forsworenne 7 trywleasne clypode buton he þa forewarda geheolde, oððe þider ferde 7 hine þær betealde þær seo forewarde ær wæs gewroht 7 eac gesworen. Ða ferde se cyng to Hæstingan to þa*m* Candelmæssan; 7 onmang þa*m* þe he þær wederes abad, he let halgian þ*et* mynster æt þære Bataille; 7 10 Herbearde Losange þa*m* b*iscope* of Þeotfordan his stæf bena*m*; 7 þæræft*er* to midlengtene ofer sæ for into Normandige. Syððan he þider co*m*, he 7 his broðer Rodbeard se eorl gecwæðan þ*et* hi mid griðe togædere cuman sceoldan; 7 swa dydon; 7 gesemede beon ne mihtan. Syððan eft hi togædere coman mid 15 þa*m* ilcan mannan þe ær þ*et* loc makedon 7 eac þa aðas sworen; 7 ealne þon*e* bryce uppon þone cyng tealdon, ac he nolde þæs geþafa beon ne eac þa forewarde healdan; 7 forþa*m* hi þa mid mycelon unsehte tocyrdon. And se cyng syððan þon*e* castel æt Bures gewann 7 þes eorles men þærinne gena*m*: þa sume ihyder 20 to lande sende. Ðærtogeanes, se eorl mid þes cynges fultume of France gewann þone castel æt Argentses 7 þearinne Rogger Peiteuin gena*m* 7 seofen hundred þes cynges cnihta mid hi*m*; 7 syððan þon*e* æt Hulme. 7 Oftrædlice heora ægðer uppon oðerne tunas bærnde 7 eac menn læhte. Ða sende [se] cyng 25 hider to lande 7 het abeodan ut xx þusenda engliscra manna / him to fultume to Normandig. Ac þa hi to sæ coman, þa het f. 70r

1093/40 *MS.* mænu 1094/24 *MS.* sende cyng

hi man cyrran 7 þ*et* feoh syllan to þæs cynges behofe þe hi genumen hæfdon, þet wes ælc man healf punda; 7 hi swa dydon.
30 7 Se eorl innon Normandig æft*er* þison, mid þa*m* cynge of France, 7 mid eallon þan þe hi gegaderian mihton, ferdon towardes Ou, þær se cyng W*illelm* inne wæs, 7 þohtan hine inne to besittanne; 7 swa foran oð hi coman to Lungeuile. Ðær wearð se cyng of France þurh gesmeah gecyrred; 7 swa syððan eal seo
35 fyrding tohwearf. Her onmang þison se cyng W*illelm* sende æfter his broðer Heanrige, se wæs on þa*m* castele æt Damfront, ac forþi þe he mid friðe þurh Normandig faran ne mihte, he hi*m* sende scipon æfter 7 Hugo eorl of Ceastre. Ac þa ða hi towardes Ou faran sceoldan þær se cyng wæs, hi foran to Engle-
40 lande 7 up coman æt Hamtune on Ealra Halgena mæsseæfne; 7 her syððon wunedon, 7 to Cr*ist*esmæssan wæron on Lunden. Eac on þisu*m* ylcan geare þa wylisce menn hi gegaderodon, 7 wið þa frencisce þe on Walon oððe on þære neawiste wæron 7 hi ær belandedon gewinn up ahofon, 7 manige festena 7 castelas
45 abræcon 7 men ofslogon. An[d] syððan heora gefylce weox, hi hi on ma todældon: wið sum þæra dæle gefeaht Hugo eorl of Scrobscire 7 hi aflymde; ac þeahhweðer þa oðre ealles þæs geares nanes yfeles ne geswicon þe hi don mihton. Ðises geares eac þa Scottas heora cyng Dunecan besyredon 7 ofslogan, 7 heo*m*
50 syððan eft oðre syðe his fæderan Dufenal to cynge genamon, þur[h] þes lare 7 totihtinge he wearð to deaðe beswicen.

Mill*esi*mo xcv. On þisu*m* geare wæs se cyng Will*el*m to Cr*ist*esmæssan þa feower forewarde dagas on Hwitsand; 7 æfter þa*m* feorðan dæge hider to lande for 7 upp com æt Doferan. And Heanrig þes cynges broðer her on lande oð /
f. 70v lengten wunode; 7 þa ofer sæ for to Normandig mid mycclon
6 gersuman on þæs cynges heldan uppon heora broðer Rodbeard eorl; 7 gelomlice uppon þone eorl wann 7 him mycelne hearm ægðer on lande 7 on mannan dyde. And þa to Eastran heold se cyng his hired on Winceastre. 7 Se eorl Rodbeard of Norð-
10 hymbran nolde to hirede cuman, 7 se cyng forðan wearð wið hine

1094/45 *MS.* An 1094/51 *MS.* þur

swiðe astyrod 7 him to sænde 7 heardlice bead, gif he griðes
weorðe beon wolde, þet he to Pentecosten to hired come. On
þisum geare wæron Eastron on viii° *Kalendarum* Apr*ilis*; 7 þa
uppon Eastron on S*anct*e Ambrosius mæsseniht, þ*et* is ii[i]
No*narum* Apr*ilis*, wæs gesewen forneah ofer eall þis land, 15
swilce forneah ealle þa niht, swiðe mænifealdlice steorran of
heofenan feollan, naht be anan oððe twam, ac swa þiclice þ*et*
hit nan mann atellan ne mihte. Heræft*er* to Pentecosten wæs
se cyng on Windlesoran, 7 ealle his witan mid hi*m*, butan þa*m*
eorle of Norðhymbran, forþa*m* se cyng him naþer nolde ne 20
gislas syllan ne uppon tryw ðan geunnon þ*et* he mid griðe cumon
moste 7 faran. 7 Se cyng forþi his fyrde bead 7 uppon þon*e*
eorl to Norðhymbran for. 7 Sona þes þe he þider co*m*, he
manege 7 forneah ealle þa betste of þes eorles hirede innan
anan fæstene gewann 7 on hæftene gedyde, 7 þon*e* castel æt 25
Tinemuðan besæt oððet he hine gewann 7 þæs eorles broðer
þærinne 7 ealle þa þe hi*m* mid wæron; and syððan ferde to
Bebbaburh 7 þon*e* eorl þærinne besæt. Ac þa ða se cyng geseah
þ*et* he hine gewinnan ne mihte, þa het he makian ænne castel
toforan Bebbaburh 7 hine on his spæce "Malueisin" het—þ*et* 30
is on englisc "Yfel nehhebur"—7 hine swiðe mid his mannan
gesætte; 7 syððan suðweard for. Ða sona æft*er* þam þe se cyng
wæs suð afaren, feorde se eorl anre nihte ut of Bebbaburh
towardes Tinemuðan. Ac þa þe innan / þam niwan castele f. 71[r]
wæron his gewær wurdon, 7 him æft*er* foran 7 onfuhton, 7 hine 35
gewundedon 7 syððan gelæhton, 7 þa þe mid hi*m* wæron sume
ofslogan, sume lifes gefengon. Onman[g] þison wearð þa*m*
cynge cuð þ*et* þa wylisce men on Wealon sumne castel heafdon
tobroken, Muntgum[r]i hatte, 7 Hugon eorles men ofslagene
þe hine healdon sceoldan. 7 He forþi oðre fyrde het fearlice 40
abannan, 7 æft*er* S*anct*e Michaeles mæsse into Wealan ferde 7
his fyrde toscyfte 7 þ*et* land eall þurhfor swa þ*et* seo fyrde eall
togædere co*m* to Ealra Halgena to Snawdune. Ac þa wylisce
atoforan into muntan and moran ferdan þ*et* heo*m* man to cuman

14 *MS.* ii. 30 *MS.* hine *altered from* his 37 *MS.* onman
39 *MS.* muntgumni

45 ne mihte; 7 se cyng þa ha*m*weard gewende forþa*m* he geseah þ*et*
he þær þes wintres mare don ne mihte. Ða þa se cyng ongean
co*m*, þa het he niman þon*e* eorl Rotbeard of Norðhymbran 7 to
Bæbbaburh lædan 7 ægðer eage ut adon buton þa þe þærinne
wæron þon*e* castel agyfan woldan: hine heoldan his wif 7
50 Moreal se wæs stiward 7 eac his mæg. Ðurh þis wearð se castel
þa agyfen. 7 Moreal wearð þa on þes cynges hirede, 7 þurh
hine wurdon manege, ægðer ge gehadode 7 eac læwede, geypte,
þe mid heora ræde on þes cynges unheldan wæron. Þa se cyng
sume ær þære tide het on hæftneðe gebringan; 7 syððan swiðe
55 gemahlice ofer eall þis land beodan þ*et* ealle þa þe of þa*m* cynge
land heoldan, eallswa hi friðes weorðe beon woldan, þ*et* hi on
hirede to tide wæron. And þone eorl Rotbert het se cyng to
Windlesoran lædan 7 þær innan þa*m* castele healdan. Eac on
þis ylcan geare togeanes Eastron co*m* þæs Papan sande hider to
60 lande—þ*et* wæs Waltear bisceop, swiðe god lifes man of Albin
þære ceastre—7 þa*m* arceb*iscope* Ansealme uppon Pentecosten
of þæs Papan healfe Urban*us* his palliu*m* geaf, 7 he hine under-
f. 71[v] feng æt his arcestole on Cantwarabyrig. / And se biscop Waltear
her on lande þæs geares syððan lange wunode, 7 man syððan
65 þ*et* Romgesceot be hi*m* sende swa man manegan gearan æror
ne dyde. Ðises ylcan eac geares wæron swiðe untidgewidera, 7
forþi geond eall þis land wurdon eorðwæstmas eall to medem-
68 lice gewende.

An*no* M*illesimo* xcvi. On þison geare heold se cyng Will*el*m his
hired to Cr*ist*esmæssan on Windlesoran. 7 Will*el*m bisco*p* of
Dunholme þær forðferde to geares dæge. And on Octab*as*
Epyphan*ie* wæs se cyng 7 ealle his witan on Searbyrig. Þær
5 beteah Gosfrei Bainard Will*el*m of Ou, þes cynges mæg, þ*et*
he heafde gebeon on þes cynges swicdome, 7 hit hi*m* on gefeaht
7 hine on orreste oferco*m*; 7, syððan he ofercumen wæs, hi*m*
het se cyng þa eagan ut adon 7 syþðan belis[ni]an, 7 his
stiward, Will*el*m hatte, se wæs his modrian sunu, het se cyng
10 on rode ahon. Ðær wearð eac Eoda eorl of Ca*m*paine, þæs

1095/51 *MS.* on *altered from* in 1096/8 *MS.* belisman

cynges aðum, 7 manege oðre, belende. 7 Su[m]e man to Lundene lædde 7 þær spilde. Ðises geares eac to þa*m* Eastran wearð swiðe mycel styrung geond ealle þas þeode 7 fela oðra þeodan þurh Urban*us*, se wæs Papa gehaten þeah þe he þæs setles naþing næfde on Rome; 7 ferde unarimedlice folc mid wifan 7 cildan to þi þ*et* hi uppon hæðene þeodan winnan woldan. Ðurh þas fare wearð se cyng 7 his broðor Rodbeard eorl sehte, swa þ*et* se cyng ofer sæ for 7 eall Normandig æt hi*m* mid feo alisde, swa swa hi þa sehte wæron. And se eorl syððan ferde, 7 mid hi*m* se eorl of Flandran 7 se of Bunan 7 eac manege oðre heafodmen; 7 se eorl Rotbeard 7 þa þe mid him ferdon þon*e* winter on Puille wunedon. Ac þes folces þe be Hungrie for, fela þusenda þær 7 be wæge earmlice forforan, 7 fela hreowlice 7 hungerbitene ongean winter ha*m* tugon. Ðis wæs swiðe hefigtime gear geond eall Angelcyn, ægðer ge þurh mænigfealde gylda 7 eac þurh swiðe / hefigtymne hunger þe þisne eard þæs geares swiðe gedrehte. Eac on þison geare þa heafodmen þe þis land heoldan oftrædlice fyrde into Wealon sendon 7 mænig man mid ˡþa*m*ˡ swiðe g*e*drehtan, ac man þær ne gespædde, butan manmyrringe 7 feohspillinge.

15 20 25 f. 72r 30

Ann*o* M*illesimo* xcvii. Her on þison geare weas se cyng Willelm to Cr*ist*esmæssan on Normandig; 7 þa togeanes Eastron hider to lande for, forþa*m* he þohte his hired on Winceastre to healdenne, ac he wearð þurh weder gelet oððet Eastre æfen þ*et* he up co*m* ærost æt Arundel, 7 forþi his hired æt Windlesoran heold. 7 þæræft*er* mid mycclu*m* here into Wealon ferde, 7 þ*et* land swiðe mid his fyrde þurhfor, þurh sume þa wyliscean þe hi*m* to wæron cumen 7 his lædteowas wæron. 7 þærinne wunode fra*m* Middesumeran forneah oð August, 7 mycel þærinne forleas on mannan 7 on horsan 7 eac on manegan oðran þingan. Ða wylisce men, syððon hi fra*m* þa*m* cynge gebugon, heo*m* manege ealdras of heo*m*sylfan gecuron: sum þæra wæs Caduugaun gehaten þe heora weorðast wæs, se wæs Griffines broðersunu cynges. Ac þa ða se cyng geseah þ*et* he

5 10

1096/11 *MS.* sumNe

15 nan þingc his willes þær geforðian ne mihte, he ongean into
þison lande for, 7 hraðe æfter þa*m* he be þa*m* gemæron castelas
let gemakian. Ða uppon S*anct*e Michael*es* mæssan, iiii° No-
narum Octobr*is*, ætywde an selcuð steorra on æfen scynende 7
sona to setle gangende; he wæs gesewen suðweast 7 se leoma þe
20 hi*m* of stod wæs swiðe lang geþuht suðeast scinende, 7 forneah
ealle þa wucan on þas wisan ætywde: manige men leton þ*et* hit
cometa wære. Sona æft*er* þyson se arceb*iscop* Ansealm of
Cantwarbyrig leafe æt þa*m* cynge na*m*—þeah hit þa*m* cynge
ungewill wære, þæs þe men leton—7 ofer sæ for, forþa*m* him
25 þuhte þ*et* man on þisne þeodan lytel æfter rihte 7 æft*er* his
f. 72ᵛ dyhte dyde. And se cyng þæræft*er* uppon S*anct*e / Martines
mæssan ofer sæ into Normandig for; ac, þa hwile þe he wederes
abad, his hired innon þa*m* sciran þær hi lagon þon*e* mæston
hearm dydon þe æfre hired oððe here innon friðlande don
30 sceolde. Ðis wæs on eallon þingan swiðe hefigtyme gear 7 ofer-
geswincfull, on ungewederan þa man oððe tilian sceolde oððe
eft tilða gegaderian 7 on ungyldan þa næfre ne ablunnon. Eac
manege sciran þe mid weorce to Lundenne belu*m*pon wurdon
þærle gedrehte þurh þon*e* weall þe hi worhton onbutan þon*e* Tur
35 7 þurh þa brycge þe forneah eall toflotan wæs 7 þurh þæs cynges
heallegeweorc þe man on Westmynstre worhte; 7 mænige man
þærmid gedrehte. Eac on þysu*m* ylcan geare sona uppon
S*anct*e Michaeles mæssan ferde Eadgar æþeling mid fyrde þurh
þæs cynges fultu*m* into Scotlande 7 þet land mid stranglicu*m*
40 feohte gewann 7 þon*e* cyng Dufenal ut adræfde, 7 his mæg
Eadgar, se wæs Melcolmes sunu cynges 7 Margarite þære cwenan,
he þær on þæs cynges Willelmes heldan to cynge gesette, 7
sy[ðð]an ongean into Engleland for.

Mill*esimo* xcviii. On þysum geare to Cr*ist*esmæssan wæs se
cyng W*illelm* on Normandig. 7 Walcelin b*iscop* on Winceastre
7 Baldewine abb*ot* on S*anct*e Ædmund innan þære tide bægen
forðferdan. 7 On þisu*m* geare eac Turold abb*ot* of Burh forð-
5 ferde. Ðises geares eac to þan sumeran innan Barrucscire æt

1097/36 *2nd* man, a *inserted over subpuncted* e 1097/43 *MS.* syddan

Fincha*m*stæde an mere blod weoll, swa swa manige trywe men sædan þe hit geseon sceoldan. 7 Hugo eorl wearð ofslagen innan Anglesege fra*m* utwikingan; 7 his broðer Rodbert wearð his yrfenuma, swa swa he hit æt þa*m* cynge ofeode. Toforan S*anct*e Michael*es* mæssan ætywde seo heofon swilce heo forneah 10 ealle þa niht byrnende wære. Ðis wæs swiðe g*e*swincfull gear þurh manigfeal[de] ungyld; 7 þurh mycele renas þe ealles geares ne ablunnon forneah ælc tilð on mersc/lande forferde. f. 73r

Mill*esi*mo xcix. Her wæs se cyng Will*el*m to Midewintra on Normandig; 7 to Eastron hider to lande co*m*, 7 to Pentecosten forman siðe his hired innan his niwan g*e*byttlan æt Westmynstre heold. 7 þær Rannulfe his capellane þ*et* biscoprice on Dunholme geaf, þe æror ealle his gemot ofer eall Engleland draf 7 5 bewiste. 7 Sona þæræft*er* ofer sæ for 7 þon*e* eorl Elias of þære Manige adraf, 7 hy syððan on his geweald gesætte; 7 swa to S*anct*e Michael*es* mæssan eft hider to lande co*m*. Ðises geares eac on S*anct*e Martin*es* mæssedæg asprang up [to] þan swiðe sæflod 7 swa mycel to hearme gedyde swa nan man ne g*e*munet 10 þ*et* hit æfre æror dyde, 7 wæs ðæs ylcan dæges luna p*ri*ma. And Osmund biscop of Searbyrig innon Aduent forðferde.

Mill*esi*mo c. On þison geare se cyng W*illelm* heold his hired to Cr*ist*esmæssa on Gleaweceastre, 7 to Eastron on Winceastre, 7 to Pentecost*en* on Westmynstre. 7 To þa*m* Pentecost*en* wæs ˡgeˡsewen innan Barrucscire æt anan tune blod weallan of eorþan, swa swa mænige sædan þe hit g*e*seon sceoldan. And 5 þæræft*er* on morgen æft*er* Hla*m*mæsse dæge wearð se cyng Willelm on huntnoðe fra*m* his anan men mid anre fla ofsceoten, 7 syððan to Winceastre gebroht 7 on þa*m* biscoprice bebyrged: þ*et* wæs þæs þreotteðan geares þe he rice onfeng. He wæs swiðe strang 7 reðe ofer his land 7 his mænn 7 wið ealle his 10 neahheburas 7 swiðe ondrædendlic; 7 þurh yfelra manna rædas þe hi*m* æfre gecweme wæran 7 þurh his agene gitsunga, he æfre þas leode mid here 7 mid ungylde tyrwigende wæs, forþan þe

1098/12 *MS.* manigfealð 1099/9 *MS.* up to to þan 1100/6 *MS.* morgem, *with last minim subpuncted.*

on his dagan ælc riht afeoll 7 ælc unriht for Gode 7 for worulde
15 up aras. Godes cyrcean he nyðerade, 7 þa b*is*coprices 7 abb*ot*-
f. 73ᵛ rices þe þa ealdras on his dagan feollan, / ealle he hi oððe wið feo
gesealde oððe on his agenre hand heold 7 to gafle gesette, forþan
þe he ælces mannes—gehadodes 7 læwedes—yrfenuma beon
wolde, 7 swa þ*et* þæs dæges þe he gefeoll he heafde on his
20 agenre hand þ*et* arceb*iscop*rice on Cantwarbyrig 7 þ*et* bisceop-
rice on Winceast*re* 7 þ*et* on Searbyrig 7 xi abb*ot*rices, ealle to
gafle gesette. And, þeah þe ic hit læng ylde, eall þet þe Gode
wæs lað 7 ri'h'tfull*e* mannan, eall þ*et* wæs gewunelic on þisan
lande on his tyman; 7 forþi he wæs forneah ealre his leode lað 7
25 Gode andsæte, swa swa his ænde ætywde, forþan þe he on middewardan his unrihte buten behreowsunge 7 ælcere dædbote
gewat. On þæne Þunresdæg he wæs ofslagen 7 þæs on morgen
bebyrged. 7 Syðþan he bebyrged wæs, þa witan þe þa neh
handa wæron his broðer Heanrig to cynge gecuran. 7 He
30 þærrihte þ*et* bisc*op*rice on Winceast*re* Will*el*me Giffarde geaf,
7 siþþan to Lundene for; 7 on þan Sunnandæge þæræft*er*,
toforan þa*m* weofode on Westmynstre, Gode 7 eallan folce
behet ealle þa unriht to aleggenne þe on his broðer timan
wæran 7 þa betstan lage to healdene þe on æniges cynges dæge
35 toforan him stodan. And hine syððan æft*er* þa*m* se biscop of
Lundene Mauric*ius* to cynge gehalgode, 7 hi*m* ealle on þeosan
lande to abugan 7 aðas sworan 7 his men wurdon. And se cyng
sona æft*er* þa*m*, be þære ræde þe hi*m* abutan wæran, þon*e* biscop
Rannulf of Dunholme let niman 7 into þa*m* Ture on Lundene let
40 gebringon 7 þær healdan. Ða toforan S*anct*e Michael*es* mæssan
co*m* se arcebiscop Ansealm of Cantwarbyr*ig* hider to lande, swa
swa se cyng Heanrig be his witena ræde hi*m* æft*er* sende, forþan
þe he wæs ut of þis lande gefaren for þan mycelan unrihte þe
se cyng Will*el*m him dyde. And siðþan sona heræft*er* se cyng
45 gena*m* Mahalde hi*m* to wife, Malcolmes cynges dohter of Scot-
f. 74ʳ lande 7 Margareta þære goda / cwæne, Eadwardes cynges
magan, 7 of þan rihtan Ænglalandes kynekynne; 7 on S*anct*e

16 *MS.* Ealle, *with capital* E *beginning new page.* 23 *MS.* ri'h'tfułł
40 *MS.* Michaeł, *with* e *altered from* l

Martines mæssedæg heo wearð him mid mycelan weorðscipe forgifen on Westmynstre, 7 se arcebisc*op* Ansealm hi hi*m* bewæddade 7 siððan to cwene gehalgode. And se arceb*iscop* 50 Thomas of Eoferwic heræft*er* sona forðferde. Ðeoses ylces geares eac innan hærfest co*m* se eorl Rotbert ham into Normandi, 7 se eorl Rotb*ert* of Flandr*an* 7 Eustati*us* eorl of Bunan fra*m* Ierusale*m*. 7 Sona swa se eorl R*otbert* into Normandig com, he wearð fra*m* eallan þa*m* folce bliþelice underfangen, butan 55 þa*m* castelan ðe wæron g*e*sætte mid þæs cynges Heanriges manna[n], togeanes þan he manega gewealc 7 gewinn hæfde.

Mill*esi*mo ci. Her on þisu*m* geare to Cr*ist*esmæssan heold se cyng Heanrig his hired on Westmynstre, 7 to Eastran on Winceastre. 7 þa sona þæræfter wurdon þa heafodmen her on lande wiðerræden togeanes þa*m* cynge, ægðer ge for heor[a] agenan mycelan ungetrywðan 7 eac þurh þon*e* eorl Rodbert 5 of Normandig, þe mid unfriðe hider to lande fundode. And se cyng sy[ðð]an scipa ut on sæ sende his broðer to dære 7 to lættinge; ac hi sume æft æt þære neode abruðon 7 fra*m* þa*m* cynge gecyrdon 7 to þa*m* eorle Rotb*er*te gebugan. Ða to Middesumeran ferde se cyng ut to Pefenesæ mid eall his fyrde 10 togeanes his broðer 7 his þær abad. Ac onmang þison co*m* se eorl Rotb*ert* up æt Portesmuðan xii nihtan toforan Hlafmæssan; 7 se cyng mid ealre his fyrde hi*m* togeanes co*m*. Ac þa heafodmen heo*m* betwenan foran 7 þa broðra gesehtodan on þa gerad þet se cyng forlet eall þ*et* he mid streangðe innan Normandig 15 togeanes þa*m* eorle heold, 7 þ*et* ealle þa on Englelande heora land ongean heafdon þe hit ær þurh þone eorl forluron, 7 Eustaties eorl eac eall his fæder land her on lande, 7 þet se eorl Rotb*er*t ælce geare sceolde of Englalande / þreo þusend marc f. 74v seolfres habban, 7 lochweðer ˡþæra geˡbroðra oðerne oferbide 20 wære yrfeweard ealles Englalandes 7 eac Normandiges buton se forðfarena yrfenuman heafde be rihtre æwe: 7 þis þa mid aðe gefestnodan xii þa hihste of ægðre healfe. And se eorl syððan oððet ofer S*anct*e Michael*es* mæsse her on lande wunode, 7 his

1100/57 *MS.* manna. 1101/4 *MS.* heoran 1101/7 *MS.* syddan

25 men mycel to hearme æfre gedydon swa hi geferdon þa hwile þe se eorl her on lande wunode. Ðises geares eac se b*iscop* Rannulf to þa*m* Candelmæssan ut of þa*m* Ture on Lunden nihtes oðbærst þær he on hæftneðe wæs, 7 to Normandige for, þurh þes macunge mæst 7 tospryttinge se eorl Rotb*er*t þises geares þis land mid 30 unfriðe g*e*sohte.

Mill*esi*mo cii. On þisu*m* geare to Natiuiteð wæs se cyng Heanrig on Westmynstre, 7 to Eastron on Winceastre. 7 Sona þæræft*er* wurdon unsehte se cyng 7 se eorl Rotb*er*t of Bælæsme, se hæfde þon*e* eorldo*m* her on lande on Scrobbesbyrig þe his 5 fæder Roger eorl ær ahte, 7 micel rice þærto, ægðer g*e* beheonon sæ ge begeondon. 7 Se cyng ferde 7 besæt þon*e* castel æt Arundel, ac, þa he hine swa hraðe gewinnan ne mihte, he let þærtoforan castelas gemakian 7 hi mid his mannan gesette, 7 syððan mid ealre his fyrde ferde to Brigge 7 þær wunode oððet 10 he þone castel hæfde, 7 þone eorl Rotbert belænde 7 ealles benæmde þes he on Englalande hæfde. 7 Se eorl swa ofer sæ gewat, 7 se fyrde syððan ha*m* cyrde. Ða þæræft*er* to S*anct*e Michaele*s* mæssen wæs se cyng æt Wæstmynstre, 7 ealle þa hæfodmen on þis lande, g*e*hadode 7 læwede. 7 Se arceb*iscop* 15 Ansealm heold g*e*hadodra manna sinoð, 7 hi þær manega beboda setton þe to Cr*ist*endome belimpað 7 ægðer manige, frencisce 7 englisce, þær heora stafas 7 rice forluron þe hi mid unrihte begeaton o[ðð]e mid woge þæron lifedon. 7 On ðisu*m* ylcan f. 75ʳ geare on Pentecosten mæssan wuce, þa coman / þeofas, sum of 20 Aluearnie, su*m* of France, 7 su*m* of Flandres, 7 breokan þa mynstre of Burh 7 þærinne naman mycel to gode on golde 7 on seolfre, þet wæron roden 7 calicen 7 candelsticcan.

Mill*esi*mo ciii. Her on þisu*m* geare to Midewintra wæs se cyng Heanrig æt Westmynstre. 7 þæræft*er* sona ferde se b*iscop* Willelm Giffard ut of þis land forþan þe he ongean riht nolde his hades onfon æt þa*m* arceb*iscope* Girarde of Eoferwic. 7 5 þa to þan Eastran heold se cyng his hired on Winc*eastre*. 7 þæræft*er* ferde se arceb*iscop* Ansealm of Cantwarbyrig to Rome,

1102/18 *MS.* odde

swa swa hi*m* 7 þa*m* cynge gewearð. Ðises geares eac co*m* se
eorl Rotbert of Normandig to sprecene wið þone cyng her on
lande, 7 ær he heonne ferde he forgeaf þa þreo þusend marc þe
hi*m* seo cyng Heanrig be foreweard ælce geare gifan sceolde. 10
On þisum geare eac æt Heamstede innan Barrucscire wæs
gesewen blod of eorðan. Ðis wæs swiðe gedeo'r'fsum gear her
on lande, þurh mænifealde gyld, 7 þurh orfcwealm 7 wæstma
forweorþenesse ægðer ge on corne 7 eac on eallon treowwæst-
man. Eac on morgen uppon S*anct*e Laurent*ius* mæssedæg 15
gedyde se wind swa mycel to hearme her on lande on eallon
westman swa nan man ne gemunde þ*et* æfre ænig ær gedyde.
On ðisum ylcan geare Mathias abb*ot* of Burh forðferde, se ne
lyfode na leng þa*n* an geare syððan 'he' abb*ot* wæs: æft*er*
S*anct*e Michael*es* mæssan on xii K*alendarum* Nov*embris* he wæs 20
mid procession underfangan to abb*ote*, 7 on ða*m* ylcan dæge þes
oðres geares he wearð dead on Gleawceastre 7 þær bebyrged.

Mill*esi*mo ciiii. Her on þisu*m* geare to Cr*ist*esmæssan heold
se cyng Heanrig his hired æt Wæstminstre, 7 to Eastron on
Winceastre, 7 to Pentecosten eft on Westmynstre. Ðises geares
wæs se forma Pentecostes dæg on No*nas* Iuni*i*, 7 on þam / 4
Tiwæsdæge þæræft*er* ætywdan feower circulas to þa*m* middæge f. 75v
onbutan þære sunnan hwites hiwes, ælc under oðran gebroiden
swylce hi gemette wæron: ealle þe hit gesawon wundredon,
forþan hi næfre ær swilce ne gemundon. Heræft*er* wurdon sehte
se eorl Rotb*er*t of Normandig 7 Rotb*er*t de Bælesme, þe se cyng
Heanri æror belænd hæfde 7 of Englalande adrifen. 7 þurh 10
heora sehte wurdon wiðerræde se cyng of Englalande 7 se eorl
of Normandig. 7 Se cyng his folc ofer sæ into Normandig
sende 7 þa heafodmen þær on lande hi underfengon 7 on heora
hlafordes þæs eorles swicdome into heora castelan gelogodan,
þanon hi manige gedrecednissa on hergunga 7 on bærninge þam 15
eorle gedydon. Eac þises geares Willelm eorl of Moretoin
heonon of lande into Normandig for; ac syððan he afaren wes
he wið þone cyng geworhte, forhwan hine se cyng ealles
benæmde 7 belænde þæs þe he her on lande hæfde. Nis eaðe to

20 asecgenne þises landes earmða þe hit to þysan timan dreogende wæs, þurh mistlice 7 mænigfealdlice unriht 7 gyld þæ næfre ne geswican ne ne ateorodon; 7 æfre ealswa se cyng for, full hergung þurh his hired uppon his wreccea folc wæs, 7 þæronmang foroft bærneta 7 manslihtas:

25 eall þis wæs God mid to gremienne,
7 þas arme leode mid to tregienne.

Mill*esi*mo cv. On þisu*m* geare to Natiuiteð heold se cyng Heanrig his hired æt Windlesoran. 7 þæræft*er* to þa*m* lengtene he for ofer sæ into Normandig uppon his broðer Rotbert eorl; 7 onmang þa*m* þe he þær wunode he gewann of his broþer Caþum
5 7 Baius, 7 mæst ealle þa castelas 7 þa heafodmen þær on lande hi*m* wurdon underþeodde. 7 Se [cyng] syððan to herfest eft ongean hider to lande co*m*; 7 þ*et* he on Normandig g*e*wunnen hæfde syððan on sibbe 7 hi*m* gebygle wunode, butan þa þe þa*m*
f. 76r eorle Will*el*me of Mortoin ahwær neah wunedon, þa he ge/lom-
10 lice geswæncte swa he swiðost mihte for his landlyre her on lande. And þa toforan Cr*ist*esmessan co*m* Rotb*er*t de Bælesme hider to lande to þa*m* cynge. Ðis wæs swiðe gedyrfsum gear her on lande, þurh wæstma forwordenessa 7 þurh þa mænigfealde gyld þe næfre ne geswican ær se cyng oferfore 7 þa hwile þe he
15 þær wæs 7 eft syððan he ongean com.

Mill*esi*mo cvi. Her on þyson geare wæs se cyng Henrig to Natiuiteð on Westmynstre, 7 þær his hired heold. 7 Uppon þære tide Rotbert de Bælesme mid unsehte fra*m* þa*m* cynge ut of þison lande into Normandige for. Ða heræft*er* onforan læng-
5 tene wæs se cyng æt Norðha*m*tune; 7 se eorl Rotbert his broðer of Normandig þyder to hi*m* co*m*, 7, forþa*m* se cyng hi*m* nolde agifan þ*et* þe he on Normandig*e* uppon hi*m* genumen hæfde, hi mid unsehte tohwurfon, 7 se eorl ferde ofer sę sona eft ongean. On þære forman længtenwucan, on þon*e* Frigedæg ˡi. xiiii
10 K*alendarum* Ma*rtii*ˡ, on æfen ætywde an ungewunelic steorra, 7 lange stunde þæræft*er* wæs ælce æfen gesewen hwile scinende. Se steorra ætywde innon þ*et* suðwest: he wæs litel geþuht and

1105/6 *MS.* 7 se syððan 1105/12 her *preceded by subpuncted* o

deorc, ac se leoma þe hi*m* fra*m* stod wæs swiðe beorht, 7 swilce ormæte beam geþuht norðeast scinende, 7 su*m*ne æfen wæs gesæwen swilce se beam ongeanweardes wið þes steorran ward 15 fyrcliende wære. Gehwylce sædon þ*et* hig ma on þison timon uncuðra steorra gesawon, ac we hit openlicor ne awriton forþa*m* þe we hit sylfe ne sawon. On þa niht þe on morgen wæs Cena D*omi*ni, þ*et* is se þunresdæg toforan Eastran, wæron gesewen twegen monan on þære heofonan toforan þam dæge, oðer be 20 eastan 7 se oðer be westan, begen fulle; 7 þæs ylcan dæges wæs se mona xiiii[a]. To Eastran wæs se cyng æt Baðan, 7 to Pentecosten æt Searbyrig, forþa*m* þe he nolde on his fundunge ofer sæ hired healdan. Ðæræfter to/fora˥n˥ August ferde se cyng ofer f. 76v sæ into Normandig. 7 Ealle mæst þe þær on lande wæron hi*m* 25 on his willan to gebugon, wiðuton Rotb*er*t de Bælesme 7 þa*m* eorle of Moretoin 7 feawa oðre of þa*m* heafodmannan þe mid þa*m* eorle of Normandige þe gyt heoldan. 7 Forþan se cyng syððan mid fyrde for 7 besæt þæs eorles ænne castel of Moretoin, Tenercebrai hatte. Onmang þa*m* þe se cyng þon*e* castel 30 besæt, co*m* se eorl Rotb*er*t of Normandig on S*anct*e Michaele*s* mæsseæfen uppon þone cyng mid his fyrde, 7 mid hi*m* Rotb*er*t de Bælesme 7 Willelm eorl of Moretoin 7 ealle þa þe mid heo*m* woldan. Ac seo streongðe 7 se sige wearð þæs cynges. Ðær wearð se eorl of Normandig gefangen, 7 se eorl of Moretoin 7 35 Rotb*er*t de Stutteuile, 7 to Englalande syððan gesende 7 on hæftneðe gebrohte. Rotb*er*t de Bælesme þær wearð aflymed, 7 Will*el*m Crispin g*e*læht, 7 manige forð mid. Eadgar æþeling, þe litle ær fra*m* þa*m* cynge to þa*m* eorle wæs gefaren, þær wæs eac gefangen; þone let se cyng syððan sacleas faran. Syððan 40 geeode se cyng eall þ*et* on Normandige wæs, 7 hit on his willan 7 geweald gesette. Ðises geares eac wæron swiðe hefige 7 sinlice gewinn betwux þa*m* Casere of Sex˥l˥ande 7 his sunu; 7 onmang þa*m* g*e*winnan se fæder forðferde 7 se sunu feng to þam rice. 45

Mill*esi*mo cvii. On þisu*m* geare to Cr*ist*esmæssan wæs se cyng Henri on Normandig, 7 þ*et* land on his g*e*weald dihte 7 sette;

7 þæræft*er* to længtene hider to lande co*m*, 7 to Eastran his hired on Windlesoran heold, 7 to Pentecosten on Westminstre;
5 7 syððan eft to Augustes anginne on Westmynstre wæs, 7 þær þa biscopricen 7 abbodric*en* geaf 7 sette þe on Englelande oððe on Normandige buton ealdre 7 hyrde [wæron]: ðera wæron swa fela swa nan man næs þe gemvnde þ*et* æfre ær swa fela togædere
f. 77r gyfene wæron. 7 Æt þes ylcan / sy[ð]e, onmang þa o[ð]re þe
10 abb*od*rices underfengon, Ernulf, þe ær wæs prior on Cantwarbyrig, feng to þa*m* abb*od*rice on Burh. Đis wæs rihtlice ymbe vii gear þæs þe se cyng Henri cynedomes onfeng, 7 wæs þ*et* an and fowertigeðe gear þæs þe Francan þises landes weoldan. Manege sædon þet hi on þa*m* monan þyses geares
15 mistlice tacna gesawon 7 ongean cynde his leoman wexende 7 waniende. Đises geares forðferdon Mauric*ius* biscop on Lunden 7 Rotb*er*t abb*ot* on S*anct*e Eadmundes byrig 7 Ricard abb*ot* on Elig. Đises geares eac forðferde se cyng Eadgar on Scotlande Id*us* Ian*uarii*, 7 feng Alexander his broðer to þa*m* rice
20 swa se cyng Henri hi*m* geuðe.

Mill*esi*mo cviii. Her on þisu*m* geare wes se cyng Henri to Natiuiteð on Westmynstre, 7 to Eastron on Winceastre, 7 to Penteco*sten* eft on Westmynstre. 7 þæræft*er* toforan Aug*ust* he ferde into Normandig. 7 Se cyng of France Philipp*us*
5 forðferde No*nis* Aug*usti*, 7 feng his sunu Loðewis to þa*m* rice. 7 Wurdon syððon manege gewinn betwux þa*m* cynge of France 7 þa*m* of Englelande þa hwile þe he on Normandig wunode. On þisu*m* geare eac forðferde se arceb*iscop* Girard of Eoferwic
9 toforan Pentecost*en* 7 wearð syððan Thomas þærto gesett.

Mill*esi*mo cix. Her on þison geare wæs se cyng Henri to Cr*ist*esmæssan 7 to Eastron on Normandig; 7 toforan Pente*costen* hider to lande co*m*, 7 his hired on Westmynstre heold. Đær wurdon þa forewarda full worhte 7 þa aðas gesworene his
5 dohter þa*m* Casere to gifene. Đises geares gewurdon swiðe fela þunra, 7 þa swiðe ægeslice. And se arceb*iscop* Ansealm of

1107/7 *MS*. hyrde. Đera 1107/9 *MS*. syde 1107/9 *MS*. odðre

Cantwarabyrig forðferde on þa*m* dæge xi K*alendarum* Apr*ilis*. 7 Wæs se forma Easterdæg on Letania Maior. 8

Mill*esi*mo cx. On þisu*m* geare heold se cyng Henri his hired to Cr*ist*esmæssan æt Westmynstre, 7 to Eastron / he wæs æt Mærlebeorge, 7 to Pentec*osten* forman siþe his hired on þa*m* niwan Windlesoran heold. Đises geares sende se cyng toforan længtene his dohter mid mænigfealdan madman ofer sæ 7 hi þam Casere forgeaf. On þære fiftan nihte on Maies monðe ætywde se mona on æfen beorhte scinende, 7 syððan litlan 7 litlan his leoht wanode swa þ*et* he sona nihtes to þa*m* swiðe mid ealle acwanc þ*et* naþer ne leoht ne trændel ne nan þing mid ealle of hi*m* wæs gesæwen, 7 swa þurhwunode fullneah oð dæg, 7 syðþan full 7 beorhte scinende ætywde: he wæs þæs ylcan dæges feowertyne nihta eald. Ealle þa niht wæs seo lyft swiðe clene 7 þa steorran ofer eall þa heofon swiðe beorhte scinende; 7 tr˹e˺owwæstmas wurdon þære nihte þurh forste swiðe fornumene. Đæræft*er* on Iunies monðe ætywde an steorra norðan eastan, 7 his leoma stod toforan hi*m* on þet suðwest; 7 þus manega niht wæs gesæwen, 7 furðor nihtes syððan he ufor astah he wæs g*e*sewen on bæc on þ*et* norðwest gangende. Đises geares wurdon belænde Philipp*us* de Brause 7 Will*el*m Malet 7 Will*el*m Bainart. Eac þises geares forðferde Elias eorl þe þa Mannie of þa*m* cynge Heanri geheold 7 onc[n]eow; 7 æft*er* his forsiðe feng to se eorl ˹of˺ Angeow, 7 hi togeanes þa*m* cynge heold. Đis wæs swiðe gedeorfsu*m* gear her on lande þurh gyld þe se cyng nam for his dohter gyfte, 7 þurh ungewædera for hwan eorðwestmas wurdon swiðe amyrde 7 treowwestmas ofer eall þis land forneah eall forwurdon. Đises geares me began ærost to weorcenne on þa*m* niwan mynstre on Ceortesæge.

f. 77v (margin) — line numbers 5, 10, 15, 20, 25

Mill*esi*mo cxi. On þison geare ne bær se kyng Henri his coronan to Cr*ist*esmæssan, ne to Eastron, ne to Pentec*osten*; 7 innan August he ferde ofer sæ into Normandig for unsehte þe wið hi*m* hæfdon sume be þa*m* gemæran of France, 7 swiðost for þa*m* eorle of Angeow þe þa Mannie togeanes him heold. And / 5

1110/21 *MS.* oncweow

f. 78r syððan he þyder ofer co*m*, manega unrada 7 bærnetta 7 hergunga hi heo*m* betweonan gedydan. On þison geare forðferde se eorl Rotbert of Flandran, 7 feng his sunu Baldewine þærto. Ðises geares wæs swiðe lang wint*er* 7 hefigtyme 7 strang, 7 þurh þ*et*
10 eorðwæstmas wurdon swiðe amyrde 7 g*e*wearð se mæsta orfcwealm þe ænig mann mihte gemunan.

Mill*esi*mo cxii. Eall þis gear wunode se cyng Henri on Normandig for þære unsehte þe he hæfde wið France 7 wið þon*e* eorl of Angeow, þe þa Mannie togeanes hi*m* heold. 7 Onmang þa*m* þe he þær wæs, he belænde þon*e* eorl of Eureus 7 Will*el*m
5 Crispin, 7 ut of Normandi adraf, 7 Philippe de Braus his land ageaf, þe ær wæs belænd; 7 Rotb*er*t de Bælesme he let niman 7 on prisune don. Ðis wæs swiðe god gear 7 swiðe wistfull on wudan 7 on feldan, ac hit wæs swiðe hefigtyme 7 sorhfull þurh
9 ormætne mancwealm.

Mill*esi*mo cxiii. Her on þison geare wæs se cyng Henri to Natiuiteð 7 to Eastron 7 to Penteco*sten* on Normandig. 7 þæræft*er* to sumeran he sænde hider to lande Rotb*er*t de Bælesme into þam castele to Wærha*m*, 7 hi*m*sylf sona þæræft*er*
5 hider to lande com.

Mill*esi*mo cxiiii. On þison geare heold se cyng Henri his hyred to Natiuiteð on Windlesoran 7 þæs geares syððan he ne heold hired nan oftar. And to Middansumeran he ferde mid fyrde into Wealon, 7 þa wyliscean coman 7 wið þon*e* cyng griðedon,
5 7 he let þærinne castelas weorcean. 7 þæræft*er* innan September he for ofer sæ into Normandig. Ðises geares on æfteward Mai wæs gesewen an selcuð steorra mid langan leoman manege niht scinende. Eac on þis ylcan geare wæs swa mycel ebba æghwær anes dæges swa nan man æror ne g*e*munde 7
10 swa þ*et* man ferde ridende 7 gangende ofer Tæmese be eastan þære brigge on Lunden. Þises geares wæron swiðe mycele windas on Octobr*is* monðe, ac he wæs ormæte mycel on þa niht
f. 78v Octabę S*an*ct*i* Martini, 7 þ*et* gehwær on wudan 7 on / tunan gecydde. Eac on þisu*m* geare se cyng geaf þet arceb*iscop*rice on

Cantwarabyrig Raulfe, se wæs æror biscop on Hrofeceastre. 15
And se arceb*iscop* on Eoferwic, Thomas, forðferde, 7 feng
Turstein þærto, se wæs æror þæs cynges capelein. On þæs
ylcan tyme feorde se cyng toweard þon*e* sæ 7 ofer wolde, ac
wæder hi*m* lætte. Þa hwile þa sende he his writ æft*er* þon*e*
abb*ot* Ernulf of Burh 7 bebead hi*m* þ*et* he efeostlice scolde to 20
hi*m* cuman, forþi þ*et* he wolde sprecon mid hi*m* dærne sprece.
Ða he to hi*m* co*m*, þa neodde he hi*m* to þa*m* biscoprice of
Hrofeceastre, 7 þa arc*e*biscopes 7 biscopes 7 þ*et* dugeð þ*et* wæs
on Englalande forð mid se cyng. 7 He lange wiðstod, ac hit ne
forheol[d] naht, 7 se cyng þa bebead þon*e* arc*e*b*iscop* þ*et* he 25
sceolde hi*m* læden to Cantwarabyrig 7 blætson hi*m* to b*iscop*,
wolde he nolde he. Þis wæs don on þære tuna þa man cleopa[ð]
Burne, þ*et* wæs þes dæges xvii K*alendarum* Octobr*is*. Ða þe
munecas of Burch hit herdon sægen, þa wæron hi swa sari swa
hi næfre ær ne wæron, forði þ*et* he wæs swiðe god 7 softe man 30
7 dyde mycel to gode wiðinnan 7 wiðutan þa hwile þe he þær
wunode—God ælmihtig wunie æfre mid hi*m*! Ða sona þæræft*er* þa geaf se cyng þon*e* abb*ot*rice an munec of Sæis, Iohan
wæs g*e*haten, þurh þæs arceb*iscopes* gearnunge of Cantwarbyrig.
7 Sona þæræft*er* sende se cyng hi*m*, 7 se arceb*iscop* of Cantwar- 35
b*yrig*, to Rome ˈæft*er* þes ærceb*iscopes* palliu*m*ˈ 7 an ˈmunecˈ mid
hi*m*, Warner wæs gehaten, 7 þon*e* ærcediæcne Iohan, þes
arceb*iscopes* neafe; 7 hi þær well spæddon. Ðis wæs don þes
dæges xi K*alendarum* Octobr*is* on þone tuna þe man cleopað
Rugenore; 7 þes ylces dæges codc se cynˈgˈ on scipa on 40
Portesmuðe.

Mill*esi*mo cxv. Her wæs se cyng Henri to Natiuiteð on Normandig; 7 onmang þa*m* þe he þær wæs, he dyde þ*et* ealle þa
heafodmæn on Normandig dydon manræden 7 holdaðas his
sunu Will*el*me þe he be his cwæne hæfde; 7 æft*er* þan syððan
innon Iulies monðe hider into lande co*m*. Ðises geares wæs swa 5
strang wint*er* mid snawe 7 mid forste swa nan man þe þa

1114/25 *MS.* forheol 27 *MS.* cleopad 36 æft*er* þes ærceb*iscopes* palliu*m* *inserted above the line in a different ink;* munec *inserted in right margin in a different ink.* 37 wæs *inserted in different ink over subpuncted* is

f. 79r lifode / ær þan nan strengre ne *ge*munde, 7 wearð þurh þ*et* ungemæte orfcwealm. On þison geare sænde se Papa Paschal*is* Raulfe ærceb*iscope* on Cantwarabyrig palliu*m* hider to lande, 7
10 he his onfeng mid mycelan wurðscipe æt his arcestole on Cant*wara*byrig; hine brohte Ansealm abb*ot* of Rome, se wæs nefa Ansealmes ærceb*iscopes*, ˡ7 se abb*ot* Iohan of Burh.ˡ

Mill*esi*mo cxvi. On þison geare wæs se cyng Henri to Natiuiteð æt S*anct*e Albane, 7 þær let þ*et* mynster halgian, 7 to Eastron on Wudiham. 7 Wes eac þyses geares swiðe hefigtyme winter 7 strang 7 lang, wið orf 7 wið ealle þing. And se cyng æft*er*
5 Eastron sona ferde ofer sæ into Normandig. 7 Wurdon manega unrada 7 ræfunga 7 castelas *ge*numene betwux France 7 Normandig. Mæst þis unsehte wæs forþan þe se cyng Henri fylste his nefan þa*m* eorle Tædbalde de Blais, þe þa wyrre hæfde togeanes his hlaforde þa*m* cynge of France Loðewis. Ðis wæs
10 swiðe *ge*swincfull gear 7 byrstfull on eorðwæstman, þurh þa ormæte reinas þe coman sona onforan August 7 swiðe gedrehton 7 geswencton þe gyt þe co*m* Candelmæssan. Eac þis gear wæs swa gæsne on mæstene swa þ*et* on eallon þison lande ne eac on Wealon ne *ge*hyrde me of nanan segcean. Ðis land 7 þas leodan
15 wurdon eac þyses geares oftrædlice sare geswencte þurh þa gylˡdˡ þe se cyng na*m* ægðer ge binnan burgan 7 butan. On þisu*m* ylcan geare bærnde eall þ*et* mynstre of Burh 7 eallæ þa husas butan se captelhus 7 se slæpperne, 7 þærtoeac bærnde eall þa mæste dæl of þa tuna. Eall þis bela*m*p on an Frigdæg,
20 þ*et* wæs ii No*narum* Aug*usti*.

Mill*esi*mo cxvii. Eall þis gear wunode se cyng Henri on Normandig for þes cynges unsehte of France 7 his oðra nehhebura. 7 þa to ðan sumeran co*m* se cyng of France 7 se eorl of Flandra
4 mid hi*m* mid fyrde into Normandig, 7 ane niht. þærinne wunedon
f. 79v 7 on morgen butan gefeohte on/gean ferden. 7 Normandig wearð swiðe gedreht ægðer *ge* þurh gyld ge þurh fyrde þe se cing Henri þærongean gaderode. Eac þeos þeode þurh þis ylce, þurh manigfealde gyld, wearð strange geswenct. Ðises geares

1115/27 7 se abb̄ Iohan of burh *inserted in the margin in a paler ink.*

eac on þære nihte K*alend*ę Decemb*ris* wurdon ormætlica wædera mid þunre 7 lihtinge 7 reine 7 hagole. And on þære 10
nihte iii° Id*us* Dec*embris* wearð se mona lange nihtes swylce he eall blodig wære, 7 syððan aðistrode. Eac on þære nihte xvii K*alendarum* Ian*uarii* wæs seo heofon swyðe read gesewen swylce hit bryne wære. And on Octab*as* S*anc*t*i* Ioh*anni*s Eu*angelist*ę wæs seo mycele eorðbyfung on Lumbardige, for hwan manega 15
mynstras 7 turas 7 huses gefeollon 7 mycelne hearm on mannan gedydon. Ðis wæs swyðe byrstful gear on corne þurh þa renas þe forneh ealles geares ne geswicon. And se abb*ot* Gilebert of Westmynstre forðferde viii Id*us* Dec*embris*; and Farits abb*ot* of Abbandune vii K*alendarum* Martii. And on þisum ylcan 20
geare * * * * * * * * * * * *
* * * * * * * * *

Mill*esi*mo cxviii. Her eall þis gear wunode se cyng Henri on Normandig for þes cynges wyrre of France 7 þæs eorles of Angeow 7 þæs eorles of Flandran. 7 Se eorl of Flandra warð innan Normandig gewundod, 7 swa gewundo[d] into Flandran
for. Ðurh þisra unsehte wearð se cyng swyðe gedreht 7 mycel 5
forleas ægðer ge on feoh 7 eac on lande; 7 mæst hine dryfdon his agene mæn þe hi*m* gelome fra*m* bugon 7 swicon 7 to his feondan cyrdon 7 heo*m* to þæs cynges hearme 7 swicdome heora castelas ageafon. Eall þis strange gebohte Englaland þurh
þa mænigfealdlice gyld þe ealles þises geares ne geswicon. On 10
þison geare on þære wucon Theophanie wæs anes æfenes swyðe mycel lihtinge 7 ungemetlice slæge þæræft*er*. And seo cwen
Mahald / forðferde on Westmynstre þæs dæges K*alend*ę Mai f. 80r
7 þær wæs bebyrged; and se eorl Rotbert of Mellent þises
geares eac forðferde. Eac on þison geare to S*anc*t*e* Thomas 15
mæsse wæs swa swiðe ungemetlice mycel wind þ*et* nan man þe þa lifode nænne maran ne gemunde, 7 þ*et* wæs æghwer geseone ægðer ge on husan 7 eac on treowan. Ðises geares eac forðferde se Papa Paschal*is* 7 feng Iohan of Gaitan to þa*m* Papdome, þa*m*
wæs oðer nama Gelasius. 20

1117/21 ylcan geare *begins line; the rest of the line and the following one are left blank.* 1118/4 *MS.* gewundon

Mill*esi*mo cxix. Ðis gear eall wunode se cyng Henri on Normandig; 7 wæs þurh þæs cynges wyrre of France 7 eac his agenra manna, þe hi*m* mid swicdome fra*m* wæron abugon, oftrædlice swyðe gedreht oððet þa twegen cyngas innan Nor-
5 mandige mid heor[a] folcan coman togædere. þær wearð seo cyng of France aflymed 7 ealle his betste mæn genumene. 7 Syððan þæs cynges mæn Heanriges manega hi*m* to gebugen 7 wið hine acordedan þe æror mid heora castelan hi*m* togeanes wæron; 7 sume þa castelas he mid strengðe gena*m*. Ðises
10 geares ferde Willelm, þæs cynges sunu Heanriges 7 þære cwene Mahalde, into Normandige to his fæder, 7 þær wearð hi*m* forgifen 7 to wife beweddod þæs eorles dohter of Angeow. On S*anct*e Michael*es* mæsseæfen wæs mycel eorðbifung on suman steodan her on lande, þeah swyðost on Gloweceastrescire 7 on
15 Wigreceastrescire. On þis ylcan geare forðferde se Papa Gelasius on þas halfe þære muntan, 7 wæs on Clunig bebyrged; 7 æft*er* hi*m* se arceb*iscop* of Uiana wearð to Papan gecoren, þam wearð nama Calixtus, se syððan to S*anct*e Lucas mæssan Eu*an*gelista co*m* into France to Ræins, 7 þær heold conciliu*m*.
20 7 Se arceb*iscop* Turstein of Eoferwic þyder ferde, 7 forþi þe he togeanes rihte 7 togeanes þa*m* arcestole on Cantwarabyrig 7 togeanes þæs cynges willan his had æt þam Papan underfeng, him wiðcwæð se cyng ælces geanfares to Englalande; 7 he þus
f. 80v his arceb*iscop*rices þærnode 7 mid ðam / Papan towardes Rome
25 for. Eac on þison geare forðferde se eorl Baldewine of Flandran of þa*m* wundan þe he innan Normandige gefeng; 7 æfter hi*m* feng Carl his faðasunu to þam rice, se wæs Cnutes sunu þæs haligan cynges of Denmarcan.

Mill*esi*mo cxx. Ðises geares wurdon sehte seo cyng of Englelande 7 se of France; 7 æfter heora sehte acordedan ealle þæs cynges Heanriges agene mæn wið hine innan Normandige, 7 se eorl of Flandran 7 se of Puntiw. Syððan heræfter sætte
5 se cyng Henrig his castelas 7 his land on Normandi æfter his willan, 7 swa toforan Aduent hider to lande for. 7 On þam

1119/3 *MS.* wæron mid abugon, *with* mid *subpuncted.* 1119/5 *MS.* heoran 1119/13 *MS.* michaeł, *with* e *altered from* l

fare wurdon adr[u]ncene þæs cynges twegen sunan Willelm 7 Ricard, 7 Ricard eorl of Ceastre 7 Ottuel his broðor 7 swyðe manega of þæs cynges hired—stiwardas 7 burþenas 7 byrlas 7 of mistlicean wican—7 ungerim swyðe ænlices folces forð mid. 10 Ðysra deað wæs heora freondan twyfealdlic sar: an þet hi swa fearlice þises lifes losedan; oðer þet feawa heora lichaman ahwær syððan fundena wæron. Ðises geares com þet leoht to Sepulchrum Domini innan Ierusalem twiges, ænes to Eastron and o[ð]re siðe to Assumptio Sanctę Marie, swa swa geleaffulle 15 sædon þe þanon coman. An[d] se arcebiscop Turstein of Eoferwic wearð ˡþurhˡ þone Papan wið þone cyng acordad, 7 hider to lande com 7 his biscoprices onfeng, þeah hit þam arcebiscope of Cantwarabyrig swyðe ungewille wære. 19

Millesimo cxxi. Her wæs se cyng Henri to Cristesmæssan on Bramtune; 7 þæˡrˡæfter toforan Candelmæssan on Windlesoran [wearð] him to wife forgyfen Aðelis 7 syððan to cwene gehalgod, seo wæs þæs heretogan dohtor of Luuaine. And se mona 4 aþystrodc on þære nihte Nonę Aprilis / 7 wæs xiiii luna. And f. 81ʳ se cyng wæs to Eastran on Beorclea; and þæræfter to Pentecosten he heold mycelne hired on Westmynstre; and syððan þæs sumeres mid ferde into Wealan for, 7 þa wyliscean him ongean coman 7 æfter þes cynges willan hi wið hine acordedan. Ðises geares com se eorl of Angeow fram Ierusalem into his 10 lande; 7 syððan hider to lande sende 7 his dohter let feccean, seo wæs Willelme þes cynges sune æror to wife forgyfan. And on þære nihte Uigilia Natalis Domini wæs swyðe mycel wind ofer eall þis land, 7 þet wearð on manegan þingan swyðe gesene. 14

Millesimo cxxºiiº. On þis geare wæs se king Heanri on Cristesmæssan on Norhtwic, 7 on Pasches he weas on Norhthamtune. 7 On þone lententyde þærtoforen forbearn se burch on Gleawecestre. Þa hwile þe þa munecas sungen þære messe 7 se dæcne hafde ongunnan þone godspel "Preteriens Iesus", þa com se 5 fir on ufenweard þone stepel 7 forbearnde ealle þe minstre 7

1120/7 *MS.* adrncene 1120/15 *MS.* odre 1120/16 *MS.* An
1121/3 *MS.* on windlesoran him to wife

ealle þa gersumes þe þærbinnen wæron, foruton feawe bec 7 iii messehakeles: þet wes ˈþesˈ dæies viii Id*us* M*artii*. 7 **þ**æræfter þe Tywesdæi æfter Palmes Sunendæi wæs swiðe micel wind on
10 þ*et* dæi xi K*alendarum* Apr*ilis*. **þ**æræfter comen feale tacne wide hwear on Engleland, 7 feole dwild wearen geseogen 7 geheord. 7 **þ**es niht viii K*alendarum* Aug*usti* wæs swiðe micel eorðdyne ofer eal Sumersetescire 7 on Gleawecestrescire. Siððon on þæs dæi vi Id*us* Sept*embris*, þet wæs ˈonˈ S*anc*te
15 Mariȩ messedæi, þa wearð swiðe micel wind fra*m* þa undern dæies to þa swarte nihte. **þ**eos ilce geares forðferde Raulf seo ærcebiscop of Cantwarbyrig, þ*et* wæs on þæs dæies xiii° K*alendarum* Nouemb*ris*. **þ**æræfter wæron feole scipmen on sæ 7 on wæter, 7 sædon þ*et* hi sægon on norðeast fir micel 7 brad
f. 81v wið þone eorðe; 7 weax on lengþe up onan to þam / wolcne, 7 se
21 wolcne undide on fower healfe and faht þærtogeanes swilc hit scolde acwencen, 7 se fir weax naþama up to þe heouene. **þ**æt fir hi seagon in ðe dæirime, and læste swa lange þ*et* hit wæs liht
24 ofer eall: þet wæs þæs dæies vii° Idus Decemb*ris*.

Mill*esi*mo cxx°iii°. On þyssum geare wæs se king Henri on Cristestyde at Dunestaple. 7 **þ**ær comen þes eorles sandermen of Angeow to him. 7 **þ**eonen he ferde to Wudestoke, 7 his biscopes 7 his hird eal mid him. **þ**a tidde hit on an Wodnesdei
5 —þet wæs on iii° Id*us* Ian*ua*rii—þet se king rad in his derfald, and se biscop Roger of Seresbyrig on an half him and se biscop Rotbert Bloet of Lincolne on oðer half him; 7 riden þær s[pr]ecende. **þ**a aseh dune se biscop of Lincolne 7 seide to þam kyng, "Laferd kyng, ic swel**te**." 7 Se kyng alihte dune of
10 his hors 7 alehte hine betwux his earmes 7 let hine beran ham to his inne; 7 wearð þa sone dead; 7 man ferode hine to Lincolne mid micel wurðscipe 7 bebyrigde hine toforen S*anc*tȩ Mariȩ wefod, 7 hine bebyrigde se b*iscop* of Ceastre, Rotbert Pecceþ wæs gehaten. Ða sone þæræfter sende se kyng hise
15 write ofer eal Englalande 7 bed hise biscopes 7 hise abbates 7 hise þeignes eallc þet hi scolden cumen to his gewitenemot on

1123/8 *MS.* sˈrˈpecende.

Candelmesse deig to Gleawceastre him togeanes: 7 hi swa diden. Ða hi wæran þær gegaderod, þa bed se kyng heom þæt hi scoldon cesen hem ærcebiscop to Cantwarabyrig swa hwam swa swa hi woldon 7 he hem hit wolde tyþian. Ða spræcon ða biscopas 20 hem betwenan and sæden þæt hi næfre mare ne wolden hafen munec/hades man to ercebiscop ofer hem, ac iedon ealle samod- f. 82r lice to þone kyng and ieornden *þet* hi mosten cesen of clerchades man swa hwam swa swa hi wolden to ercebiscop; 7 se kyng hit hem tidde. Ðis wæs eall ear gedon ðurh se biscop of Seresbyrig 25 7 þurh se biscop of Lincolne ær he wære dead, forði þet næfre ne luueden hi munece regol ac wæron æfre togænes muneces 7 here regol. And se p*ri*or 7 se munecas of Cantwarabyrig 7 ealle þa oðre þe ðær wæron munechades men hit wiðcwæðen fulle twa dagas: ac hit naht ne beheld, for se biscop of Særesbyrig 30 wæs strang 7 wealde eall Engleland 7 wæs þærtogeanes eall *þet* he mihte 7 cuðe. Ða cusen hi an clerc—Willelm of Curboil wæs gehaten, he was canonie of an mynstre Cicc hatte—7 brohten him toforen se kyng. 7 Se kyng him geaf ðone ærcebiscoprice, 7 ealle þa biscopas him underfengen. Him wið- 35 cwæðen muneces 7 eorles 7 þeignes ealle mest þe þær wæron. On þa ilca tyma ferden þes eorles sandermen mid unsæhte fra*m* [þone] kyng, na of his gyfe naht ne rohton. On þa ilca tyma com an legat of Rome—Henri wæs gehaten, he wæs abbot of S*ancte* Ioh*anni*s mynstre of Anieli, 7 he co*m* æfter þe Romescot 40 —7 he sæde þone kyng *þet* hit wæs togeanes riht *þet* man scolde setten clerc ofer muneces 7 swa swa hi hæfden cosen ærcebiscop æror in her˹e˺ capitele æfter rihte: ac se kyng hit nolde undon, for þes b*iscopes* luuen of Særesbyrig. Ða ferde se ærcebiscop sone þæræfter to Can˹t˺warabyrig 7 wæs þær underfangan, 45 þæh hit wære here unþancas, 7 was þære sone gebletsod to biscop / fram se biscop of Lundene 7 se b*iscop* Ernulf of f. 82v Roueceastre 7 se b*iscop* Will*el*m Gifard of Winceastre 7 se b*iscop* Bernard of Wales 7 se b*iscop* Roger of Searesbyrig. Ða sone in þe lenten ferde se ærcebiscop to Rome æfter his palliu*m*, 50 7 mid him ferde se b*iscop* Bernard of Wales 7 Sefred abbot of

37–8 *MS.* fra*m* kyng

Gleastingbyrig 7 Anselm abbot of S*ancte* Ædmund 7 Iohan ærcedæcne of Cantwarabyrig 7 Gifard wæs þes kinges hirdclerc. On þa ilca tima ferde se ærcebiscop Ðurstan of Eoferwic
55 to Rome þurh þes Papes hese; 7 com þider ðre dagas ær se ærceb*iscop* of Cantwarabyrig come, 7 wæs þære underfangan mid micel wurðscipe. Ða co*m* se ærceb*iscop* of Cantwarabyrig 7 wæs ðære fulle seoueniht ær he mihte cumen to þes Papes spræce: þ*et* wæs forþan þ*et* hit wæs don ðone Pape to under-
60 standen þ*et* he hæfde underfangen ðone ær[c]ebiscoprice togeanes þa muneces of þe mynstre 7 togeanes rihte. Ac þ*et* oferco*m* Rome þet ofercumeð eall weoruld—þ*et* is gold 7 seolure; 7 se Pape sweðolode 7 gaf hi*m* his pallium—7 se ærceb*iscop* swor him underþeodnysse of ealle ða þing þ*et* se Papa
65 hi*m* onleide on S*ancte* Petres [w]euod and S*ancte* Paules—7 sende him ha*m* ða mid his bletsunge. Ða hwile þ*et* se ærceb*iscop* wæs ut of lande, geaf se kyng ðone biscoprice of Baðe þes cwenes canceler—Gode'f'reið wæs gehaten, he wæs boren of Luuein: þ*et* wæs þes dæiges Annuntiatio S*ancte* Marie at
70 Wudestoke. Ða sone þæræ[f]ter ferde se king to Winceastre, 7 wæs eall Eastrentyde þære. 7 þa hwile þ*et* he þær wæs, þa geaf he þone biscoprice of Lincolne an clerc—Alexander wæs gehaten, he wæs þes biscopes nefe of Searesbyrig: þis he dyde eall for þes biscopes luuen. Ða ferde se kyng þenen to Portes-
75 muðe 7 læi þære eall ofer Pentecostewuce. Þa sone swa he
f. 83r hæfde wind, swa ferde he ofer / into Normandie; 7 betæhte þa 'eall' Engleland to geamene 7 to wealden þone b*iscop* Roger of Searesbyrig. Ða wæs se kyng eall þes geares in Normandie. 7 Weax þa micel unfrið betwux him 7 hise þeignas, swa þ*et*
80 se eorl Walaram of Mellant 7 Hamalri 7 Hugo of Mundford 7 Will*el*m of Romare and fela oðre wendan fra*m* him 7 helden here castles him togeanes. 7 Se kyng held stranglice he*m* togeanes, 7 þes ylces geares he wan of Walaram his castel Punt Aldemer, 7 of Hugo, Mundford; 7 siððen he spedde æfre leong
85 þe bet. Ðes ylce geares, ær se biscop of Lincolne co*m* to his b*iscop*rice, forbearn eall meast se burh of Lincolne, 7 micel

60 *MS.* ærebiscoprice 65 *MS.* heuod 70 *MS.* þær ærter

ungerime folces—wæpmen 7 wimmen—forburnen; 7 swa mycel hearm þær wæs gedon swa nan man hit cuðe oþer secgen: þet wæs þes dæges xiiii° K*alendarum* Iunii. 89

Mill*esi*mo c°xx°iiii°. Eall þis gear wes se king Heanri on Normandi: þ*et* wes for se miccle unfrið þ*et* he heafde wið se king Loðewis of France 7 wið se eorl of Angeow 7 wið his agene men alremest. Þa gelamp hit on þes dæges Annuntiatio S*anct*ę Marie þ*et* se eorl Waleram of Mellant ferde fra*m* his an castel, 5 Belmunt het, to his an oðer castel Watteuile; mid hi*m* ferde þes kinges stiward of France, Amalri, 7 Hugo Gerueises sunu 7 Hugo of Munford 7 fela oðre godre cnihte. Þa comen ˡhemˡ togeanes þes kinges cnihtes of ealla þa casteles ða þærabuton wæron 7 fuhton wið hem 7 aflcmden he*m* 7 namen þone eorl 10 Waleram 7 Hugo Gerueises sunu 7 Hugo of Mundford 7 fif 7 twenti oðre cnihtes 7 brohton he*m* to þone kinge. 7 Se king let don þone eorl Waleram 7 Hugo Gerueises sunu on heftnunge on ðone castel on Roðem, 7 Hugo of Mundford he sende to Engˡlˡeland 7 let hine don on / ifele bendas on þone castel on f. 83ᵛ Gleucestre, 7 of þa oðre swa fela swa hi*m* þuhte he sende norð 16 7 suð to hise casteles on heftnunge. Ða siððon ferde se king 7 wan calle þes eorles casteles Walera*m* þa wæron on Normandi 7 ealla þa oðre þa his wiðrewines healden hi*m* togeanes. Eall ˡwasˡ þes unfrið for þes eorles sunu Rotbert of Normandi, Willelm 20 het. Se ilce Will*el*m hefde numen Fulkes eorles gingre dohter to wife of Angeow, 7 forði se king of France 7 ealle þas eorles heolden mid hi*m* 7 ealle þa rice men, 7 sæidon þet se king heold his broðer Rotbert mid wrange on heftnunge 7 his sunu Will*el*m mid unrihte aflemde ut of Normandi. Ðes ilces geares wæron 25 fæla untime on Englelande on corne 7 on ealle westme, swa þ*et* be[t]weonen Cristesmesse 7 Candelmesse man sælde þ*et* acersæd hwæte—þ*et* is twegen sedlæpas—to six scillingas, 7 þ*et* bærlic—þ*et* is þre sedlæpas—to six scillingas, 7 þ*et* acersæd aten—þ*et* ˡisˡ feower sedlæpas—to feower scillingas. Þet wæs 30 forþi þ*et* corn wæs litel 7 se penig wæs swa ifel þ*et* se man þa

1124/13 *MS.* heftnunge, *with* u *above subpuncted* i 1124/27 *Between* be *and* tweonen, *half an* o

hæfde at an market an pund, he ne mihte cysten þærof for nan
þing twelfe penegas. On þes ilces geares forðferde se eadig
biscop Ernulf of Roueceastre, se æror wæs abbot on Burch: þet
35 wæs þes dæies Id*us* Martii. 7 Þæræft*er* forðferde se king Alexander of Scotlande on þes dæies ix K*alendarum* Mai; 7 Dauid
his broðer, þa wæs eorl on Norðhamtunescire, feng to rice and
hæfde ða baðe togedere þone kinerice on Scotlande 7 þone
eorldom on Englelande. 7 On þæs dæies xix K*alendarum*
40 Ian*uarii* forðferde se Pape on Rome, Calistus wæs gehaten, 7
f. 84r Honorius / feng to Papedom. Ðes ilces geares æft*er* S*ancte*
Andreas messe toforen Cristesmesse held Raulf Basset 7 þes
kinges ðæines gewitenemot on Leþecæstrescire at Hundehoge,
7 ahengen þær swa fela þefas swa næfre ær ne wæron: þet
45 wæron on þa litle hwile ealles feower 7 feowerti manne 7 six men
spilde of here ægon 7 of here stanes. Fela soðfeste men sæidon
þ*et* þær wæron manege mid micel unrihte gespilde; oc ure
Laford God ælmihtig, þa eall digelnesse seð 7 wat—he seoð þ*et*
man læt þ*et* ærme folc mid ealle unrihte: ærost man hem
50 beræfoð her eahte and siþðon man he*m* ofslæð. Ful heui gær
wæs hit: se man þe æni god heafde—him me hit beræfode mid
strange geoldes 7 mid strange motes; þe nan ne heafde stærf of
53 hungor.

MILLESIMO c°xxv°. On þis gær sende se king Henri toforen
Cristesmesse of Normandi to Englalande 7 bebead þet man
scolde beniman ealla þa minetere þe wæron on Englelande
heora liman—þ*et* wæs here elces riht hand 7 heora stanen
5 beneðan: þ*et* wæs for se man ðe hafde an pund, he ne mihte
cysten ænne peni at anne market. 7 Se biscop Roger of Særesbyrig sende ofer eall Englalande 7 bebead hi ealle þ*et* hi scolden
cumen to Winceastre to Cristesmesse. Þa hi ðider coman, ða
nam man an 7 an 7 benam ælc ðone riht hand 7 þa stanes
10 beneðan. Eall þis wæs gedon wiðinnon þa twelf niht, 7 þ*et* wæs
eall mid micel rihte, forði þ*et* hi hafden fordon eall þ*et* land mid
here micele fals þ*et* hi ealle abohton. On þes ilces gæres sende
se Papa of Rome to ðise lande an cardinal, Iohan of Creme wæs

gehaten. He / com first to þone king on Normandi; 7 se king f. 84v
hine underfeng mid micel wurðscipe, beteahte hine siððon þone 15
ærceb*iscop* W*illelm* of Cantwarabyrig; 7 he hine ledde to
Cantwarabyrig; 7 he wæs þær underfangen mid micel wurðscipe
7 mid micel processione*m*, 7 he sang ðone heh messe on Eastren-
dæi æt Cristes wefod. 7 Siððon he ferde ofer eall Englalande to
ealle þa biscoprices 7 abbotrices þa wæron on þis lande, 7 ofer 20
eall he wæs underfangen mid wurðscipe 7 ealle hine iæfen
micele gife 7 mære. 7 Siððon he heold his concilie on Lundene
fulle þreo dagas on Natiuitas S*anct*ę Marię on Septemb*er* mid
ærcebiscopes 7 mid leodbisc*opes* 7 abbotes 7 læred 7 lawed;
7 bead þær þa ilce lagas þa ANSELM ærceb*iscop* hæfde æror 25
beboden, 7 feala ma—þeah hit litel forstode. 7 Þeonon he for
ofer sæ sone æft*er* S*anct*e Michaeles messe, 7 swa to Rome;
7 se ærceb*iscop* W*illelm* of Cantwarabyrig 7 se ærceb*iscop*
T*urstein* of Eferwic 7 se bisc*op* A*lexander* of Lincolne 7 se
b*iscop* of Loþene I*ohan* 7 se abbot of S*anct*e Alban G*osfreið*; 30
7 wæran þær underfangen of þone Pape Honori*us* mid micel
wurðscipe, 7 wæron þære eall þone wintre. On ðes ilces geares
wearð swa micel flod on S*anct*e Laurent*ius* messedæig þ*et* feola
tunes 7 men weorðan adrencte, 7 brigges tobrokene, 7 corn 7
mædwe spilt mid ealle, 7 hunger 7 cwealm on men 7 on erue; 35
7 on ealle westme swa micel untime wearð swa hit ne wæs feola
gear ær. 7 Þes ilces geares forðferde se abbot I*ohan* ˡof Burch
on ii Id*us* Octobris.

Mill*esimo* c°xxvi. Eall þis gear wæs se kyngˡ Heanri on Normandi eall to æft*er* heruest. Þa co*m* he to þis lande betwyx
Natiuit*as* S*anct*e Marie 7 Michaeles messe. Mid hi*m* co*m* se
cwen 7 his dohter þ*et* he æror hafde giuen þone Kasere Heanri 4
of Loherenge to wife. 7 He brohte mid him / þone eorl Waleram f. 85r
7 Hugo Gerueises sunu, 7 þone eorl he sende to Brigge on
hestnunge 7 þeonon he sende hi*m* to Walingeforde siððon, 7
Hugo to Windlesofra 7 let hine don on harde bande. 7 Þa

1125/25 *MS.* ilce, *with* l *altered from* c 1125/37–1126/1 of burch . . . se kyng *inserted over an erasure, in ink like that of 1126 b and in lines running over on to margins.* 1126/5 *MS.* onf, *with* n *blurred out.*

æft*er* Michaeles messe com se Scotte kyng Dauid of Scotlande
10 hider to lande; 7 se king Heanri underfeng hine mid micel
wurðscipe, 7 he wunode þa eall þet gear on þis lande.

On þes ilces geares let se kyning nimen his broðer Rotbert
fra*m* þone biscop Roger of Særesbyri 7 betahte hine his sune
Rotbert eorl of Gleucæstre, 7 let hine læden to Bricstowe 7
15 þær diden on þone castel : þæt wæs eall don ðurh his dohtres
ræd, 7 þurh se Scotte kyng Dauid, hire eam.

Mill*esi*mo c°xxvii°. Đis gear heald se kyng Heanri his hird æt
Cristesmæsse on Windlesoure. Þær wæs se Scotte kyng Dauid
7 eall ða heaued, læred 7 læuued, þ*et* wæs on Engleland. 7
Þær he let swere˹n˺ ercebiscopes 7 biscopes 7 abbotes 7 eorles
5 7 ealle þa ðeines ða þær wæron his dohter Æðelic Englaland 7
Normandi to hande æfter his dæi, þe ær wæs ðes Caseres wif
of Sexlande; 7 sende hire siððen to Normandi, 7 mid hire ferde
hire broðer Rotbert eorl of Gleucestre 7 Brian þes eorles sunu
Alein Fergan, 7 lett hire beweddan þes eorles sunu of Angeow,
10 Gosfreið Martæl wæs gehaten: hit ofþuhte naþema ealle frencisc 7 englisc, oc se kyng hit dide for to hauene sibbe of se eorl
of Angeow 7 for helpe to hauene togænes his neue Will*el*m. Đes
ilces gæres on þone lententide wæs se eorl Karle of Flandres
ofslagen on ane circe þær he læi 7 bæd hine to Gode tofor þone
15 we˹o˺fede amang þane messe fra*m* his agene manne. 7 Se kyng
of France brohte þone eorles sunu Will*el*m of Normandi, 7 iæf
f. 85v hine þone / eorldom, 7 þet landfolc him wið toc. Þes ilce
Will*el*m hæfde æror numen ðes eorles dohter of Angeow to wife,
oc hi wæron siððen totweamde for sibreden: þet wes eall ðurh
20 þone kyng Heanri of Engleland. Siððen þa na*m* he þes kynges
wifes swuster of France to wife; 7 forþi iæf se kyng him þone
eorldom of Flandres. Đes ilce gæres he gæf þone abbotrice
of Burch an abbot, Heanri wæs gehaten, of Peitowe, se hæfde
his abbotrice S*ancte* Ioh*anni*s of Angeli on hande. 7 Ealle
25 þa ærcebiscopes 7 biscopes seidon þ*et* hit wæs togeanes riht,
7 þ*et* he ne mihte hafen twa abbotrices on hande. Oc se ilce

1126/12 *Here there is a distinct change to much paler ink.* 1127/9 *MS.* lett *altered from* leot

Heanri dide þone king to understandene *þet* he hæfde læten his abbotrice for *þet* micele unsibbe *þet* wæs on *þet* land, 7 *þet* he dide ðurh þes Papes ræd 7 leue of Rome 7 ðurh þes abbotes of Clunni 7 þurh þæt he wæs legat of ðone Romescott: oc hit 30 ne wæs naðema eallswa, oc he wolde hauen baðe on hande, 7 swa hafde swa lange swa Godes wille wæs. He wæs on his clærchade biscop on Scesscuns; siððan warð he munec on Clunni, 7 siððon p*ri*or on þone scolue minstre; 7 siððon he wærð p*ri*or on Sauenni. Þaræftor, þurh *þet* he wæs ðes kynges mæi of Engle- 35 land 7 þes eorles of Peitowe, þa geaf se eorl him þone abbotrice of S*ancte* Ioh*anni*s minstre of Angeli. Siððon, þurh his micele wrences, ða beiæt he þone ærcebiscoprice of Besencun, 7 hæfde hit þa on hande þre dagas; þa forlæs he *þet* mid rihte, forþi *þet* he hit hæfde æror beieten mid unrihte. Siððon þa 40 beiet he þone biscoprice of Seintes, *þet* wæs fif mile fra*m* his abbotrice; *þet* he hæfde fulneah seoueniht on hande; þenon brohte se abbot him of Clunni, swa swa he æror dide of Besencun. Þa beþohte he him *þet* gif / he mihte ben rotfest on f. 86r Engleland *þet* he mihte habben ˡeˡal his wille. Besohte þa ðone 45 kyng 7 sæide hi*m* *þet* he wæs eald man 7 forbroken man, 7 *þet* he ne mihte ðolen þa micele unrihte 7 þa micele unsibbe ða wæron on here land, 7 iærnde þa þurh hi*m* 7 ðurh ealle his freond na*m*cuðlice þone abbotrice of Burhc. 7 Se kyng hit hi*m* iætte, forði *þet* ˡheˡ wæs his mæi 7 forþi *þet* he wæs an hæfod ða 50 að to swerene 7 witnesse to berene þær ða eorles sunu of Normandi 7 þes eorles dohter of Angeow wæron totwemde for sibreden. Þus earmlice wæs þone abbotrice gifen betwix Cristesmesse 7 Candelmesse at Lundene. 7 Swa he ferde mid þe cyng to Wincestre. 7 Þanon he co*m* to Burch. 7 Þær he 55 wunede eallriht swa drane doð on hiue: eall *þet* þa beon dragen toward, swa frett þa drane 7 dragað fraward—swa dide he: eall *þet* he mihte tacen, wiðinnen 7 wiðuten, of læred 7 of læwed, swa he sende ouer sæ; 7 na god þær ne dide ne na god ðær ne læuede. Ne þince man na sellice *þet* we soð seggen; for 60 hit wæs ful cuð ofer eall land *þet* swa radlice swa he þær co*m*— *þet* wæs þes Sunendæies *þet* man singað "Exurge, q*ua*re

obdormis, D*omine*?"—þa son þræfter þa sægon 7 herdon fela men feole huntes hunten. Ða huntes wæron swarte 7 micele 7
65 ladlice, 7 here hundes ealle swarte 7 bradegede 7 ladlice, 7 hi ridonc on swarte hors 7 on swarte bucces. Þis wæs segon on þe selue derfald in þa tune on Burch 7 on ealle þa wudes ða wæron fra*m* þa selua tune to Stanforde; 7 þa muneces herdon ða horn blawen þ*et* hi blewen on nihtes. Soðfeste men heo*m*
70 kepten on nihtes; sæidon, þes þe heo*m* þuhte, þ*et* þær mihte wel ben abuton twenti oðer þritti hornblaweres. Þis wæs sægon 7 herd fra*m* þ*et* he þider co*m* eall þ*et* lente[n]tid onan to
f. 86ᵛ Eastren. / Þis was his ingang: of his utgang ne cunne we iett
74 noht seggon. God scawe fore!

Mill*esi*mo c°x°x°viii. Eall þis geare weas se kyng Heanri on Normandi, for þone unfrið þ*et* wæs betwenen him 7 his nefe ðone eorl of Flandres. Oc se eorl wearð gewunded at an gefiht fram anne swein; 7 swa gewundod he for to S*ancte* Berhtines
5 minstre, 7 sone þear wearð munec 7 liuode siððon fif dagas; 7 he wearð þa dæd 7 þær bebyriged. God geare his sawle! Þ*et* wæs ðes daies vi K*alendarum* Aug*usti*. Ðes ilces geares forðferde se biscop Randulf Passefla*m*bard of Dunholme 7 þære bebyriged on No*nas* Sept*embris*. 7 Þes ilces geares ferde
10 se forensprecene abbot Henri ha*m* to his agen minstre to Peitou be þes kynges leue. He dide ðone king to understanden þ*et* he wolde mid alle forlæten þone minstre 7 þ*et* land 7 þær wunien mid hi*m* on Englalande 7 on ðone mynstre of Burh. Oc hit ne was naðema swa: he hit dide forði þ*et* he wolde þurh his micele
15 wiles ðear beon, wær it tweolf monð oððe mare, 7 siððon ongeon cumen. God ælmihtig haue his milce ofer þ*et* wrecce stede! Ðes ilces geares co*m* fra*m* Ier*usal*em Hugo of þe Te*m*ple to ðone kyng on Normandig; 7 se kyng hi*m* underfeng mid micel wurðscipe 7 micele gersumes hi*m* geaf on gold 7 on silure: 7
20 siððon he sende hi*m* to Englalande. 7 Þær he wæs underfangen of ealle gode men, 7 ealle hi*m* geauen gersume, 7 on Scotlande ealswa, 7 be hi*m* senden to Ier*usal*em micel eahte mid ealle on

1127/72 *MS.* lented tid

gold 7 on silure. 7 He bebead folc vt to Ier*usa*lem; 7 þa for
mid hi*m* 7 æfter hi*m* swa micel folc swa næfre ær ne dide siððon
þ*et* se firste fare was on Vrbanes dæi Pape, þeah hit litel 25
behelde. He seide þ*et* fulle feoht was sett betwenen ða Cristene
7 þa heðene: þa hi þider comen, ða ne was hit noht buton
læsunge. Þus earmlice wear[ð] ˡeallˡ þ*et* folc ˡswengt.ˡ / 28

Mill*esi*mo c°xx°ix°. On ðis gear sende se kyng to Englaland f. 87r
æfter þone eorl Walera*m* 7 æft*er* Hugo Gerueises sunu; 7 þær
hi gisleden hem; 7 Hugo ferde ha*m* to his agen land to France,
7 Waleram belaf mid þone kyng 7 se kyng hi*m* geaf eall his land
buton his castel ane. Siððon, þa co*m* se kyng to Englaland 5
innon heruest, 7 se eorl co*m* mid hi*m*; 7 wurðon þa alswa gode
freond swa hi wæron æror feond. Ða sone, be þes kynges ræd
7 be his leue, sende se ærceb*iscop* Will*el*m of Cantwarbyrig ofer
eall Englaland 7 bead biscopes 7 abbotes 7 ærcedæcnes 7 ealle
þa p*ri*ores, munecces 7 canonias þa wæron on ealle þa cellas on 10
Englaland, 7 æft*er* ealle þa þet Cristendome hæfdon to begemen
7 to locen, 7 þ*et* hi scolden ealle cumen to Lundene at Michaeles
messe 7 þær scolden sprecon of ealle Godes rihtes. Þa hi ðider
comen, þa began þ*et* mot on Monendæig 7 heold onan to ðe
Fridæig. Þa hit eall co*m* forð, þa weorð hit eall of earcedæcnes 15
wifes 7 of preostes wifes, þ*et* hi scolden hi forlæten be S*ancte*s
Andreas messe, 7 se þe þ*et* ne wolden done forgede his circe
7 his hus 7 his ham 7 neframa nan clepunge þærto na hafde
mare. Þis bebæd se ærceb*iscop* Will*el*m of Cantwarabyrig 7
ealle þa leodbiscopes ða [þ]a wæron on Englalande. 7 Se kyng 20
hem geaf ealle leue ha*m* to farene; 7 swa hi ferdon ha*m*. 7 Ne
forstod noht ealle þa bodlaces: ealle heoldon here wifes be þes
kynges leue swa swa hi ear didon. Ðis ilces geares forðferde
se biscop Will*el*m Giffard of Winceastre 7 þear bebyriged on viii
K*alendarum* Febr*uarii*. 7 Se kyng Henri geaf þone biscoprice 25
æft*er* Micheles messe þone abbot Henri his nefe of Glasting-
byri, 7 he wæs gehalgod to biscop fra*m* þone ærceb*iscop* Will*el*m
of Cantwarabyri þes dæies xv K*alendarum* Dece*m*b*ris*. Þes

1128/28 *MS.* weard 1129/18 *MS.* nan *altered from* nen 20 *MS.* wa

ilces geares forðferde Honor*ius* Papa. Ær he wære wel ded, þa
f. 87v wære þær coren twa papes. / Se an wæs gehaten Petr*us*; he wæs
31 munec of Clunni 7 weas boren of þa ricceste men of Rome. Mid
hi*m* helden ða of Rome 7 se duc of Sicilie. Se oðer het Grego-
ri*us*; he wæs clerc 7 wærð flemd ut of Rome fra*m* þon oðer pape
7 fra*m* his cinnesmen. Mid hi*m* held se Kasere of Sexlande 7
35 se kyng of France 7 se kyng He'a'nri of Engleland 7 ealle þa be
þis half þa muntes. Nu wærð swa mycel dwyld on Cristendom
swa it næfre ær ne wæs. Crist sette red for his wrecce folc! Đis
ilces geares on S*ancte* Nicholaes messeniht litel ær dæi wæs
39 micel eorðdine.

M*illesimo* c°xxx°. Đis geares wæs se mynstre of Cantwarabyri
halgod fra*m* þone ærceb*iscop* Will*el*m þes dæies iiii° No*narum*
Mai. Đær wæron þas biscopes Iohan of Roueceastre, Gilebert
Uniu*er*sal of Lundene, He'a'nri of Winceastre, Alexander of
5 Lincolne, Roger of Særesbyri, Simon of Wigorceastre, Roger of
Couentre, Godefreith of Bathe, Eourard of Noruuic, Sigefrid
of Cic[ea]stre, Bernard of S*ancte* Dauid, Audoen*us* of Euereus
of Normand*i*, Iohan of Sæis. Þes feorðe dæges þæræft*er* wæs
se king He'a'nri on Roueceastre; 7 se burch forbernde ælmæst;
10 7 se ærceb*iscop* Will*el*m halgede S*ancte* Andreas mynstre 7 ða
forsprecon bisc*opes* mid hi*m*. 7 Se kyng Heanri ferde ouer sæ
into Normandi on heruest. Đes ilces geares co*m* se abbot
Heanri of Angeli æft*er* Æsterne to Burch, 7 seide þ*et* he hæfde
forlæten þone mynstre mid ealle. Æft*er* him co*m* se abbot [of]
15 Clunni, Petr*us* gehaten, to Englelande bi þes kynges leue, 7
wæs underfangen ouer eall swa hwar swa he co*m* mid mycel
wurðscipe. To Burch he co*m*, 7 þær behet se abbot Heanri hi*m*
þ*et* he scolde beieton hi*m* þone mynstre of Burch þ*et* hit scolde
beon underðed into Clunni: oc man seið to biworde, "Hæge
20 sitteð þa aceres dæleth!" God ælmihtig adylege iuele ræde! 7
Sone þæræft*er* ferde se abbot of Clunni ham to his ærde.

f. 88r Mill*esi*mo cxxxi. / Đis gear æfter Cristesmesse on an Moneniht
æt þe forme slæp wæs se heouene o ðe norð half eall swilc hit

1130/7 *MS.* cic'a'estre 1130/14–15 *MS.* se abbot clunni

wære bærnende fir, swa þ*et* ealle ðe hit sægon wæron swa offæred swa hi næfre ær ne wæron: þ*et* wæs on iii Id*us* Ian*uarii*. Ðes ilces geares wæs swa micel oˡrˡfcwalm swa hit næfre ær ne wæs on manne gemynd ofer eall Engleland: þ*et* wæs on næt 7 on swin swa þ*et*, on þa tun þa wæs tenn ploges oðer twelfe gangende, ne belæf þær noht an; 7 se man þa heafde twa hundred oðþe ðre hundred swin, ne beleaf him noht an. Þæræft*er* swulten þa hennefugeles. Þa scyrte ða flescmete 7 se ceose 7 se butere. God hit bete þa his wille beð! 7 Se kyng Heanri co*m* ha*m* to Engleland toforen heruest æft*er* S*ancte* Petres messe þe firrer. Ðes ilces geares for se abbot Heanri toforen Eastren fram Burch ofer sæ to Normandi; 7 þær spreac mid þone kyng, 7 sæide hi*m* þet se abbot of Clunni heafde hi*m* beboden þ*et* he scolde cumen to hi*m* 7 betæcen hi*m* þone abbotrice of Angeli, 7 siðþen he wolde cumen ha*m* be his læfe. 7 Swa he ferde ha*m* to his agen mynstre 7 þær wunode eall to Midsumer Dæi. 7 Ðes oðer dæies æfter S*ancte* Ioh*anni*s messedæi, cusen þa muneces abbot of he*m*self and brohten hi*m* into cyrce mid p*ro*cessione*m*; sungen "Te D*eu*m Laud*amus*", ringden þa belle, setten hi*m* on þes abbotes settle, diden hi*m* ealle hersu*m*nesse swa swa hi scolden don here abbot. 7 Se eorl 7 ealle þa heafedmenn 7 þa muneces of þa mynstre flemden se oðer abbot Heanri ut ˡofˡ þa mynstre. Hi scolden nedes: on fif 7 twenti wintre ne biden hi næfre an god dæi. Her hi*m* trucode ealle his mycele cræftes: nu hi*m* behofed þ*et* he crape in his mycele codde in ælc hyrne, gif þær wære hure an unwreste wrenc þ*et* he mihte get beswicen anes Crist 7 eall Cristene folc. Þa ferde he into Clunni, 7 þær man hi*m* held þ*et* he ne mihte na east na west. Sæide se abbot of Clunni / þ*et* hi heafdon forloron S*ancte* Ioh*anni*s mynstre þurh hi*m* 7 þurh his mycele sotscipe. Þa ne cuþe he hi*m* na betre bote bute behet hem 7 aðes swor on halidom þ*et*, gif he moste Engleland secen, þet he scolde begeton he*m* ðone mynstre of Burch, swa þ*et* he scolde setten þær p*ri*or of Clunni 7 circeweard 7 hordere 7 reilþein, 7 ealle þa ðing þa wæron wiðinne mynstre 7 wiðuten, eall he scolde he*m* betæcen. Þus he ferde

9 *MS.* ðre, *with* ð *altered from* t

into France, 7 þær wunode eall þ*et* gear. Crist ræde for þa wrecce muneces of Burch 7 for þ*et* wrecce ˡstedeˡ! Nu he*m*
40 behofeð Cristes helpe 7 eall Cristenes folces!

M*illesimo* cxxxii. Ðis gear co*m* Henri king to þis land. Þa co*m* Henri abbot 7 uureide þe muneces of Burch to þe king forþi ð*at* he uuolde underþeden ð*at* mynst*re* to Clunie, sua ð*at* te king was welneh bepaht 7 sende eft*er* þe muneces. 7 þurˡhˡ Godes
5 milce 7 þurˡhˡ þe b*iscop* of Seresb*yr*i 7 te b*iscop* of Linc*ol* 7 te oþre rice men þe þer wæron, þa wiste þe king ð*at* he feorde mid suicdo*m*. Þa he na*m*mor ne mihte, þa uuolde he ð*at* his nefe sculde ben abb*ot* in Burch: oc Crist it ne uuolde. Was it noht suithe lang þereft*er* þat te king sende eft*er* hi*m* 7 dide hi*m* gyuen
10 up ð*at* abb*ot*rice of Burch 7 faren ut of lande. 7 Te king iaf ð*at* abb*ot*rice an p*ri*or of S*ancte* Neod, Martin was gehaten; he co*m* on S*ancte* Pet*res* messedei mid micel wurscipe into the minstre.

M*illesimo* cxxxv. On þis gære for se king H*enri* ouer sæ æt te La*m*masse. 7 Ð*at* oþer dei þa he lai an slep in scip, þa þestrede þe dæi ouer al landes 7 uuard þe sunne suilc als it uuare thre niht ald mone, an st*er*res abuten hi*m* at middæi. Wurˡþˡen
5 men suiðe ofuundred 7 ofdred, 7 sæden ð*at* micel þing sculde cum*en* hereft*er*: sua dide, for þat ilc gær warth þe king ded ð*at* oþer dæi eft*er* S*ancte* Andreas massedæi on Norm*andi*. Þa þestre[den] sona þas landes, for æuric man sone ræuede oþer þe mihte. Þa namen his sune 7 his frend 7 brohten his lic to
10 Engle*land* 7 bebirie[den] in Reding*e*. God man he wes 7 micel æie wes of hi*m*: durste nan man misdon wið oðer on his time. Pais he makede men 7 dær. Wua sua bare his byrthen gold 7
f. 89ʳ sylure, durste na*n* man sei to hi*m* naht bute god. / Enmang þis was his nefe cumen to Engle*land*, Stephne de Blais; 7 co*m* to
15 Lundene; 7 te lundenisce folc hi*m* underfeng 7 senden ęft*er* þe ærceb*iscop* Will*el*m Curbuil; 7 halechede hi*m* to kinge on Midewintre Dæi. On þis kinges time wes al unfrið 7 yfel 7 ræflac, for agenes hi*m* risen sona þa rice men þe wæron swikes, alre fyrst Balduin de Reduers; 7 held Execestre agenes hi*m* 7 te

1132/8 *MS.* xpist 1135/7–8 *MS.* Þa þestre sona 10 *MS.* bebiriend

king it besæt, 7 siððan Bald*uin* acordede. Þa tocan þa oðre 7 20
helden her castles agenes hi*m*. 7 Dauid king of Scotland toc to
uuerrien hi*m*. Þa, þohuuethere þat, here sandes feorden betwyx
heo*m* 7 hi togædere comen, 7 wurðe sæhte, þoþ it litel forstode. 23

M*illesimo* cxxxˈviiˈ. Đis gære for þe ˈk*ing*ˈ Steph*ne* ofer sæ to
Normandi; 7 ther wes underfangen, forþi ð*at* hi uuenden ð*at*
he sculde ben alsuic alse the eo*m* wes, 7 for he hadde get his
tresor; ac he todeld it 7 scatered sotlice. Micel hadde Henri
k*ing* gadered gold 7 syluer, 7 na god ne dide me for his saule 5
tharof. Þa ˈþeˈ king S*tephne* to Engla*land* co*m*, þa macod he his
gadering æt Oxeneford. 7 Þar he na*m* þe b*iscop* Roger of Sere-
b*yri*, 7 Alex*ander* b*iscop* of Lincol 7 te canceler Rog*er*, hise
neues, 7 dide ælle in p*ri*sun til hi iafen up here castles. Þa the
suikes undergæton ð*at* he milde man was 7 softe 7 god, 7 na 10
iustise ne dide, þa dideˈnˈ hi alle wunder. Hi hadden hi*m*
manred maked 7 athes suoren, ac hi nan treuthe ne heolden.
Alle he wæron forsworen 7 here treothes forloren, for æuric
rice man his castles makede 7 agænes hi*m* heolden; 7 fylden þe
land ful of castleˈsˈ. Hi suencten suyðe þe uurecce men of þe 15
land mid castelweorces; þa þe castles uuaren maked, þa fylden
hi mid deoules 7 yuele men. Þa namen hi þa men þe hi wenden
ð*at* ani god hefdeˈnˈ, bathe be nihtes 7 be dæies, carlmen 7
wi*m*men, 7 diden heo*m* ˈin p*ri*sunˈ 7 pined heo*m* eft*er* gold 7
syluer untellendlice pining; for ne uuæren næure nan martyrs 20
swa pined alse hi wæron. Me henged up bi the fet 7 smoked
heo*m* mid ful smoke. Me henged bi the þu*m*bes other bi the
hefed 7 hengen bryniges on ˈherˈ fet. Me dide cnotted strenges
abuton here / hæued 7 uurythen it ð*at* it gæde to þe ˈhˈærnes. f. 89v
Hi diden heo*m* in quarterne þar nadres 7 snakes 7 pades wæron 25
inne, 7 drapen heo*m* swa. Sume hi diden in crucethur—ð*at* is,
in an cęste þat was scort 7 nareu 7 undep—7 dide scærpe stanes
þerinne 7 þrengde þe man þærinne ð*at* hi*m* bræcon alle þe
limes. In mani of þe castles wæron lof 7 gri*n*: ð*at* wæron
rachenteges ð*at* twa oþer thre men hadden onoh to bæron onne, 30

1137/19–20 *MS.* diden heo*m* ˈin p*ri*sunˈ éft*er* gold 7 syluer 7̇ pined heo*m* / untellendlice pining. 29 *MS.* lof 7 grī.

þat was sua maced, ð*at* is, fæstned to an beom—7 diden an
scærp iren abuton þa mannes throte 7 his hals, ð*at* he ⸌ne⸍ myhte
nowiderwardes, ne sitten ne lien ne slepen, oc bæron al ð*at*
iren. Mani þusen hi drapen mid hungær. I ne can ne I ne mai
35 tellen alle þe wunder ne alle þe pines ð*at* hi diden wrecce men
on þis land; 7 ð*at* lastede þa xix wintre wile Stephne was king,
7 æure it was uuerse 7 uuerse. Hi læiden g[æ]ldes o⸌n⸍ the tunes
æure u*m* wile, 7 clepeden it "tenserie". Þa þe uurecce men ne
hadden na*m*more to gyuen, þa ræueden hi 7 brendon alle the
40 tunes, ð*at* wel þu myhtes faren al a dæis fare, sculdest thu neure
finden man in tune sittende ne land tiled. Þa was corn dære, 7
fle[s]c 7 cæse 7 butere, for nan ne wæs o þe land. Wrecce men
sturuen of hungær. Sume ieden on ælmes þe waren su*m* wile
rice men. Sume flugen ut of lande. Wes næure gæt mare
45 wre⸌c⸍cehed on land ne næure hethen men werse ne diden þan
hi diden; for ouer sithon ne forbaren ⸌hi⸍ nouther circe ne
cyrceiærd, oc nam*en* al þe god ð*at* þarinne was 7 brenden
sythen þe cyrce 7 al tegædere. Ne hi ne forbaren b*iscopes* land
ne abb*otes* ne preostes, ac ræueden munekes 7 clerekes, 7 æuric
50 man other þe ouermyhte. Gif twa men oþer iii coman ridend
to an tun, al þe tunscipe flugæn for heo*m*, wenden ð*at* hi wæron
ræueres. Þe biscopes 7 lered men heo*m* cursede æure, oc was
heo*m* naht þarof, for hi uueron al forcursæd 7 forsuoren 7 forloren. War sæ me tilede, þe erthe ne bar nan corn, for þe land
55 was al fordon mid suilce dædes. 7 Hi sæden openlice ð*at* Crist
slep, 7 his halechen. Suilc, 7 mare þanne we cunnen sæin, we
f. 90r þol[ed]en xix wintre ⸌for ure sinnes.⸍ / On al þis yuele time heold
Martin abbot his abbotrice xx wint*re* 7 half gær 7 viii dæis mid
micel suinc; 7 fand þe munekes 7 te gestes al þat heo*m* behoued
60 7 heold mycel carited in the hus, 7 þoþwethere wrohte on þe
circe 7 sette þarto landes 7 rentes 7 goded it suythe 7 læt it refen,
7 brohte heo*m* into þe neuuæ mynst*re* on S*ancte* PETRES mæsse-
dæi mid micel wurtscipe: ð*at* was anno ab Incarn*atione* D*omini*
M*illesimo* cxl, a co*m*bustio*n*ę loci xxiii. 7 He for ⸌to⸍ Rome, 7
65 þær wæs wæl underfangen fra*m* þe Pape Eugenie; 7 begæt thare

37 *MS.* gæildes 42 *MS.* flec 55 *MS.* xpist 57 *MS.* þolenden

p*ri*uilegies, an of alle þe landes of þabbotrice 7 an oþer of þe landes þe lien to þe circewican, 7, gif he leng moste liuen, alse he mint to don of þe horderwycan. 7 He begæt in landes þat rice men hefden mid strengthe: of Will*el*m Malduit, þe heold Rogingha*m* þæ castel, he wan Cotingha*m* 7 Estun; 7 of Hugo of Walt*er*uile he uuan Hyrtlingb*yri* 7 Stanewig 7 lx sol of Aldewingle ˡælc gærˡ. 7 He makede manie munek*es*, 7 plantede winiærd, 7 makede mani weorkes 7 wende þe tun betere þan it ær wæs; 7 wæs god munec 7 god man, 7 forþi hi*m* luueden God 7 gode men. 70 75

Nu we willen sægen su*m* del wat belamp on Steph*nes* kinges time. On his time þe Iudeus of Noruuic bohton an Cristen cild beforen Estren, 7 pineden hi*m* alle þe ilce pining ð*at* ure Drihten was pined, 7 on Lang Fridæi hi*m* on rode hengen for ure Drihtines luue 7 sythen byrieden hi*m*; wenden ð*at* it sculde ben forholen. Oc ure Dryhtin atywede ð*at* he was hali m*artyr*; 7 t[e] munekes hi*m* namen 7 bebyried hi*m* heglice in þe minst*re*. 7 He maket þur[h] ure Drihtin wunderlice 7 manifældlice miracles; 7 hatte he S*anct* Willelm. 80 84

M*illesimo* cxxxviˡiiˡ. On þis gær co*m* Dauid king of Scotl*and* mid ormete færd to þis land; wolde winnan þis land. 7 Hi*m* co*m* togænes Will*el*m eorl of Albamar, þe þe king adde beteht Euorwic, 7 t[e] other æuez men mid fæu men; 7 fuhten wid heo*m*, 7 fle*m*den þe king æt te Standard, 7 sloghen suithe micel of his genge. / 5

M*illesimo* cxl. On þis gær wolde þe king Steph*ne* tæcen Rodb*er*t eorl of Gloucestre, þe kinges sune Henries; ac he ne myhte, for he wart it war. Þerefte*r* [i] þe lengten þestrede þe sunne 7 te dæi abuton nontid dæies, þa men eten, ð*at* me lihtede candles to æten bi; 7 þat was xiii K*alendarum* Ap*rilis*: wæron men suythe ofwundred. Þerefte*r* fordfeorde Will*elm* ærcebi*scop* of Cantwarb*yri*; 7 te king makede Teodbald ærcebi*scop*, þe was abbot in the Bec. Þerefte*r* wæx suythe micel uuerre betuyx þe f. 90ᵛ 5

1137/77 *MS.* xpisten 80 *MS.* byrieden, *with* d *altered from* n 82 *MS.* to 83 *MS.* þur 1138/4 *MS.* to f. 90ᵛ *From this point on the manuscript is badly rubbed.* 1140/3 *MS.* hi þe lengten

king 7 Randolf eorl of Cæstre: noht forþi ð*at* he ne iaf hi*m* al
10 ð*at* he cuthe axen hi*m*, alse he dide alle othre; oc æfre þe mare
he iaf heo*m*, þe wærse hi wæron hi*m*. Þe eorl heold Lincol
agænes þe king 7 bena*m* hi*m* al ð*at* he ahte to hauen. 7 Te king
for þider 7 besætte hi*m* 7 his brother Will*el*m de Ro[m]are in
þe castel. 7 Te æorl stæl ut 7 ferde eft*er* Rodb*er*t eorl of
15 Glou[c]estre 7 brohte hi*m* þider mid micel ferd, 7 fuhten suythę
on Ca[nd]elmasse Dæi agenes heore lauerd, 7 namen hi*m*—for
his m[en h]i*m* suyken 7 flugæn—7 læd hi*m* to Bristowe 7 diden
þar in p*ri*sun 7 [in fe]teres. Þa was al Englel*and* styred mar þan
ær wæs; 7 al yuel wæ[s i]n lande. Þereft*er* co*m* þe king*es* doht*er*
20 Henries, þe hefde ben emp*er*ic[e in] Alamanie 7 nu wæs cun-
tesse in Angou; 7 co*m* to Lundene, 7 te lundenissce folc hire
wolde tæcen, 7 scæ fleh 7 forles þar mic[el]. Þereft*er* þe biscop of
Wincestre, Henri þe king*es* brother Steph*nes*, spac wid Rodb*er*t
eorl 7 wyd þe*m*p*er*ice 7 suor heo*m* athas ð*at* he neure ma mid
25 te king his brother wolde halden 7 cursede alle þe men þe mid
hi*m* heoldon, 7 sæde heo*m* ð*at* he uuolde iiuen heo*m* up Wincestre 7 dide heo*m* cumen þider. Þa hi þærinne wæren, þa co*m*
þe king*es* cuen mid al hire strengthe 7 besæt heo*m*, ð*at* þer wæs
inne micel hungær. Þa hi ne leng ne muhten þolen, þa stal[en]
30 hi ut 7 flugen. 7 Hi wurthen war widuten 7 folecheden heo*m*,
7 namen Rodb*er*t eorl of Glouc*estre* 7 ledden hi*m* to Rouecestre
7 diden hi*m* þare in p*ri*sun. 7 Te emp*er*ice fleh into an minstre. /
f. 91r Þa feorden þe wise men betwyx þe kinges freond 7 te eorles
freond, 7 sahtlede sua ð*at* me sculde leten ut þe king of p*ri*sun
35 for þe eorl 7 te eorl for þe king: 7 sua diden. Sithen þereft*er*
sa[ht]leden þe king 7 Randolf eorl at Stanford, 7 athes suoren
7 treuthes fæston ð*at* her nouþer sculde besuyken other; 7 it ne
forstod naht. For þe king hi*m* sithen na*m* in Ha*m*tun þurhc
wicci ræd 7 dide hi*m* in p*ri*sun; 7 efsones he let hi*m* ut þurhc
40 wærse red, to ð*at* forewarde ð*at* he suor on halido*m* 7 gysles fand
þat he alle his castles sculde iiuen up. Sume he iaf up, 7 sume
ne iaf he noht; 7 dide þanne wærse þanne he hær sculde. Þa

13 *etc. Where not otherwise stated, bracketed letters fill lacunae.* 29 *MS.* stali 36 *MS.* sa|t|hleden 37 *MS.* besuyken, *with* y *altered from* i

was Engleland suythe todeled: sume helden mid te king, 7
sume mid þe*m*p*er*ice; for þa þe king was in p*ri*sun, þa wenden
þe eorles 7 te rice men þat he neure mare sculde cum*en* ut, 45
7 sæhˈtˈleden wyd þe*m*p*er*ice 7 brohten hire into Oxenford 7
iauen hire þe burch. Þa þe king was ute, þa herde ð*at* sægen 7
toc his feord 7 besæt hire in þe tur. 7 Me læt hire dun on niht
of þe tur mid rapes, 7 stal ut 7 scæ fleh 7 iæde on fote to
Walingford. Þærefte*r* scæ ferde ouer sæ. 7 Hi of Normandi 50
wenden alle fra þe king to þe eorl of Angæu, sume here þankes
7 sume here unþankes; for he besæt heo*m* til hi aiauen up here
castles, 7 hi nan helpe ne hæfden of þe k*ing*. Þa ferde Eustace
þe king*es* sune to France 7 na*m* þe king*es* suster of France to
wife; wende to bigæton Normandi þærþurh. Oc he spedde 55
litel, 7 be gode rihte, for he was an yuel man; for warese he
[com he d]ide mare yuel þanne god: he reuede þe landes 7
læide mic[ele gelde]s on. He brohte his wif to Engleland, 7
dide hire in þe caste[l on Can]teb*yri*. God wi*m*man scæ wæs,
oc scæ hedde litel blisse mid hi*m*. 7 Crist ne wolde ð*at* he sculde 60
lange rixan; 7 wærd ded, 7 his moder beien. 7 Te eorl of Angæu
wærd ded, 7 his sune Henri toc to þe rice. 7 Te Cuen of France
todælde fra þe king; 7 scæ co*m* to þe iunge eorl Henri, 7 he toc
hire to wiue 7 al / Peitou mid hire. Þa ferde he mid micel færd f. 91v
into Engleland, 7 wan castles. 7 Te king ferde agenes hi*m* mid 65
micel mare ferd. 7 Þoþwæthere fuhtten hi noht, oc ferden þe
ærcebi*scop* 7 te wise meˈnˈ betwyx heo*m* 7 makede ð*at* sahte
ð*at* te king sculde ben lauerd 7 king wile he liuede 7 æfte*r* his
dæi ware Henri king; 7 he heldˈeˈ hi*m* for fader 7 he hi*m* for
sune; 7 sib 7 sæhte sculde ben betwyx heo*m* 7 on al Engle- 70
land. Þis, 7 te othre foruuardes þet hi makeden, suoren to
halden þe king 7 te eorl 7 te b*iscopes* & te eorles 7 rice men
alle. Þa was þe eorl underfangen æt Wincestre 7 æt Lundene
mid micel wurtscipe; 7 alle diden hi*m* manred 7 suoren
þe pais to halden; 7 hit ward sone suythe god pais sua ð*at* 75
neure was her*ere*. Þa was þe k*ing* strengere þanne he æue[r]

57, 58, 59 *Across these three lines there is a rectangular hole 7 or 8 letters wide.*
60 *MS.* xpist 76 *MS.* herˈe (*u.v.r. photograph*); æuert

her was. 7 Te eorl ferde ouer sæ; 7 al folc hi*m* luuede, for he
78 dide god iustise 7 makede pais.

M*illesimo* cliiii. On þis gær wærd þe king Steph*ne* ded 7 bebyried
þer his wif ˈ7 his suneˈ wæron bebyried æt Fauresfeld; þæt
minst*re* hi makeden. Þa þe king was ded, þa was þe eorl
beionde sæ; 7 ne durste nan man don oþer bute god for þe
5 micel eie of hi*m*. Þa he to Engleland co*m*, þa was he underfangen mid micel wurtscipe, 7 to king bletcæd in Lundene on
þe Sunnendæi beforen Midwint*re* Dæi, 7 held þære micel curt.
Þat ilce dæi þat Mart*in* abb*ot* of Burch sculde þider faren,
þa sæclede he, 7 ward ded iiii No*narum* Ian*uarii*. 7 Te munek*es*
10 innen dæis cusen oþer of heo*m*sælf, Will*el*m de Walt*er*uile is
gehaten, god clerc 7 god man 7 wæl luued of þe k*ing* 7 of alle
gode men; 7 on [morg]en byrie*den* þabb*ot* hehlice. 7 Sone þe
cosan ab*bot* ferde, 7 te muneces m[id hi*m*, to] Oxenforde to
þe k*ing*; [7 he] iaf hi*m* þat abb*ot*rice. 7 He ferde hi*m* son[e to
15 Linco]l, 7 wæs þær bletcæd to abbot ær he ham come; 7 sithen
was underfangen mid micel wurtscipe at Burch mid micel
p*ro*cessiun; 7 sua he was alsua at Ramesæie, 7 at Torn*eie*, 7 at
Crul*and* 7 Spall*ding*, 7 at S. Albanes 7 F . . . . 7 Nu is abbot 7
19 fair haued begunnon: Xpist hi*m* unne þ[us] enden!

1154/12, 13, 15–16 *The rectangular hole affects these lines.* 1154/18 *MS.* F . . . : *see Notes.*

COMMENTARY

1070

1. *se eorl Walþeof*: son of Earl Siward of Northumbria (see table, *EHD* 990); his career is treated by F. S. Scott, 'Earl Waltheof of Northumbria', *Archaeologia Aeliana*, 4th ser. xxx (1952), 149–215. He first submitted to the Conqueror, whom he accompanied to Normandy in 1067 (1066 D; also William of Poitiers, 244), then in 1069 joined the Danish forces invading the Humber (see *infra* 3 n.), distinguishing himself in the fighting at York (*s.a.* D; *Gest. Reg.* ii. 311). Although married to the Conqueror's niece Judith, he was again involved in rebellion in 1075 (see 1075, 1076).

2. *se cyng let hergian*: compare Florence, ii. 5: *rex Willelmus monasteria totius Angliæ perscrutari, et pecuniam, quam ditiores Angli, propter illius austeritatem et depopulationem, in eis deposuerant, auferri et in ærarium suum jussit deferri.*

3. *Swegn cyng*: Sveinn Estrithson, king of Denmark; for his interest in the English throne, see table, *EHD* 984. In 1069 his brother Ásbjörn and several of his sons, including the future St. Canute of Denmark (see 1087/150 n.), had landed in Yorkshire and led the rising which provoked the Conqueror's second and decisive wasting of that county (*s.a.* DE; also Florence, ii. 3).

4. *of Denmarcan*: i.e. 'from Denmark'.

10. *Hereward*: already by the mid twelfth century a legendary figure, as in the *Gesta Herwardi* (ed. T. D. Hardy and C. T. Martin, *Lestorie des Engles*, 2 vols., R.S., 1888–9, i. 339–404, see also ii, pp. xxxiii–xxxv), compiled by a man who claimed to have met maimed survivors of his band and preserved in the Peterborough Register of Robert of Swaffham, and also in the related *Liber Eliensis* (ed. Blake, 173 et seq., see also xxxiv–xxxvi); the former refers (ii. 339–40) to an older version *Anglice conscriptum* of which only a few mouldy shreds remained. For the significance of these legends, see M. Keen, *The Outlaws of Medieval Legend*, 1961, 9–38. All that is certain about Hereward is that he was a tenant of Peterborough Abbey, see J. H. Round, 'The Knights of Peterborough', *Feudal England*, 132–7, also E. A. Freeman, *The History of the Norman Conquest of England*, 5 vols., Oxford, 1867–76, iv. 804–12.

12. *an frencisce abbot*: compare Hugo, 77, *cuidam monacho Normanno.* Although invariably distinguishing between *Normandige* and *Franc-*

land, France (see *infra* 1076/7 n., 1087/38 n.), *ASC* uses *frencisc* for 'Norman', according to a usage common at this time and indeed regular in documents from the Anglo-Norman royal chancery, see ' "France" and "French" in *The Anglo-Saxon Chronicle*', *Leeds Studies in English*, N.S. iii (1969), 35–45.

Turolde: previously abbot of Malmesbury, where the monks were much relieved when the Conqueror moved him to Peterborough so that his martial skills might find scope in the rebellious Fens (*Gest. Pont.* 420). For a Peterborough view of his character, see Hugo, 84–5.

15. *Ywære*: true to the character he is given here, after the sack he set off for Denmark to recover what relics he could (Hugo, 82).

24. *Bolhiðe geate*: 'The Bolhithegate was presumably at the East end of the Abbey . . . as at this period the road through Peterborough crossed the river by a ford and passed the East end of the Abbey' (C. and W. T. Mellows, transs., *The Peterborough Chronicle of Hugh Candidus*, 1941, 39, n. 3).

27. *kynehelm*; 28. *fotspure*: the *nimbus* and *suppedaneum* usual with a medieval crucifix (P. Gradon, *RES* N.S. xi (1960), 64; relevant illustrations may be found in D. Talbot Rice, *English Art 871–1100*, Oxford, 1952, plates 13, 31, 53b, 64b, 74 a and b, 79a, 82a).

30. *hæcce*: 'altar frontal'; *magnam tabulam . . . que solebat esse ante altare*, presumably that given by Abbot Leofric (Hugo, 66, 78–9).

34. *gersumas . . . on bokes*: Eadmer, 74–5, lists gospel-books among financial assets. Book-covers were often encrusted with gold, silver, and jewels, as with the tenth-century German *Sion Gospels*; see, for instance, *Exeter Riddle* 26 (G. P. Krapp and E. v. K. Dobbie, eds., *The Exeter Book*, 1936, 193), the colophon of the *Lindisfarne Gospels* (E. G. Millar, *The Lindisfarne Gospels*, 1923, 3 and plate xxxvi, compare 5), the reference in the Thorney *Liber Vitae* to 'two ores of weighed gold, which is wired on to the outside of this book' (Whitelock, *Saga-Book of the Viking Society*, xii (1937–45), 128), and also B. Colgrave, ed. and trans., *The Life of Bishop Wilfrid by Eddius Stephanus*, Cambridge, 1927, 164–5. Pre-Conquest Peterborough (*Gildene Burh*, 1066 E) had possessed at least three such volumes, for Bishop Athelwold had presented *an Cristes boc mid sylure berenod* (A. J. Robertson, ed., *Anglo-Saxon Charters*, no. XXXIX), Abbot Leofric, *texta euuangeliorum et multas alias res, similiter omnia ex auro et argento* (Hugo, 66), and Archbishop Cynesige, *textum euangelii optime paratum de auro* (Hugo, 73).

35. *for ðes mynstres holdscipe*: 'from loyalty to the abbey', thus, Hugo, 79, *dixerunt quia pro fidelitate ecclesie hoc facerent, et melius illa Dani seruarent ad opus ecclesie quam Franci*, adding, *et* [*Hereuuardus*] *sepe postea iurauit se bona intencione hoc fecisse quia putabat illos uincere*

Willelmum regem; cf. 1048 E *for þes cynges swicdome* 'because of treachery towards the king'.

36. *geden heom*: the reflexive dative may be due to contamination from the following *ferden heom*, a common construction.

36–9. In the manuscript this passage is pointed thus:

'ferden heom to elig betæhtan þær þa ealla þa gærsume þa denescæ menn wændon ꝥ hi sceoldon ofer cumen. þa frencisca men þa todrefodon ealle þa munekes. beleaf . . .'

Some adjustment is needed: it was Hereward and his men who drove all the monks away, not the Frenchmen, who have not yet arrived and whose coming will be the signal for their return (*infra*, lines 58–9). Plummer removed the stop after *cumen* and added one after *frencisca men*; his text has been variously translated: 'The Danes expected that they were going to overcome the Frenchmen' (Whitelock *et alii*), 'the Danes, thinking they would get the better of the French' (Garmonsway), or, 'The Danes thought that they would forestall the Frenchmen' (Rositzke). Hugo, 79, says, however, *nauigauerunt festinantes, quia timebant ne superuenirent Normanni*, and a few lines later the English text itself says, *þa wæron þa utlagas ealle on flote, wistan þet he* [Turold] *scolde þider cumen*. Probably, therefore, the sense required for the disputed passage is, 'thinking that the Frenchmen would catch up with them', with *ofercuman* in its sense 'overtake' and inverted word-order, object–verb–subject; so I put a stop after *denescæ menn*, none after *cumen*, and a full stop after *frencisca men*. Further, *þa denescæ menn* is the indirect object of *betæhtan*, compare Hugo, *Et cum uenissent ad Eli, commendauerunt omnia ipsis Danis*: Hereward's own men are 'outlaws'. So translate: 'Thinking the Normans would catch them, they went away to Ely and there they handed all the treasure over to the Danes. They drove away all the monks.'

todrefodon ealle þa munekes: some, including Athelwold, the prior, to whom the Danes offered a bishopric, were taken to Ely. Athelwold managed to steal back the arm of St. Oswald (brought from Bamborough to Peterborough by a certain Winegotus, see Hugo, 70), which he first hid in the straw of his bed and then sent secretly to Ramsey for safe keeping. After peace was restored it took a divine vision, and Abbot Turold's threat of burning the abbey over their heads, to persuade the monks of Ramsey to return this relic to Peterborough (Hugo, 79–83).

40. *Leofwine lange*: for a possible identification, see F. E. Harmer, *Anglo-Saxon Writs*, Manchester, 1952, 254.

45. *iiii^o^* Nonarum *Iunii*: for the expansion, compare f. 12^r^ (*s.a.* 616) *iiii^o^ nonarū feƀ.*

61. *Ægelric biscop*: see also 1072 E (=1073 D); bishop of Durham from 1041 until he retired to Peterborough in 1056 (*s.a.* D; also *Hist. Eccl. Dun.* 91–2); arrested in 1069, probably for complicity in rebellion,

at the same time as Ægelwine (see 1071/4 n.), his brother and successor at Durham, was outlawed (*s.a.* DE; Hugo, 74, 82; and *Hist. Eccl. Dun.* 92, 105), and now imprisoned at Westminster. 1072 DE says, *He wæs to biscop hadod to Eoferwic, ac hit wæs mid unrihte him of genumon, 7 man geaf him þet biscoprice on Dunholme*; Hugo, 73–4, agrees, attributing his loss of York to the traditional hostility of secular chapters to monastic bishops. This story, although thus accepted by twelfth-century Peterborough authorities, cannot be true, as no compatible vacancy occurred at York. It probably arose from misunderstanding of 1041 D, *Her man hadode Ægelric biscop to Eoferwic*, where *to Eoferwic* could mean either 'to the see of York' or 'at York (to some other see)' (see Plummer, ii. 220), combined with the fact that Ægelric was deposed from Durham after three years and recovered that see only by bribery of Earl Siward (*Hist. Eccl. Dun.* 91–2). His character is enigmatic: for Hugo he was a saintly old man abandoning his see *pro amore Dei* in order to spend his last years as a simple monk; for Symeon, who makes similar charges against Ægelwine too, he was a greedy opportunist forcing himself on an unwilling chapter and stealing the diocesan treasures in order to play the benefactor at Peterborough (*Hist. Eccl. Dun.* 94, 105).

65. *Baldewine eorl*: Baldwin VI of Flanders, son of Baldwin V and of Adela, daughter of Robert I of France, and so brother of the Conqueror's wife Matilda (table, *EHD* 999).

66. *Willelm eorl*: William FitzOsbern, earl of Hereford, the Conqueror's *dapifer* and in 1067 his regent in England (1066 D; also William of Poitiers, 238, 240, 262, 264); for his family connections, see table, *EHD* 991, and also D. C. Douglas, 'The Ancestors of William Fitz-Osbern', *EHR* lix (1944), 62–79. For the present events and a character-sketch, see *Gest. Reg.* ii. 314–15; also Ordericus, ii. 234–7.

Franca cyng: Philip I. Baldwin V of Flanders, his uncle by marriage, had acted as regent during his minority (A. Fliche, *Le Règne de Philippe Ier, roi de France (1060–1108)*, Paris, 1912, 7).

67. *Rodbriht eorl*: brother of Baldwin VI, surnamed 'the Frisian' because of his marriage to the widow of Florent I of Holland (Ordericus, ii. 234); Philip of France later married his stepdaughter Bertha. See also *infra* 1079/6 n., 1085/3 n., and C. Verlinden, *Robert Ier le Frison, comte de Flandre*, Ghent, 1935, esp. 46–70. The battle took place at Cassel (*dép.* Nord).

1071

1. *Ædwine eorl 7 Morkere eorl*: sons of the Earl Ælfgar of Mercia who had a stormy career during the Confessor's reign, and so grandsons of Earl Leofric and brothers of the Edith who married Harold Godwinson (table, *EHD* 989). Edwin had succeeded his father as earl of Mercia; Morcar had been chosen by the Northumbrians to

succeed the outlawed Tostig (E *s.a.* 1064, D, correctly, 1065). After Hastings (at which they were not present, having exhausted their resources at the battle of Fulford) they joined Edgar the Atheling (see 1074/2 n.) and later submitted with him to the Conqueror, whom they accompanied to Normandy the following spring (1066 D; William of Poitiers, 236, 244). When slain, Edwin had been on his way to Malcolm of Scotland (Florence, ii. 9; compare 1072/4 n.). Morcar survived to be freed by the Conqueror on his death-bed, together with Siward Barn (see *infra*, 5 n.), Roger of Hereford (see 1075/9 n.), and others, only to be straightway reimprisoned by Rufus (Florence, ii. 20).

4. *Egelwine*: brother of Ægelric (see 1070/61 n.) and his successor at Durham; outlawed in 1069 (*s.a.* DE), he had joined Edgar the Atheling in Scotland (*Hist. Ecc. Dun.* 105; *Hist. Reg.* ii. 190, 102). For his imprisonment at Abingdon, see also J. Stevenson, ed., *Chronicon Monasterii de Abingdon*, 2 vols., R.S., 1858, i. 485–6.

5. *Siward Bearn*: compare Florence, ii. 9, *Siwardus, cognomento Barn*; in 1069 he had been one of Edgar the Atheling's party of refugees to Scotland (*Hist. Reg.* ii. 190). Although evidently a magnate, he cannot be firmly identified. He is probably the *Siward bar* who figures in Domesday as the *TRE* antecessor of Henry of Ferrières (ancestor of the earls of Derby, see *Complete Peerage*, iv. 190–1 and *VCH Derby*, i. 299–303) in Derbyshire, Warwickshire (see Round in *VCH Warks.* i. 282 et seq.), Lincolnshire (as 'Seubar', see C. W. Foster *et alii*, eds. and transs., *The Lincolnshire Domesday*, 1924, 100, also 223), Nottinghamshire (see *VCH Notts.* i. 234, 283) and Berkshire (see *VCH Berks.* i. 347, 348, 349). Le Prévost identified him also in the *Siwardus et Aldredus, filii Ædelgari, pronepotes regis*, listed by Ordericus among those submitting to the Conqueror at Barking (ii. 166 and n.); but this *Siwardus* also appears as a benefactor to Shrewsbury Abbey (ii. 416), with a known career incompatible with that of Siward Barn (see *VCH Salop*, i. 300 and Chibnall, ed., *Orderic Vitalis*, ii. 194 n.)

7. *brycge gewrohte*: compare Florence, ii. 9, *pontem . . . duorum milliarorum longum fieri jussit* (and for a later bridging operation there, *Gest. Steph.* 66). Ely was then a true island, lying in the angle made by the confluence of the Cam with the Ouse and cut off on the other sides by fens (see H. C. Darby, *The Medieval Fenland*, 106–14). Unfortunately, the long account of this siege in *Liber Eliensis* is wholly unreliable (see Blake, op. cit. liv–lvii).

1072

1. *lædde scipfyrde 7 landfyrde to Scotlandė*: the extant writ commanding Abbot Ægelwig of Evesham (see 1077/5 n.) to assemble all his knights at Clarendon (calendared by H. W. C. Davis, ed., *Regesta Regum Anglo-Normannorum*, I: 1066–1100, Oxford, 1913, as no. 63) is usually

connected with this expedition, see Round, *Feudal England*, 238; compare also the undated reference to a Scottish expedition in *Chronicon Monasterii de Abingdon*, ii. 9–10.

3. *æt þam Gewæde*: D *ofer þæt wað*, *WA Scodwade*; compare Reginald of Durham, *Vita S. Oswaldi*: *Scotwad, quod in Scottorum lingua Forth nominatur* (in *Sym. Dun. Opera*, i. 339). The Forth, representing the northernmost boundary of Anglian colonization, was at this time often regarded by the English as the southern boundary of Scotland, no matter where the political frontier of the moment happened to lie (compare 1091/34 *Loðene on Englaland*).

4. *Se cyng Melcolm*: Malcolm Canmore. He had made repeated incursions into northern England (*Hist. Reg.* ii. 190–6), and in 1067 and again in 1069 had sheltered Edgar the Atheling (see 1074/2 n.), whose sister Margaret he married (1067 D; compare *Hist. Reg.* ii. 191–2). See also 1093/26 n.

5. *gislas sealde*: evidently including his eldest son Duncan, see 1093/33–5.

7 *his man wæs*: the significance of the Pact of Abernethy has been much disputed; see Stenton, 598, and, for a Scottish view, R. L. Graeme Ritchie, *The Normans in Scotland*, Edinburgh, 1954, 29–38, 386.

6. *Egelric*: see 1070/61 n. He died and was buried in his fetters, *sperans se pro hoc martirio in gloria resurrecturum* (Hugo, 74).

1073

2. *Mans*: for the Conqueror's acquisition of the overlordship of Maine and his struggles to retain it, see R. Latouche, *Histoire du comté du Maine pendant le xe et le xie siècle*, Bibliothèque de l'Ecole des Hautes Études, clxxxiii, Paris, 1910, 31–8, and also Stenton, 577, 599–600.

1074

2. *Eadgar cild*: Edgar the Atheling, son of Edmund Ironside's son Edward the Exile and of his wife, a kinswoman of the Emperor (1067 D, compare 1057 D; table, *EHD* 982). Regarded by many as the true heir to the English throne (1066 D; William of Poitiers, 214), he had, in spite of an early submission to the Conqueror (1066 D; William of Poitiers, 236, 238), been involved since the Conquest in several risings (1068 DE, 1069 E), taking refuge in the intervals with Malcolm of Scotland, who married his sister Margaret (St. Margaret of Scotland, see 1093/26 n.). 1075 D, the corresponding annal, adds that, having been shipwrecked while on his way to enlist under Philip of France, Edgar made this present peace at Malcolm's prompting. From time to time during the next thirty years he played minor parts in Anglo-Norman and Scottish affairs, becoming a close friend

of Robert Curthose, whom he accompanied on the Crusade (see 1086/14, 1091 *passim*, 1093/4, 1097/38, 1106/38; *Gest. Reg.* ii. 309–10; Ordericus, iv. 70). William of Malmesbury, speaking of him as still alive *c.* 1125, calls him so 'simple' as to be contemptible, but Orderic takes a kinder view.

1075

1. *Willelm cyng geaf. . .*: but Florence, ii. 10, says that the marriage was made *contra præceptum regis Willelmi.*

Raulfe eorle: earl of Norfolk and Suffolk, son of Ralph the Steallere (see *infra*, 3 n.); surnamed 'of (G)uader' (Ordericus, ii. 222) or 'of Gaël' (*dép.* Ille-et-Vilaine) from the Breton estates he held (also *Radulphus Brito*, Ordericus, ii. 262, iii. 484); see G. H. White, *The Complete Peerage*, ix, 1936, 571–4.

Willelmes dohtor Osbearnes sunu: for William FitzOsbern, see 1070/66 n.

3. *bryttisc*: 'Breton', likewise 13 *infra*, *Bryttas*='Bretons'; compare 1076, where Dol-de-Bretagne is in *Brytlande* and defended by *Bryttas*, also *ASC* 890, *Sant Laudan* [Saint-Lo], *þæt is betueoh Brettum Francum*. On the other hand, in 1087/98 and 1088/22 *Brytland*='*Wales*', just as in OE *Bryttas* regularly='Welshmen'. An ambiguity seems to persist at least till the end of the Middle Ages (*MED*; but for a possible distinction between Latin *Britones/Britanni*, see R. S. Loomis, *Arthurian Literature in the Middle Ages: A Collaborative History*, Oxford, 1959, 55). For the high proportion of Bretons among the 'Norman' settlers, see Stenton, *English Feudalism*, 25–8.

his fæder wæs englisc: for Ralph the Steallere, *dapifer*, *minister*, of the Confessor, see G. H. White, op. cit. 568–71, where his charter attestations and the Domesday references to him are collected; he preceded his son as earl of Norfolk and Suffolk, probably by the Conqueror's gift. His unEnglish name suggests that *ASC* may be wrong about his nationality, compare the description of his son as *Brito ex patre* (*Gest. Reg.* ii. 313); but he may be the *Radulphus anglicus* who attested certain Breton charters in 1031–2.

9. *Roger eorl*: Roger of Breteuil, earl of Hereford, the bride's brother (table, *EHD* 991, which also shows why, 23 below, he is called the Conqueror's kinsman). Letters Lanfranc wrote to him on hearing of the conspiracy, together with others to the Conqueror and to Walchere of Durham, are calendared in Davis, *Regesta* I, as nos. 78–83.

Walþeof eorl: see 1070/1 n.

11. *gecydd þam cynge*: Florence, loc. cit., says that Waltheof, forced into the plot against his will, repented, confessed to Lanfranc and then revealed the treason to the Conqueror, throwing himself on his mercy, so likewise D, *Walþeof eorl . . . wreide hine sylfne 7 bæd*

forgyfenysse 7 bead gærsuman; but Ordericus, ii. 265, *per delationem Judith uxoris suæ accusatus est*.

16. *wearð gelet*: Florence, ii. 11, describes how he was cut off by forces led not only by the Norman castellans Urse of Abetôt and Walter de Lacy but also by the English prelates Wulfstan of Worcester (see 1088/26 n.) and Ægelwig of Evesham (see 1077/5 n.).

17. *castelmen*: including Odo of Bayeux and Geoffrey, bishop of Coutances (Florence, loc. cit.).

19. *for to scipe*: Florence, loc. cit., *ascensa navi de Anglia ad minorem Brytanniam fugit*, but Ordericus, ii. 263, and Hen. Hunt. 206, both say he went first to Denmark for help (compare *infra*, 26 n.). Ordericus adds that Ralph and his wife were both to die while following Robert of Normandy on the First Crusade (ii. 264, iii. 484).

26. *Cnut Swægnes sunu*: see also 1070/3 n., 1085/2, 1087/150 n. Hen. Hunt., loc. cit., says Ralph of Gaël was with this fleet.

28. *Eadgið seo hlæfdige*: the Confessor's widow and Earl Godwine's daughter (see table, *EHD* 988).

32. *fordyde*: D *fordemde*, *WA judicati sunt*, presumably the original reading; but E has not been emended since it makes sense as it stands. The rhymes suggest that the D text of the following verses is also superior to E's.

1076

1. *Swægn cyng*: see 1070/3 n.

4. *Walþeof eorl wes beheafdod*: the *W* is rubricated as for the obit of a martyr. Florence, ii. 12, outspokenly condemns this execution, likewise Ordericus, ii. 290, who adds that the Conqueror never afterwards enjoyed a day's peace. For Waltheof's later reputation as a saint, see *Vita et Passio Waldevi Comitis* and *Miracula Sancti Waldevi Gloriosi Martyris* (ed. F. Michel, *Chroniques anglo-normandes*, 3 vols., Rouen, 1836–40, ii. 99–142); also *Gest. Pont.* 321–2 (compare *Gest. Reg.* ii. 312); Ordericus, ii. 265–7, 286–90.

6. *Dol*: as Florence, ii. 12, speaks of *castellum Radulfi comitis, quod Dol nominatur*, Ralph of Gaël may have been present, even though Dol was not in his own lands.

7. *se cyng*: Philip I, at this time constantly intent on curbing Norman pretensions, see Fliche, *Philippe Ier*, 269–74, also R. Fawtier, *Les Capétiens et la France*, Paris, 1942, 22.

of Francland: 'from France'; until 1094 the title is always *Franca cyng, Francena cyng*. The sense is the narrow one, 'French royal domain', see *Leeds Studies in English*, N.S. iii. 37–8.

1077

2. *Englalandes cyng*: this formula, replacing *Engla cyng* (e.g. 1066 D), etc., is first recorded in I Cnut (F. Liebermann, ed., *Die Gesetze der Angelsachsen*, 3 vols., Halle, 1903–16, i. 278).

5. *Ægelwig*: 1078 D, *se woruldsnotra abbot*. Appointed in 1058, he was, with Wulfstan of Worcester (see 1088/26 n.), one of the longest surviving Anglo-Saxon prelates. A contemporary *Life* of him is embedded in *Chronicon Abbatiæ de Evesham* (ed. W. D. Macray, R.S., 1863), see R. R. Darlington, 'Æthelwig, Abbot of Evesham', *EHR* xlvii (1933), 1–22, 177–98.

7. *Hereman*: a Fleming who had been chaplain to the Confessor, see *Gest. Pont.* 182–3, also F. Barlow, ed. and trans., *The Life of King Edward*, 1962, xlvii. Appointed in 1045 to the see of Ramsbury (*s.a.* CDE), in 1058 he obtained that of Sherborne also; and about 1075 moved the united see from Sherborne to Salisbury (i.e. Old Sarum, see *VCH Wilts.* vi. 51–67, esp. 60 et seq.).

1079

2. *þam twam Mariam mæssan*: i.e. the Assumption (15 August) and the Nativity (6 September).

6. *gefeaht togeanes his sunu Rotbearde*: D is fuller, saying that Robert resented his father's refusal to allow him real authority in the duchy of Normandy with which he had been formally invested; see also Ordericus, ii. 377–90; *Gest. Reg.* ii. 316–17; and Florence, ii. 12.

7. *Gerborneð*: Gerberoy (*dép.* Oise), *quod ei rex Philippus præstiterat* (Florence, ii. 13; likewise Ordericus, ii. 386; see also *Gest. Reg.* ii. 316); but an extant charter shows Philip I temporarily allied with the Conqueror at the siege here (Davis, *Regesta* I, no. 115a).

8. *gewundod*: D and Florence (ii. 13) give fuller (but not wholly compatible) accounts, telling how Robert Curthose himself wounded his father but then allowed him to escape (compare also *Gest. Reg.* ii. 317).

1080

1. *Walchere*: Ægelwine's successor at Durham and since Waltheof's fall also 'earl' in Northumbria. The assembly where the mob killed him had been summoned to consider the murder, allegedly instigated by his chaplain Leofwine, of his chief adviser, the thane Ligulf (Florence, ii. 13–16, and *Hist. Eccl. Dun.* 116–17, both giving the place as *Ad Caput Capræ*, Gateshead; also *Gest. Pont.* 271–2 and *Gest. Reg.* ii. 330–1). Edith, the Confessor's widow, is said to have prophesied Walchere's end by exclaiming at his consecration, 'Pulchrum hic martirem habemus!'

3. *on Hloðeringa*: Walchere had been a clerk at Liège (*Hist. Reg.* ii. 195), in Lower Lorraine, which, as the frontier ran along the Scheldt, was then in the German Empire (see A. Longnon, *La Formation de l'unité française*, Paris, 1922, 41, and F. Barlow, *The English Church 1000–1066*, 1963, map on 12–13; and compare 1126/4, *þone kasere Heanri of Loherenge*).

1081

1. *into Wealan*: where unrest was being caused by Gruffydd ap Cynan, a former king of Gwynedd, whom the marcher earls now succeeded in imprisoning (J. E. Lloyd, *A History of Wales from the Earliest Times to the Edwardian Conquest*, 2 vols., 3rd edn. 1939, ii. 385; also B. G. Charles, *Old Norse Relations with Wales*, Cardiff, 1934, chap. ii).

1082

1. *Odan biscop*: Odo of Bayeux, the Conqueror's half-brother (see table, *EHD* 983); earl of Kent, and regularly given vice-regal powers in England (compare 1087/86 et seq.; see also D. C. Douglas, *The Domesday Monachorum of Christ Church Canterbury*, 1944, 27 et seq., and F. West, *The Justiciarship in England 1066–1232*, Cambridge, 14–16). His career has been summarized by S. E. Gleason, *An Ecclesiastical Barony of the Middle Ages: The Bishopric of Bayeux, 1066–1204*, Harvard, 1936, 8–17. Some contemporary historians attributed this imprisonment to his having tried to entice Norman magnates to follow him in an expedition to seize the Papacy (*Gest. Reg.* ii. 34; Ordericus, iii. 189–92). Freed by the dying Conqueror (Ordericus, iii. 247, with a character-sketch put into the king's mouth), he straightway rebelled against Rufus (1088 *passim*).

1083

1. *seo ungeþwærnes on Glæstingabyrig*: compare the account by Florence, ii. 16–17, and the three versions by William of Malmesbury, in *Gest. Reg.* ii. 329–30, in *Gest. Pont.* 197, and in *De Antiquitate Glastoniensis Ecclesiæ* (ed. T. Hearne, *Adami de Domerham Historia, etc.*, 2 vols., Oxford, 1727, i. 110–11, 113–16); this last version, the longest and most dramatic, has verbal resemblances both to our text and to Florence (see *infra*, 3 n., 26 n.; J. Armitage Robinson, *Somerset Historical Essays*, 1921, 1–25, deals with some problems concerning *De Ant. Glast.*, but not with this episode).

2. *þurstane*: a former monk of Caen. Although banished to Normandy in punishment for this affair, he bought the abbey back from Rufus for £500.

3. *misbead his munecan . . .*: compare Florence, ii. 16: *Hic inter cætera stultitiæ suæ opera, Gregorianum cantum aspernatus, monachos cœpit*

compellere, ut, illo relicto, cujusdam Willelmi Fescamnensis cantum discerent et cantarent (also, in the same words, *De Ant. Glast.* 114, and, more briefly, Ordericus, ii. 226; William 'of Fécamp' is the monastic reformer, William of Volpiano, more often known as William of Dijon, who in 1001 undertook the reform of Fécamp, see Knowles, *Monastic Order*, 554–5). William of Malmesbury also gives Thurstan's monks less academic cause to hate him, saying he robbed and starved them (*Gest. Pont.* 197).

26. *ðet blod com . . .*: in *De Ant. Glast.* the flowing of blood *de altari usque ad gradus, de gradibus usque ad terram* is linked with the wounding of the crucifix (*suprà*, 19–20) to give the miracle which is the core of this version of the story.

27. *þreo . . . eahteteone*: Florence and Malmesbury both say two killed and fourteen wounded; Florence adds that the monks, defending themselves with stools and candlesticks, injured some of the men-at-arms.

32. *peanega*: for an approximate valuation of the 'penny' at a somewhat earlier time, see H. R. Loyn, 'Boroughs and Mints A.D. 900–1066', in R. H. M. Dolley, ed., *Anglo-Saxon Coins: Studies presented to F. M. Stenton*, 1961, 123–4:

'There is much to be said for thinking of an Anglo-Saxon penny more in terms of a pre-1914 half-sovereign; that is to say, of a coin of considerable value, not lightly to be spent or lost, rather than in terms of any silver coin familiar to us.'

1085

2. *Cnut*: for his previous attempts against the Conqueror, see 1070/3 n., 1075/26; see also 1087/150 for his death. For the context of this threatened invasion, see Stenton, *English Feudalism*, 149–51.

3. *Rodbeardes eorles*: Robert 'the Frisian' (see 1070/67 n.), who had already shown hostility by harbouring Edgar the Atheling (1075 D) and the rebellious Robert Curthose (1079 D). For this Dano-Flemish alliance, compare 1075/28 and see *Gest. Reg.* ii. 315–20, also Verlinden, *Robert Ier le Frison*, 108–12.

8. *of Francrice and of Brytlande*: 'from the king of France's lands and from Brittany', compare Hen. Hunt. 207, and Florence, ii. 18. *Chronicon Monasterii de Abingdon*, ii. 11, describes the gathering and quartering of this army of *solidarios*.

21. *Mauricius*: a former royal chancellor, responsible for the rebuilding of (Old) St. Paul's after the fire of 1087 (*Gest. Pont.* 145–6; see also W. R. Matthews and W. M. Atkins, eds., *A History of St. Paul's Cathedral*, 1957, 19, 66).

22. *Rodbeard*: one of the Conqueror's worst choices, who kept his monks in subjection by allowing them neither food nor instruction (*Gest. Pont.* 309). He moved the see from Chester to Coventry.

23. *mycel geþeaht . . . ymbe þis land*: the Domesday Survey. For summaries of the motives and methods of the Survey, see Stenton, 609–10, 644–9, also the bibliography on 693–5; *EHD* gives bibliography on 803–4 and 810–11, and on 847–78 an introduction to Domesday Book and extracts from it; note the other contemporary descriptions of the survey on 851–5, 882, 889, especially the closely similar but fuller note in a Worcester compilation (*EHD* 853 and Liebermann, *Ungedruckte AN. Geschichtsquellen*, 21–2).

26. *lett agan ut*: *agān* 'come forth'.

35. *sceame to tellanne*: a more impersonal but no less telling record of public indignation occurs in the note made by Robert, bishop of Hereford, in a copy of the *Chronicle* of Marianus Scotus: *Et vexata est terra multis cladibus ex congregatione regalis pecuniae procedentibus* (W. H. Stevenson, 'A Contemporary Description of the Domesday Survey', *EHR* xxii (1907), 74, also *EHD* 851; compare Florence, ii. 19).

1086

The scribe repeats the number *Millesimo lxxxv*, numbering the next three annals also a year behind; the correct date at 1087/2 proves the error is merely graphic.

3. *dubbade . . . to ridere*: the earliest extant reference to knighthood in England.

6. *þe ahtes wæron*: WA, *qui alicujus pretii erant*; for interpretation of this phrase, see Stenton, *English Feudalism*, 112–14.

8. *holdaðas*: see H. A. Cronne, 'The Salisbury Oath', *History*, xix (1934–35), 248–52, and also Stenton, 610–11.

14. *Eadgar æþeling*: see 1074/2 n.; Florence, ii. 19, adds, *et Apuliam adiit*.

18. *swiðe hefelic gear*: like comets and eclipses, storms and pestilences were seen eschatologically, for the end of the world, still much in men's minds (one date forecast had been 1065), was to be heralded by plagues, famines, and earthquakes, as well as by falling stars and by eclipses of the sun and moon (Matthew xxiv, also Mark xiii and Luke xxi); compare Wulfstan's sermon *Secundum Lucam* (D. Bethurum, ed., *The Homilies of Wulfstan*, Oxford, 1957, 125, also notes 278 et seq.).

1087

12. *fordrifene*: 'exhausted', perhaps with a grim pun on *drif* 'fever' in line 7.

22. *sealde his land . . . to male*: for the high proportion of royal manors recorded in Domesday as 'at farm', see R. Lennard, *Rural England 1086–1135*, Oxford, 1959, 123–4; and for similar practices by Rufus, see Eadmer, 26. The general fiscal activities of the Norman sheriff are treated by W. A. Morris, 'The Office of Sheriff in the Early Norman Period', *EHR* xxxiii (1918), 145–75 (=ch. iii of *The Medieval English Sheriff to 1300*, Manchester, 1927), esp. 156, 165–73.

38. *France*: the royal domain as distinct from the great fiefs such as Normandy, compare 1076/7 n. For this last campaign of the Conqueror's, see Ordericus, iii. 222–6, and *Gest. Reg.* ii. 336–7.

40. *Maðante*: Mantes, capital of the French Vexin, the disputed territory.

49. *Sancte Stephanes mynstre*: Saint-Étienne de Caen, founded, together with La Trinité de Caen, as penance for the Conqueror's uncanonical marriage to Matilda of Flanders (*Gest. Reg.* ii. 327).

50. *Eala, hu leas . . .*: the Conqueror's death and burial (the fullest account is by Ordericus, iii. 248–65) furnished an apt occasion for such reflections, since as he lay dead he was robbed and then deserted by his attendants. Thus, Ordericus, iii. 249 (compare iii. 254–5):

'O sæcularis pompa, quam despicabilis es! quia nimis vana et labilis es! . . . Ecce potentissimus heros, cui nuper plus quam centum milia militum serviebant avide, et quem multæ gentes cum tremore metuebant, nunc a suis turpiter in domo non sua spoliatus est, et a prima usque ad tertiam supra nudam humum derelictus est.' Likewise Eadmer, 24:

'Quem enim conditio sortis humanæ non moveat ad pietatem, cum auditum fuerit regem istum qui tantæ potentiæ in vita sua extitit, ut in tota Anglia, in tota Normannia, in tota Cinomanensi patria, nemo contra imperium ejus manum movere auderet, mox ut in terram spiritum exhalaturus positus est, ab omni homine . . . derelictum, cadaver ejus sine omni pompa per Sequanam in naucella delatum . . .'

53. *seofon fotmæl*: even that was disputed, for in the middle of the funeral a certain *Ascelinus, Arturi filius*, stepped forward to claim that the land on which Saint-Étienne was built had been stolen from his father (Ordericus, iii. 252; also Eadmer, loc. cit., and *Gest. Reg.* ii. 337).

59. *hu gedon mann*: for other contemporary character-sketches, see *Gest. Reg.* ii. 326, 331, 335–6, and the Anonymous Monk of Caen (J. Marx, ed., *Guillaume de Jumièges: Gesta Normannorum Ducum*,

147–8). It has been suggested that this use of *gedon*, of which this is the earliest extant record, may be a calque on OFr. *confait* (see G. Karlberg, *The English Interrogative Pronouns*, Stockholm, 1954, 172, 226–7), but the existence of similar usages in other Germanic languages makes this unlikely.

67. *mære mynster*: for Battle Abbey, to be dedicated in 1094 (*s.a.*, 10), see Rose Graham, *English Ecclesiastical Studies*, 1929, 188–208. It had the earliest church built in England on an ambulatory plan (A. W. Clapham, *English Romanesque Architecture after the Conquest*, Oxford, 1934, 37; also Rice, *English Art 871–1100*, 74).

69. *mynster on Cantwarbyrig*: the cathedral at Canterbury, burnt in 1067 (*s.a.* E; *Gest. Pont.* 69; Eadmer, 13), had been rebuilt by Lanfranc after the model of his former abbey of Saint-Étienne at Caen, on a triapsidal plan such as had been seen before in England only in the Confessor's great church at Westminster (Clapham, op. cit. 36, and idem, *Romanesque Architecture in Western Europe*, Oxford, 1936, 141).

71. *afylled mid munecan*: for the fresh impetus in English monasticism at this time, see Knowles, *Monastic Order*, esp. 126–7.

74. *bær his cynehelm*: for these crown-wearings, accompanied by religious solemnity, see H. G. Richardson, 'The Coronation in Medieval England', *Traditio*, xvi (1960), esp. 126–31.

79. *þegnas 7 cnihtas*: *WA*, *barones totius Angliæ*; for these terms, see Stenton, *English Feudalism*, 115–51, esp. 132–6. This is one of the earliest examples of *cniht* denoting rank (compare 1086/4, where *chevaler*—*ridere*).

90. *faran ofer his rice* . . . : compare 1135/12–14. The archetype of such 'traditional and proverbial' expressions (Plummer, ii. 274) may be Bede's characterization of Edwin's reign (*Historia Ecclesiastica*, ed. Plummer, i. 118):

'Tanta autem eo tempore pax in Brittania, quaquauersum imperium regis Æduini peruenerat, fuisse perhibetur, ut, sicut usque hodie in prouerbio dicitur, etiam si mulier una cum recens nato paruulo uellet totam perambulare insulam a mari ad mare, nullo se ledente ualeret.'

For a late-tenth-century borrowing of this, see D. Whitelock, 'Wulfstan *Cantor*', in *Nordica et Anglica: Studies in Honor of Stefán Einarsson*, Paris and The Hague, 1968, 84; and compare Hen. Hunt. 210 (*puella auro onusta*); *Havelok*, ed. Skeat, EETS ES 4, lines 45–50; also J. A. W. Bennett and G. V. Smithers, eds., *Early Middle English Verse and Prose*, Oxford, 1966, 381.

94. *forleas þa limu*: as set down in the unofficial code known as *Leis Willelme* (Liebermann, *Gesetze*, i. 504–5), whereas (except for slaves) the Anglo-Saxon penalty had been monetary compensation (ibid. i. 8, 346).

98. *Brytland*: here 'Wales', as in 1088/22 (but compare 1075/3 n., 1085/8 n.). For the Conqueror's Welsh policy, see Stenton, 606–8, and J. G. Edwards, 'The Normans and the Welsh March', *PBA* xlii (1956), 155–77, esp. 157–63.

100. *Scotland*: see 1072/5 n. (the Pact of Abernethy).

102. *Mans*: see 1073/2 n. and also Latouche, *Histoire du comté du Maine*, 39.

103. *werscipe*: i.e. *wærscipe* 'astuteness'.

106. *Castelas he let . . .*: the study by B. J. Whiting, 'The Rime of King William', *Philologica: the Malone Anniversary Studies*, Baltimore, 1949, 89–96, is too insistent that the verses are the chronicler's own rather than popular and oral in origin. Rhyming passages can also be found in *ASC* at 975 D, 1036 C, 1075 E (=1076 D), 1104. Castles, at this date rarely built in stone, were an innovation of the Norman settlement, see E. S. Armitage, *The Early Norman Castles of the British Isles*, 1912, also D. F. Renn, *Norman Castles in Britain*, 1968; and for the military system they represent, Stenton, *English Feudalism*, 192–217.

117. *deorfrið*: for an estimate of the devastation involved in making the deer-forests, see H. C. Darby and E. M. J. Campbell, *The Domesday Geography of South-East England*, Cambridge, 1962, 324–37.

144. MS. *forleon*: most probably, as both Thorpe and Plummer suggested, an error for *forfleon*, compare *Utan forfleon geornlice man 7 morðor 7 manslihtas* (D. Bethurum, ed., *Homilies of Wulfstan*, 231), and *Uton forði ælc yfel forfleon* (B. Thorpe, ed., *Homilies of Ælfric*, i. 602).

Ordericus draws a similar moral from the Conqueror's end (iii. 255):

'Nolite ergo confidere in principibus falsis, o filii hominum; sed in Deo vivo et vero, qui creator est omnium. Veteris et novi Testamenti seriem revolvite, et exempla inde multiplicia vopis capessite, quid cavere, quidve debeatis appetere. Nolite sperare in iniquitate . . .'

150. *Cnute cynge*: see 1070/3 n., 1075/26 n., 1085/2 n. An English monk of Odensee (a daughter-house of Evesham) wrote a *Life* of *Protomartyr Danorum Kanutus*: *Ælnothi Monachi Historia ortus, vitæ, et passionis S.Canuti Regis Daniæ* (J. Langebek, *et alii*, eds., *Scriptores Rerum Danicarum*, 9 vols., Copenhagen, 1772–1878, iii. 325–90). Canute's son Charles of Flanders (see table, *EHD* 999) was also murdered in a church (1127/13 n.).

152. *on Ispanie*: a useful summary of these events occurs in P. Boissonnade, *Du nouveau sur la Chanson de Roland*, Paris, 1923, 31–5.

159. *Stigand . . . of Ciceastre*: he had moved the see to Chichester from Selsey (*Gest. Pont.* 205).

160. *se abbot of Sancte Augustine . . . of Baðon . . . of Perscoran*: Florence, ii. 19–20, supplies the names *Scollandus, Alsius, Turstanus.*

177. *unlesan ealle þa men*: compare 1071/1 n.

1088

4. *woldon habban his broðer to cynge*: for this revolt against Rufus in favour of Robert Curthose, see also Florence, ii. 21–6; Ordericus, iii. 268–78; *Gest. Reg.* ii. 360–3; *Gest. Pont.* 272–3; *Hist. Reg.* ii. 214–17.

6. *Oda biscop*: Odo of Bayeux (see 1082/1 n., 1087/84 ff.). According to Florence, his brother Robert of Mortain (see table, *EHD* 983) also took part in the revolt. Odo's present activities continued his long-standing rivalry with Lanfranc for supremacy in Kent (*Gest. Reg.* ii. 360).

Gosfrið biscop: Geoffrey of Coutances, the seventh richest baron in England, see J. H. Le Patourel, 'Geoffrey of Montbray, Bishop of Coutances, 1049–93', *EHR* lix (1944), 129–61, also West, *Justiciarship*, 7–8. He had been at Hastings (William of Poitiers, 182), and Ordericus, iii. 406, says of him, *loricatos milites ad bellandum, quam revestitos clericos ad psallendum magis erudire noverat.*

Willelm biscop: William of Saint-Calais, Walchere's successor and a great benefactor of his see (*Hist. Eccl. Dun.* 119–35): he replaced the secular canons at Durham by monks from the abbeys he had helped to refound at Jarrow and Monkwearmouth; he built much of the present cathedral, including some early ribbed vaulting as well as the early pointed vaulting (T. S. R. Boase, *English Art 1100–1216*, Oxford, 1953, 13–19 and references on 24); and he was a great collector of manuscripts (R. A. B. Mynors, *Durham Cathedral Manuscripts to the End of the Twelfth Century*, Durham, 1939, 32–45). He was, however, less admirable when he lent himself to Rufus's persecution of Anselm (Eadmer, 59 et seq.). His character remains ambiguous: Symeon portrays an ideal bishop and a father to his monks, whereas William of Malmesbury sees him as quite devoid of virtue (*Gest. Pont.* 272–3, compare Eadmer, loc. cit.); see the modern summing-up by H. S. Offler, 'William of St. Calais, First Norman Bishop of Durham', *Transactions of the Architectural and Archæological Society of Durham and Northumberland*, x/3 (1950), 258–79.

7. *be þam biscope*: ambiguous (see Plummer, ii. 276–7); probably the last-named, William of Durham, is meant. *Gest. Reg.* 360 explicitly says that Odo joined the revolt because William of Durham had now more power than he himself had, compare Florence, ii. 22, *Willelmus episcopus Dunholmensis . . . rex prædictus illius, ut veri consiliarii, fruebatur prudentia . . . ejusque consiliis totius Angliæ tractabatur respublica.*

10. *Rogere eorl*: Roger of Montgoméry (*dép.* Calvados), earl of Shrewsbury and one of the greatest Anglo-Norman magnates, see *Complete*

Peerage, xi. 683–7 and J. F. R. Mason, 'Roger de Montgomery and his Sons (1067–1102)', *TRHS*, 5th ser. xi (1963), 1–28. Ordericus, whose father had been in Montgomery service, gives him an excellent character (ii. 220).

17. *Rodbeard a Mundbræg*: Robert Mowbray (of Montbray, *dép.* Manche), nephew of Geoffrey of Coutances and earl of Northumberland (*Complete Peerage*, ix. 705–6). Ordericus, iii. 273, however, expressly excludes him from the 1088 rebels. See also 1093, 1095.

20. *Beorclea Hyrnesse*: *hyrnesse* 'that which is subject'; the earliest extant example of an alternative name, in use until the sixteenth century, for Berkeley Hundred (A. H. Smith, *The Place-Names of Gloucestershire*, Part II, EPNS xxxix, Cambridge, 1964, 206–7).

22. *Brytlande*: as in 1087/98, 'Wales' (compare *Gest. Reg.* 361, *cum Walensibus*, and Florence, ii. 24, *magno . . . Walensium exercitu*).

26. *Wlstan*: consecrated in 1062 (Florence, i. 218) and now the last surviving Anglo-Saxon prelate. A lost English *Life* by his chaplain Coleman was translated by William of Malmesbury (ed. R. R. Darlington, *The Vita Wulfstani of William of Malmesbury*, Camden Society, 1928); *Gest. Pont.* 278–89 follows this but adds the account of Wulfstan's part in suppressing this rebellion (see 1075/17 n. for him in a similar role; he conformed to Norman custom by keeping a band of household knights, *hiredmen*, see *Gest. Pont.* 281 and *Vita*, 55–6).

29. *þurh þæs biscopes geearnunga*: Florence, ii. 25–6, and *Gest. Pont.* 285 (but not *Gest. Reg.* ii. 361 or *Hist. Reg.* ii. 215) make the victory frankly miraculous, with the enemy struck blind and paralysed.

32. *Roger*: Roger Bigod, earl of Norfolk (see *Complete Peerage*, ix. 575–9); of obscure Norman origins, he had made his fortune in England.

33. *Hugo*: Hugo of Grandmesnil (*dép.* Calvados), castellan of Leicester and a great landowner in the Midlands (*Complete Peerage*, vii, notes on 524, 532, also Ordericus, ii. 222); he had fought at Hastings (William of Poitiers, 196).

37. *aweston*: 'he and his men laid waste'.

40. *englisce mannan*: all the chroniclers emphasize English loyalty to Rufus (Florence, ii. 22–3; *Gest. Reg.* ii. 362; Ordericus, iii. 271, 273; *Hist. Reg.* ii. 215), Ordericus representing the English as most vehement in demanding punishment of the traitors.

72. *Eustatius þe iunga*: Eustace III, count of Boulogne, son of the Eustace II involved in the Dover affair of 1052 (1052 D, 1048 E); for the family, see J. C. Andressohn, *The Ancestry and Life of Godfrey of Bouillon*, Bloomington, Indiana, 1947, 9 et seq., and for their estates

in England, J. H. Round, 'The Counts of Boulogne as English Lords', in *Studies in Peerage and Family History*, 1901, 147–80. See also *infra*, 1101/18 n.

76. *unniðing*: *niðing*, a Norse loan, had great pejorative force, being applied, for instance, to Swein Godwinson after his treacherous murder of his cousin Beorn (1049 C). Here it underlines that the appeal was to Englishmen, compare *Gest. Reg.* ii. 362, *nisi si qui velint sub nomine Niðing, quod nequam sonat, remanere. Angli, qui nihil miserius putarent quam hujusce vocabuli dedecore aduri* . . . (the word seems to have been felt as untranslatable, compare how the twelfth-century legal text *Quadripartitus* has *opus niðingi* as a rendering of *niðinges dæde* (Liebermann, *Gesetze*, i. 392–3)).

81. *ofer sæ ferdon*: Odo was to join the First Crusade with Robert Curthose (see 1096/17) and die on the road (*Gest. Reg.* ii. 334; Ordericus, iii. 266, 483, and iv. 16–18).

wurðscipe: possibly a vernacular equivalent of *honor* 'seignory'.

84. *forlet his biscoprice*: the tract *De Iniusta Vexatione Willelmi Episcopi* (appendix in *Symeonis Monachi Opera*, i. 170–95) purports to describe William of Durham's trial and expulsion, but H. S. Offler, *EHR* lxvi (1951), 321–41 shows that this is probably a piece of late fiction.

85. *forleton heora land*: for restoration of these forfeitures, see 1091/12.

1089

2. *Landfranc*: for contrasting contemporary views of him, see Eadmer, 12–23 (18–19 make it clear why he was specially *muneca feder 7 frouer*), and Hugh the Chantor, *History of the Church of York*, 2–5, with the strongest Yorkist bias (compare *supra*, xxx). Modern accounts include A. J. Macdonald, *Lanfranc: A Study of his Life, Work and Writing*, 2nd edn., 1944, and F. Barlow, 'A View of Archbishop Lanfranc', *Journal of Ecclesiastical History*, xvi (1965), 163–77.

The see remained vacant until Anselm's appointment in 1093 (*s.a.*, 6–8).

1090

1. *INDICTIONE XIII*: for this method of reckoning years, see R. L. Poole, *Medieval Reckonings of Time*, 1918, 29–31, and C. R. Cheney, *Handbook of Dates for Students of English History*, 1961, 2–3.

5. *þurh his geapscipe oððe þurh gærsuma*: *Gest. Reg.* ii. 363, suppressing the ironical ambiguity, *sollertia sua adquisivit, pecunia custodes corrumpens*; compare *infra*, 17 n.

6. *Sancte Waleri*: Saint-Valéry-sur-Somme.

7. *Albemare*: Aumale (*dép.* Seine-Maritime).

13. *Philippe*: *Gest. Reg.*, loc. cit., *iners, et cotidianum crapulam ructans.*

17. *for his lufan oððe for his mycele gersuma*: again *Gest. Reg.*, loc. cit., suppresses the irony (see *supra*, 5 n.), so also does Florence, ii. 27.

19. *ferde ongean*: *Gest. Reg.*, loc. cit., *convivium repetiit* (compare above 13 n.).

1091

6. *Kiæresburh*: Cherbourg. But already in 1088 Robert had sold the Cotentin, the Avranchin, and Mont-Saint-Michel to his brother Henry, in order to finance his projected invasion of England (Ordericus, iii. 267). When Henry now tried to defend his lands, his brothers besieged him in Mont-Saint-Michel until he capitulated (Ordericus, iii. 378–9; Florence, ii. 27; *Gest. Reg.* ii. 363–5).

8. *Manige*: see 1073/2 n.; for the repeated revolts against Norman overlordship since the Conqueror's death, see Latouche, *Histoire du comté du Maine*, 41 et seq.

15. *be rihtre æwe*: Robert married only on his way back from the Crusade in 1100 (Ordericus, iv. 78); Rufus never married.

23. *Melcolm*: he professed to owe homage only to the elder brother Robert, not to Rufus (Ordericus, iii. 394).

34. *Loðene on Englaland*: assuming that the Forth marked the frontier, see 1072/3 n.; compare Ordericus, loc. cit., *usque ad magnum flumen, quod Scote Watra dicitur.*

1092

2. *Cardeol*: Carlisle; for the forms of the name, see A. M. Armstrong, *et alii*, *The Place-Names of Cumberland*, Part I, EPNS xx, Cambridge, 1950, 40–2, and for the history of the region, EPNS xxii, Cambridge, 1952, xv–xxxviii. Southern settlement at this time is confirmed by place-name evidence, and among towns planted seems to be Church Brough, near Kirkby Stephen, Westmorland (M. Beresford, *New Towns of the Middle Ages*, 1967, 502–3).

3. *Dolfin*: son of Gospatric of Northumbria, he had been ruling Cumbria under the overlordship of Malcolm of Scotland.

1093

3. *7 On his broke . . .*: for a fuller account, see Eadmer, 25–43, also 359–60 (*Vita Anselmi*), and compare *Gest. Pont.* 78–83 and Ordericus, iii. 314–15.

5. *wið feo gesyllan*: i.e. commit simony, possibly with a special reference to his persistent practice of lay investiture, contrary to the Hildebrandine reforms then being enforced; compare 1100/15 n.

7. *Anselme*: see the two works by his English follower, Eadmer of Canterbury, *Historia Novorum in Anglia* (ed. Rule, R.S., 1884; compare *supra*, xxix–xxx) and *Vita Anselmi* (ibid. 305–440, also ed. and trans. R. W. Southern, 1963; see also idem, *St. Anselm and his Biographer*, 1963). Anselm's own writings have been published in a collected edition by F. S. Schmitt, 6 vols., Edinburgh, 1946–61; see also R. W. Southern and F. S. Schmitt, *Memorials of St. Anselm*, Oxford, 1969.

8. *Rodbeard*: Robert Bloet, a former royal chaplain, see *infra* 1123/7 n.
cancelere: for the function and history of the chancellorship in England, see Davis, *Regesta* I, xiii–xv, and Harmer, *Anglo-Saxon Writs*, 57–61.

11. *þære forewarde*: the 1091 agreement, of which Rufus's occupation of Cumbria had been a breach.

21. *Rodbeard*: Robert Mowbray (see 1088/17 n., 1095/9 ff.).

22. *ofsloh*: Symeon of Durham calls Malcolm's death a divine punishment for his five invasions of Northumbria (*Hist. Reg.* ii. 221–2). Ordericus, iii. 396–7, gives a variant account.

23. *Moræl*: see also 1095/50.

26. *Margarita*: St. Margaret of Scotland, sister of Edgar the Atheling (1074/2 n., also 1072/4 n.) and mother of the Matilda who became Henry I's queen (see 1100/44 ff.). D, possibly compiled after that marriage, describes Margaret's lineage and her marriage to Malcolm in great detail under 1067 (compare *Hist. Reg.* ii. 191–2). Her *Life* was written by the English monk Turgot, prior of Durham and later bishop of St. Andrews (ed. J. Pinkerton and W. M. Metcalfe, *Lives of the Scottish Saints*, Paisley, 1889, ii. 159–82; see also Ritchie, *Normans in Scotland*, 395–9).

30. *Dufenal*: Donald Bane (see table, *EHD* 997), who represented Celtic opposition to the English and Norman influences favoured by Malcolm and Margaret (Ritchie, op. cit., 60–1).

32. *Dunecan*: Malcolm's son by his first wife, Ingebjorg, daughter of Thorfinn, earl of Caithness and Orkney (table, *EHD* 997).

1094

10. *Bataille*: Battle Abbey (see 1087/67 n.).

11. *Herbearde Losange*: Herbert Losinga, originally a monk of Fécamp. Now deposed for simony but later reinstated, he moved the see to Norwich and founded the present cathedral there, see B. Dodwell, 'The Foundation of Norwich Cathedral', *TRHS*, 5th ser. vii (1957), 1–18. *The Life, Letters and Sermons of Bishop Herbert de Losinga*, ed.

and trans. E. M. Goulburn and H. Symonds, 2 vols., Oxford, 1878, is unreliable but of interest. His cognomen contemporaries refer to *ars adulationis* (*Gest. Pont.* 151–2; Florence, ii. 33), compare OFr. *losange* 'false flattery' (see G. Tengvik, *Old English Bynames*, Uppsala, 1938, 349, and Tolkien, Bibl. Fac. Philos. etc. de Liège, 1953, 63–76).

20. *Bures*: if the place which Hélie of Saint-Saëns, husband of an illegitimate daughter of Robert Curthose, held along with Arques-la-Bataille (*dép.* Seine-Maritime), then Bures-en-Bray (same *dép.*) (see Ordericus, iii. 320).

22. *Argentses*: Florence, ii. 34, *Argentinum castellum*, therefore Argentan (*dép.* Orne) (see also David, *Robert Curthose*, 85, n. 219).

Rogger Peiteuin: son of Roger Montgomery of Shrewsbury (see 1088/10 n.), surnamed 'le Poitevin' because of his marriage to a Poitou heiress (Ordericus, iii. 425–6; also *TRHS* (1963), 14–15; and for his English estates, *VCH Lancs.* i. 278 et seq., 291 et seq.).

24. *Hulme*: Le Houlme (*dép.* Seine-Maritime), defended by William Peverel (Florence, ii. 35).

28. *þet feoh syllan*: Florence, ii. 35, adds that *Rannulphus Passeflambardus* (see 1099/4 n.) collected it. For Rufus's financial straits during these campaigns, see Eadmer, 43, and compare 1090/5, 17, and *infra*, 34 n.; Suger, 8, called him *mirabilis militum mercator et solidator.*

33. *Lungeuile*: presumably Longueville (*dép.* Seine-Maritime).

34. *þurh gesmeah*: Hen. Hunt. 217, *Ingenio autem et pecunia regis Willelmi rex Francorum reversus est*; compare 1090/5, 17.

36. *Damfront*: Domfront (*dép.* Orne); for a long time Henry's headquarters.

38. *Hugo eorl of Ceastre*: Hugh of Avranches, earl of Chester (see table, *EHD* 995); a violent and self-indulgent man (Ordericus, ii. 219, iii. 4), but Eadmer, 27–9, shows him on friendly terms with Anselm.

46. *Hugo eorl of Scrobscire*: second son of Roger of Montgomery and his successor at Shrewsbury; see also 1098/7 n.

49. *Dunecan . . . Dufenal*: see the preceding annal.

1095

2. *Hwitsand*: Wissant, then the main port for English travel, see P. Grierson, 'The Relations between England and Flanders before the Norman Conquest', *TRHS*, 4th ser. xxiii (1941), 80–1.

9. *Rodbeard*: Robert Mowbray. According to Florence, ii. 38, the rebels aimed to put on the throne Stephen of Aumale, son of the Conqueror's sister Adelaide, from whom he took his title, and of Eudes of Champagne (see 1096/10 n.); but see also Ordericus, iii. 406–10.

36. *gelæhton*: for details of Earl Robert's capture, see Florence, ii. 38.

39. *Muntgum[r]i*: named from the Norman estates of the marcher earls of Shrewsbury.
Hugon eorles: i.e. of Hugh of Shrewsbury.

49. *his wif*: Matilda of Laigle (*dép.* Orne), see Ordericus, iii. 406, 409–10.

50. *Moreal*: see also 1093/23–4, and Ordericus, iii. 407, 411.

54. *ær þære tide*: i.e. before Christmas, the time of the next court; compare *WA*, *ante Natale*.

62. *of þæs Papan healfe Urbanus*: of the two claimants to the Papacy, Urban II and the Antipope Clement II invested by the Emperor Henry IV, Rufus had refused to recognize either or to allow Anselm to do so; but he had secretly sent messengers to Rome to spy out the situation and bring a pallium back for him to bestow as he wished; they brought Walter of Albano, who, once Rufus had recognized Urban, granted the pallium to Anselm (Eadmer, 40, 52–73).

65. *Romgesceot*: Peter's Pence.

1096

2. *Willelm biscop*: William of Saint-Calais (see 1088/6 n.).

5. *Gosfrei Bainard*: for the Bainard family, see Douglas, *Domesday Monachorum*, 60 et seq.
Willelm of Ou: William of Eu: see also Florence, ii. 39, and *Gest. Reg.* ii. 372–3. According to Florence (ii. 38–9, 24, 33), he had taken part in the recent Mowbray rebellion as well as in that of 1088; but Ordericus, iii. 411, attributes his downfall to private vengeance.

7. *orreste*: the judicial duel was a Norman innovation (D. M. Stenton, *English Justice between the Norman Conquest and the Great Charter, 1066–1215*, 1965, 6).

9. *stiward*: *Willelmus de Alderia . . . compater regis* (*Gest. Reg.* 372).

10. *Eoda eorl of Campaine*: Eudes, formerly count of Champagne but dispossessed by his uncle Thibaut; third husband of the Conqueror's sister, Adelaide countess of Aumale, and father of Stephen of Aumale (see 1095/9 n.; Florence, ii. 39, compare ii. 26, *castellum Odonis de Albamarno*; Ordericus, ii. 221 and iii. 319; also *Complete Peerage*, i. 350–3).

13. *swiðe mycel styrung*: the First Crusade, preached by Urban II at the Council of Clermont in November 1095, see F. Chalandon, *La Première Croisade*, Paris, 1925, and Steven Runciman, *A History of the Crusades*, 3 vols., Cambridge, 1951–4, vol. i.

Compare the opening of the eye-witness account known as *Gesta Francorum* (ed. R. Hill, 1961, 1), *facta est motio ualida per uniuersas Galliarum regiones*; also Hugo, 86.

15. *mid wifan 7 cildan*: for non-combatant pilgrims on the Crusade, see W. Porges, 'The Clergy, the Poor and the Non-Combatants on the First Crusade', *Speculum*, xxi (1946), 1–23; also Runciman, op. cit. i. 121–33.

17. *Rodbeard eorl*: for Robert of Normandy's part in the Crusade, see David, *Robert Curthose*, ch. iv; and for his mortgaging of Normandy to Rufus, in order to finance his expedition, see Florence, ii. 40; *Gest. Reg.* ii. 371; Ordericus, iii. 476. Rufus raised the money by harsh taxation, see Eadmer, 74–5, and compare *infra*, 26.

20. *eorl of Flandran*: Robert II of Flanders, son of 'the Frisian' and himself later surnamed 'of Jerusalem' (see table, *EHD* 999).

se of Bunan: Eustace III of Boulogne (see 1088/72 n.). It was his brothers, Godfrey of Bouillon and Baldwin, who were the first kings of Jerusalem, see Andressohn, *Godfrey of Bouillon*.

22. *Puille*: Apulia, then a Norman dominion under Roger of Sicily (F. Chalandon, *Histoire de la domination normande en Italie et en Sicile*, 2 vols., Paris, 1907, 287 et seq.).

28. *into Wealon*: for the Welsh unrest at this time, see Lloyd, *History of Wales*, 400 et seq., and compare 1097/6 ff.

1097

14. *Griffines broðersunu cynges*: son of Bleddyn, half-brother of the Gruffydd ap Llywelyn who had made himself overlord of all Wales before being murdered in 1063 (Lloyd, op. cit., 358–71).

22. *cometa*: a portent, see *Byrhtferth's Manual* (ed. Crawford, EETS 177, 132): *An steorra ys genemned* cometa. *þonne he ætywð, þonne getacnað he hungor oððe cwealm oððe gefeoht oððe tostencednyss þæs eardes oððe egeslice windas*. Rufus's reign was notable for portents of all kinds (*Gest. Reg.* ii. 374 et seq., esp. 376–8; Florence, ii. 45–6).

23. *leafe æt þam cynge nam*: Rufus's hostility to Anselm, dating from his appointment (Eadmer, 43–67), had broken out again (idem, 78 et seq.); Anselm repeatedly asked leave to visit Rome, and the king retaliated by exiling him (idem, 79–88). Anselm (accompanied by Eadmer) stayed abroad until recalled after Rufus's death (1100/40 ff. and Eadmer, 88–118).

27. *into Normandig*: for the Franco-Norman wars beginning now, see Suger, 6 et seq.

28. *þone mæston hearm*: for the plundering and wanton destruction habitual to Rufus's train, see Eadmer, 192; compare 1104/22.

34. *Tur*: 'the greatest stone keep yet built in Western Europe' (Boase, *English Art 1100–1216*, 69–70; also Rice, *English Art 871–1100*, 78–9).

36. *heallegeweorc*: see 1099/3 n.

1098

2. *Walcelin*: although Eadmer, 18, says he tried to replace his cathedral monks by secular canons, the Winchester annalist (who also tells a pleasant tale of how Walcelin once outwitted the Conqueror) praises him not only for asceticism but for kindness to those monks (*s.a.* 1086, 1098); *Gest. Pont.* 172 resolves the contradiction.

3. *Baldewine*: a former monk of Saint-Denis, who, having been physician to the Confessor, was appointed to Bury in 1065 (T. Arnold, ed., *Memorials of St. Edmund's Abbey*, 3 vols., R.S., 1890–6, i. 56–7; *Gest. Pont.* 156; Florence, ii. 41; also R. H. C. Davis, 'The Monks of St. Edmund, 1021–1148', *History*, xl (1955), 227–39, esp. 233–5).

4. *Turold*: see 1070/12 n. Now the monks of Peterborough bought the right of election from Rufus and elected a good man called Godric, brother of the former Abbot Brand (*ob.* 1069); but in 1102 he was deposed for simony, along with others (*s.a.*: Hugo, 86; Eadmer, 142).

6. *blod weoll*: for a prosaic explanation, see B. M. Griffiths, 'Early References to Waterbloom in British Lakes', *Proc. of the Linnean Soc. of London*, cli (1938–9), 12–19.

7. *Hugo eorl*: Hugh of Shrewsbury, killed while fighting a Viking force led by the Norwegian king, Magnus Bareleg, see Florence, ii. 42; Ordericus, iv. 26–32; F. Jónsson, ed., *Morkinskinna*, Copenhagen, 1932, 318–19. Although Florence sees his death as a judgement for his brutality to the Welsh, compare Ordericus, *Hic solus de filiis Mabiliæ mansuetus et amabilis fuit.*

8. *Rodbert*: Robert of Bellême, so named from the Norman estates he inherited from his mother, Mabel 'Talvas' (see G. H. White, 'The First House of Bellême', *TRHS*, 4th ser. xxii (1940), 67–99, also J. Boussard, 'La Seigneurie de Bellême aux xe et xie siècles', *Mélanges d'histoire du moyen âge dédiés à la mémoire de Louis Halphen*, Paris, 1951, 43–54). For a summary of his violent and treacherous career, see *Complete Peerage*, xi, 689–96, also Mason, *TRHS* (1963), esp. 24–6. For contemporary views of him, see Ordericus, iii. 300, 422–3, iv. 305, and *Gest. Reg.* ii. 476.

1099

3. *niwan gebyttlan*: Westminster Hall (see Rice, *English Art 871–1100*, 79 and references there given); Hen. Hunt. 231, records Rufus's disgust at its smallness, compare also *Gest. Reg.* ii. 374.

4. *Rannulfe*: Rannulf 'Flambard', son of a Bayeux priest; the most powerful man in Rufus's England and the most execrated by chroniclers (Ordericus, iii. 310 et seq.; *Gest. Reg.* ii. 368–9, 497; Florence, ii. 44, 46). Contemporary summaries of his career include *Hist. Eccl. Dun.* 135–41, and *Gest. Pont.* 74 (compare C. H. Talbot, ed., *The Life of Christina of Markyate*, Oxford, 1959, 40–4). The origin of his nickname, *Flambard*, also *Passeflambard*, is uncertain, but see Ordericus, loc. cit. For modern estimates of him, see R. W. Southern, 'Ranulf Flambard and the Early Anglo-Norman Administration', *TRHS*, 4th ser. xvi (1933), 95–128; also H. H. E. Craster, 'A Contemporary Record of the Pontificate of Ranulf Flambard', *Archaeologia Aeliana*, 4th ser. vii (1930), 33–56, and West, *Justiciarship*, 11.

6. *Elias*: Hélie of La Flèche, count of Maine since 1090 (see Ordericus, iii. 330–2, iv. 35–9, and for the present events, iv. 43–4, 50–3, 56–62).

12. *Osmund*: later canonized; bishop of Salisbury from 1078 (*Gest. Pont.* 183–4), and celebrated for his work on the liturgy (see W. H. Rich Jones, ed. and trans., *The Register of St. Osmund*, 2 vols., R.S., 1883–4, i, pp. xii et seq., also J. Wickham Legg, *The Sarum Missal*, Oxford, 1916, v et seq.).

1100

7. *mid anre fla ofsceoten*: Rufus's death has always remained the mystery Eadmer, 116, found it. Most contemporary chronicles allege that the arrow was, accidentally, shot by Walter Tirel, a French knight with estates at Poix (Picardy) and Pontoise (French Vexin) (Ordericus, iv. 186–7; Florence, ii. 45; *Gest. Reg.* ii. 378; Hen. Hunt. 232; see also Round, 'Walter Tirel and his Wife', *Feudal England*, 355–63); but Suger, 12 et seq., says that Tirel repeatedly affirmed his innocence. Some modern historians have argued for a murder plotted for the future Henry I's benefit, see Poole, 113–14, and references there given; an unusual approach is adopted by D. Grinnell-Milne, *The Killing of William Rufus*, 1968.

9. *He wæs swiðe strang . . .*: contemporary character-sketches include *Gest. Reg.* ii. 359, 366–74; Ordericus, iv. 9; and Hen. Hunt. 232.

15. *Godes cyrcean he nyðerade*: compare 1093/5; for Rufus's exploitation of lay investiture and systematic spoliation of the church, see Eadmer, 25–7, 49; *Gest. Reg.* ii. 369; Ordericus, iii. 312–13.

20. *arcebiscoprice on Cantwarbyrig*: while Anselm was in exile, Rufus appropriated the temporalities of the see (Eadmer, 88–9).

29. *Heanrig*: a member of the hunting party, on hearing of his brother's death he rushed to take possession of the Winchester treasury (Ordericus, iv. 87–8); compare *supra*, 7 n.

30. *Willelme Giffarde*: his consecration did not take place until 1107 (1103/3 and *s.a.*; Eadmer, 145–6; *Gest. Pont.* 109–10, 117). For his position in the investiture controversy, see G. H. Williams, *The Norman Anonymous of 1100 A.D.*, Harvard, 1951, 90 et seq. The Giffard family, from Longueville-sur-Scie (*dép.* Seine-Maritime), included Walter I, who fought at Hastings, and Walter II, created earl of Buckingham (*Complete Peerage*, ii. 386–7).

34. *þa betstan lage*: see his Coronation Charter (Liebermann, *Gesetze*, i. 520–3).

41. *Ansealm*: summoned back by Henry I (Eadmer, 118–19).

45. *Mahalde*: see also 1093/26 n. Because of assertions that Matilda, brought up in the nunnery at Wilton, was herself a nun, the marriage could not take place until a special council at Lambeth had accepted her own denials of profession (Eadmer, 121–6; compare Southern, *St. Anselm and his Biographer*, 183 et seq.).

51. *Thomas*: formerly a royal chaplain and treasurer of Bayeux. Appointed to York in 1070, from the first he opposed Canterbury pretensions to supremacy over York (Hugh the Chantor, 2–12; Eadmer, 41; *Gest. Pont.* 39–44, 62–6, 257–8). For his indignation at not having been asked to crown Henry I, see Hugh the Chantor, 10.

1101

5. *þurh þone eorl Rodbert*: for Robert of Normandy's landing at Portsmouth and its consequences, see Eadmer, 126 et seq.; Florence, ii. 48–9; *Gest. Reg.* ii. 471; Hen. Hunt. 233; Ordericus, iv. 103–5. Florence stresses that the English again remained loyal to the king.

18. *Eustaties*: Eustace III of Boulogne (see 1088/72 n.). In 1102 he was to marry Mary, sister of Henry I's queen Matilda (Florence, ii. 51); their only child Matilda became Stephen's queen (1137/14 n.).

22. *be rihtre æwe*: compare 1091/15; but this time both parties to the agreement were married and both soon had sons (William 'Adelinus' of England; William 'Clito' of Normandy).

26. *Rannulf*: Rannulf Flambard of Durham (see 1099/4 n.). Florence, loc. cit., has events in better order, with Flambard's escape preceding the invasion he instigated (compare *Gest. Reg.* ii. 471; Ordericus, iv. 109).

1102

3. *Rotbert of Bælæsme*: see 1098/8 n.; for this rebellion, see Florence, ii. 49–51; *Gest. Reg.* ii. 472–3; Ordericus, iv. 169–77.

9. *Brigge*: Bridgnorth, Salop, Æthelflæd's old citadel (Florence, loc. cit.; compare 912 C).

15. *sinoð*: see Eadmer, 141–4; Florence, ii. 51; *Gest. Pont.* 118–21. Apart from minor points of discipline, the main topics were lay investiture and clerical marriage. The former had caused friction ever since Anselm's return from exile and continued to do so until 1107 (Eadmer, 119–21, 124). For clerical marriage at this time, see C. N. L. Brooke, 'Gregorian Reform in Action: Clerical Marriage in England, 1050–1200', *Cambridge Historical Journal*, xii (1956), 1–21, also 187–8; and for further synods on this subject, 1125/25 ff. and 1129/7 ff., also Eadmer, 193–5 (1108). A similar situation obtained in Normandy (Fliche, *Philippe Ier*, 392–5).

16. *manige* . . .: for those deposed, see the authorities cited *supra*, 15 n.; they included Godric of Peterborough (see 1098/4 n.).

18. *7 On ðisum ylcan geare* . . .: a Peterborough interpolation; compare the fuller version by Hugo, 87, with, however, *Alemannia* for *Aluearnie*.

1103

4. *Girarde*: formerly a royal chancellor, then bishop of Hereford; he continued York resistance to Canterbury claims to supremacy (Hugh the Chantor, 12–14; compare *Gest. Pont.* 258–60).

6. *Ansealm*: he went to Rome to try to resolve the investiture dispute festering since 1100; the king sent William Warelwast (afterwards bishop of Exeter) to represent his own interests. Anselm stayed in exile until agreement was at last reached in 1106 (Eadmer, 148–83).

9. *þa þreo þusend marc*: see 1101/19. For the way Henry, who (says *Gest. Reg.*) never meant to pay this pension, manœuvred Robert into renouncing his claims, see Ordericus, iv. 162–3; *Gest. Reg.* ii. 462; Hen. Hunt. 234.

18. *Mathias*: according to Hugo, 87–8, a brother of Geoffrey Ridel the justiciar.

1104

10. *þurh heora sehte* . . .: see Ordericus, iv. 199–201.

16. *Willelm eorl of Moretoin*: son of the Conqueror's half-brother, Robert, count of Mortain (see J. Boussard, 'Le comté de Mortain au xie siècle', *Le Moyen Âge*, lviii (1952), 253–79) and earl of Cornwall (*Complete Peerage*, iii. 427–9), one of the greatest landholders in England. For this rebellion and his alliance with Robert of Bellême, his uncle, see Ordericus, iv. 201–2; *Gest. Reg.* ii. 473–4; Hen. Hunt. 234–5; Florence, ii. 53. Captured at Tinchebray (see 1106/33), he is said to have been blinded as well as imprisoned in perpetuity (Hen. Hunt. 255).

21. *gyld*: for this extortionate taxation, see Eadmer, 171–3.

22. *full hergung*: as in Rufus's time, compare 1097/28 n.

1105

3. *for ofer sæ*: he landed at Barfleur and was well received (Ordericus, iv. 204–10, 218–20; *Gest. Reg.* ii. 474–5; Florence, ii. 53–4; Hen. Hunt. 235; Eadmer, 165).

4. *Caþum 7 Baius*: Hen. Hunt., loc. cit., *conquisivit Cadomum pecunia, Baiocum armis*, so also (if less neatly) Florence, ii. 54; but Ordericus, iv. 219, says that Caen surrendered from fear of being burnt like Bayeux.

7. *hider to lande*: *ut copiosiori pecunia fretus, rediens anno sequenti, quod residuum erat, exhæredato fratre suo, sibi subjiceret* (Florence, ii. 54); compare lines 13–15 *infra*.

1106

5. *Rotbert . . . com*: see also Florence, ii. 54.

25. *him . . . to gebugon*: Eadmer, 165, attributes Robert's failure to hold his men to his 'piety and lack of avarice' and Henry's success to his 'gold and silver'.

30. *Tenercebrai*: Tinchebray (*dép.* Orne), the definitive battle in the struggle for Normandy, fought on the anniversary of Hastings; see Ordericus, iv. 224–33; Hen. Hunt. 235–6; *Gest. Reg.* ii. 475; Florence, ii. 54–5; also a letter from Henry I to Anselm (Eadmer, 184; *Gest. Pont.* 116–17), and H. W. C. Davis, 'A Contemporary Account of the Battle of Tinchebrai', *EHR* xxiv (1909), 728–32, and xxv. 295–6.

35. *se eorl . . . gefangen*: to spend the rest of his life a prisoner (David, *Robert Curthose*, 177–89); Hen. Hunt. 236, sees his fate as a judgement for having refused the kingdom of Jerusalem.

36. *Rotbert de Stutteuile*: from the Pays de Caux (Ordericus, iv. 214); for the family, from Etoutteville-sur-mer (*dép.* Seine-Maritime), see L. C. Loyd, *The Origins of Some Anglo-Norman Families*, 1951, 40, and G. de la Morandière, *Histoire de la maison d'Estouteville en Normandie*, Paris, 1903, esp. 19 et seq.

38. *Willelm Crispin*: brother of Gilbert Crispin, abbot of Westminster (see 1117/18 n.); for the family, see J. Armitage Robinson, *Gilbert Crispin, Abbot of Westminster*, Cambridge, 1911, 13–18, esp. 16.

43. *gewinn*: for these events, see *CMH* v. 149–51.

1107

6. *biscopricen 7 abbodricen*: with the settlement this year of the long investiture dispute (Eadmer, 184–8; Florence, ii. 55–6), William Giffard (see 1100/30 n.) and the other bishops-elect were at last consecrated.

10. *Ernulf*: a monk at Beauvais before joining Lanfranc at Canterbury; well reported on both from Canterbury and from Peterborough (Hugo, 90–1; *Gest. Pont.* 137–8; see also 1114/20 n.).

17. *Rotbert*: not the Robert, son of Hugh of Chester, deposed in 1102 (Eadmer, 142; Florence, ii. 51), but a former Westminster monk elected then and consecrated only just before his death (Eadmer, 188; also R. H. C. Davis, *History*, xl. 235–6).

Ricard: one of the Clare family (see table, *EHD* 992) and a former monk of Bec, see *Liber Eliensis*, ed. Blake, 224–7, 235–6, 413. Deposed in 1102 (Eadmer, 142; Florence, ii. 51), he seems soon to have been reinstated. In 1109, after two years' vacancy, the abbey of Ely was erected into an episcopal see (Eadmer, 195–6; Florence, ii. 60).

18. *Eadgar*: a pious and peaceful man, see Ritchie, *Normans in Scotland*, 66, 87–98, 120–1.

19. *Alexander*: see Ritchie, op. cit. 128 et seq.; according to *Gest. Reg.* ii. 476, married to one of Henry I's illegitimate daughters, for whom he did not much care.

1108

5. *Loðewis*: Louis VI 'le Gros'; see the *Life* by Abbot Suger of Saint-Denis (A. Waquet, ed. and trans., CHFMA, Paris, 1929), also A. Luchaire, *Louis VI le Gros, annales de sa vie et de son règne (1081–1137)*, Paris, 1890. Suger deals with Philip I's death and Louis's accession at 80–4.

6. *manege gewinn*: for these French wars, see Suger, 102–12.

9. *Thomas*: son of Samson bishop of Worcester and nephew of Thomas I of York (see 1100/51 n.); welcomed at York (Hugh the Chantor, 15–33). For a time he kept up resistance to the primacy of Canterbury but eventually made profession of obedience (Hugh the Chantor, loc. cit.; Eadmer, 199–211; *Gest. Pont.* 260–2, also 289).

1109

5. *dohter*: Matilda, by this marriage 'the Empress' (see 1140 *passim*), afterwards wife of Geoffrey of Anjou (see 1127/10) and mother of Henry II of England. For the political background to this marriage, see K. Leyser, 'England and the Empire in the Early Twelfth Century',

TRHS, 5th ser. x (1960), 61–83. For a modern view of the Emperor Henry V's character, see *CMH* v. 154–66.

6. *Ansealm*: for his death, see Eadmer, 206, 415–19 (*Vita*). The see remained vacant until 1114 (*s.a.*, lines 14–15).

7. *xi Kalendarum Aprilis*: Anselm died on *xi Kalendarum Maii* (21 April), see Eadmer, 417 (*Vita Anselmi*).

1110

4. *niwan Windlesoran*: *novam Windlesores quam ipse ædificaverat* (Hen. Hunt. 237); compare *VCH Berks*. iii/1. 5–6, and Beresford, *New Towns of the Middle Ages*, 395–6.

19. *Philippus de Brause*: of Briouze (*dép*. Orne); his father, William, had been a major Domesday landholder (see Douglas, *Domesday Monachorum*, 52–3; Loyd, *Origins*, 20).

Willelm Malet: for the family, see Loyd, op. cit. 56, also Robinson, *Gilbert Crispin*, 14.

20. *Willelm Bainart*: compare 1096/5 n. *Elias*: Hélie of La Flèche (see 1099/6n.); for his death, see Ordericus, iv. 103.

22. *se eorl of Angeow*: Fulk V, son of Fulk 'le Réchin' and of Bertrada of Montfort (afterwards Philip of France's mistress); son-in-law of Hélie of La Flèche. In 1128 he was to be chosen king of Jerusalem (see Runciman, *Crusades*, ii. 177–233).

27. *Ceortesæge*: for this abbey, now destroyed, see Clapham, *English Romanesque Architecture after the Conquest*, 45 and pl. facing 46.

1111

3. *unsehte*: for these French and Angevin wars, see Ordericus, iv. 303–9 and *Gest. Reg*. ii. 480–1; 'those on the French border' included Amaury of Montfort, Fulk of Anjou's uncle (see 1123/80 n.).

8. *Rotbert of Flandran*: Robert 'of Jerusalem' (see 1096/20 n.); thrown and trampled by his horse during fighting at Meaux (Ordericus, iv. 290).

1112

4. *þone eorl of Eureus*: William of Évreux, an old 'Hastings man' (Ordericus, ii. 148); for his present disgrace and exile, followed by restoration the next year, see Ordericus, iv. 279, 306.

6. *Rotbert de Bælesme*: for his imprisonment, which evidently lasted until his death, see Ordericus, iv. 304–5, and Hen. Hunt. 238, 310.

1113

2. *on Normandig*: for the settlement this year of the Franco-Angevin war against Normandy, see Suger, 170–2, and Ordericus, iv. 306–7. Fulk was granted Maine, on condition he granted it back, with his daughter's hand, to Henry I's son William 'Adelinus' (but compare 1119/10 n.).

1114

9. *ebba*: for this low tide all along the east coast, dated 10 October, see Eadmer, 225–6 (followed by Florence, ii. 67).

15. *Raulfe*: of Escures; driven from his abbacy at Séez (Sées, *dép.* Orne) about 1103 by the turmoil in Normandy, and appointed to Rochester in 1108 (Ordericus, iii. 308–9, iv. 192; Eadmer, 196; Florence, ii. 59). For his tenure of Canterbury, see Eadmer, 222–302, also *Gest. Pont.* 126–32.

17. *Turstein*: for his tenure of York, which lasted until 1140, see Hugh the Chantor, 33 to end; Eadmer, *ut supra, passim*; *Gest. Pont.* 262–6; *Hist. Reg.* ii. 302–5; also D. Nicholl, *Thurstan, Archbishop of York (1114–1140)*, York, 1964. He revived resistance to Canterbury claims to primacy, and in the consequent controversy remained unconsecrated until 1119 (see *s.a.*, 20 n.).

20. *Ernulf*: see 1107/10 n., Hugo, 96–7, and Eadmer, 225. As bishop of Rochester he probably initiated the compilation of the law-book and cartulary known as *Textus Roffensis* (ed. P. Sawyer, Early English Manuscripts in Facsimile vii and xi, Copenhagen, 1957 and 1962, i. 18).

28. *Burne*: probably Westbourne, Sussex (Whitelock, *Translation*, 184, n. 3; Garmonsway, 245, n. 1).

33. *Iohan*: see Hugo, 97–9.

35. *7 se arcebiscop . . .*: an additional subject, in apposition to *se cyng* (compare Eadmer, 226).

36. *7 an munec . . .*: compare Eadmer, loc. cit., *Warnerius monachus Cantuariensis, et Johannes clericus, filius sororis archiepiscopi* (John became archdeacon only after his return, see idem, 231). For the negotiations, see idem, 226–9; compare 1115.

40. *Rugenore*: Rowner, Hants (see *VCH Hants*, i. 492 (*Ruenore*, from Domesday), iii. 218–19).

1115

3. *manrǣden*: for this homage to William 'Adelinus', see Eadmer, 237; *Gest. Reg.* ii. 494; Hen. Hunt. 239; Florence, ii. 69.

11. *Ansealm abbot*: abbot of Santa Saba; he had helped the English envoys (Eadmer, 228). In his uncle's day he had studied at Canterbury under Ernulf, then prior there; in 1121 he became abbot of Bury St. Edmund's (see 1123/52). Modern accounts of his career are given by E. W. Williamson, *The Letters of Osbert of Clare*, Oxford, 1929, 191–200, and by Davis, *History*, xl. 236–9.

1116

2. *Sancte Albane*: see H. T. Riley, ed., *Gesta Abbatum Monasterii Sancti Albani*, 3 vols., R.S., 1867–9, i. 70–1. This new church remains the basis of the present fabric, with the only important early Anglo-Norman tower still extant (Clapham, *Romanesque Architecture in Western Europe*, 144; also *VCH Herts*. ii. 483 et seq.).

6. *unrada*...: for these French wars, see Hen. Hunt. 239–42; Ordericus, iv. 310 et seq.; Suger, 182–200. The king of France and his allies aimed to make Robert Curthose's son, William 'Clito', duke of Normandy.

8. *Tædbalde*: Thibaut IV, count of Blois and Chartres, later of Champagne also; son of Henry I's sister Adela and of Stephen count of Blois and Chartres, thus elder brother of the future Stephen of England.

13. *mæstene*: a dearth of beech-mast was calamitous because of the importance of woodland pig-farming, see Lennard, *Rural England*, 14–15, 252–60.

17. *bærnde eall þet mynstre of Burh*: first, Abbot John consigned the abbey to the Devil because some monks vexed him by tidying the refectory tables too soon; then, an impatient scullion called the Devil to blow the fire: whereat flames sprang up and consumed the best part of the abbey and of the village (Hugo, 97–8).

1117

15. *eorðbyfung*: see also Florence, ii. 70, with a further prodigy from Milan.

18. *Gilebert*: Gilbert Crispin, brother of William Crispin II (see 1106/38 n.); see J. Armitage Robinson, *Gilbert Crispin*, and also R. W. Southern, 'St. Anselm and Gilbert Crispin, abbot of Westminster', *Mediaeval and Renaissance Studies*, iii (1954), 78–115.

19. *Farits*: a Tuscan and a celebrated physician, see *Chronicon Monasterii de Abingdon*, ii. 44 et seq., and *Gest. Pont.* 192; author of a *Life of Aldhelm* severely criticized by William of Malmesbury (ibid. 330–2). In 1114 he had narrowly missed being elected archbishop of Canterbury (ibid. 126; Eadmer, 222).

20. *And on þisum ylcan geare . . .*: in the manuscript two blank lines follow. Plummer, ii. 296, suggested that the chronicler meant to note the refounding of Peterborough Abbey after the 1116 fire, compare Hugo, 98, *In alio autem anno ipse abbas inchoauit nouam ecclesiam.*

1118

3. *Se eorl . . . gewundod*: see Suger, 194–5; Ordericus, iv. 194, 316; *Gest. Reg.* ii. 479; Hen. Hunt. 242; and for his consequent death, 1119/25.

13. *Mahald*: compare 1100/45 n., also *Gest. Reg.* ii. 493–5. A pious woman, she had long lived in retirement at Westminster.

14. *Rotbert of Mellent*: a great landholder in Normandy, France, and England, being lord of Beaumont-le-Roger (*dép.* Eure), count of Meulan (*dép.* Seine-et-Oise) in the French Vexin, and earl of Leicester (*Complete Peerage*, vii. 523–6). He had fought at Hastings (Ordericus, ii. 148); under Henry I he had become one of the king's chief counsellors (Hen. Hunt. 240, *sapientissimus in rebus secularibus omnium usque in Jerusalem degentium*, compare 306–7; Eadmer, *passim*, esp. 191–2; *Gest. Reg.* ii. 482–3).

20. *Gelasius*: for Gelasius II, formerly John of Gaeta, a monk of Monte Cassino, see Ordericus, iv. 310, 311–12, 334–5; Suger, 200–2; Eadmer, 246–9; Hugh the Chantor, 61, 84–5; John of Worcester, 13; *Gest. Reg.* ii. 504–6; also *CMH* v. 105.

1119

5. *coman togædere*: at Brémule (near Les Andelys, *dép.* Eure; now the site of a farm), see Ordericus, iv. 356–63; Suger, 196–8; Hen. Hunt. 241–2.

10. *Willelm*: for his marriage, see *Hist. Reg.* ii. 257–8; *Gest. Reg.* ii. 482, 495; John of Worcester, 14; Ordericus, iv. 347 (but at iv. 306 it is linked with the 1113 peace, see 1113/2 n.).

16. *on Clunig*: Gelasius II died at Cluny (where one of the buildings still bears his name) while on his way to beg the king of France's help against the Emperor Henry V and his new Antipope Gregory VIII.

17. *arcebiscop of Uiana*: Guy of Burgundy (see references at 1118/20 n., also U. Robert, *Histoire de Pape Calixte II*, Paris, 1891). For his council at Rheims, see Ordericus, iv. 372–93; *Hist. Reg.* ii. 254–7; Eadmer, 255 et seq.; Suger, 204.

20. *Turstein*: see 1114/17 n. For his consecration from the Pope's own hands, see Hugh the Chantor, 68–74; Eadmer, 237 et seq.; *Hist. Reg.* ii. 254; *Gest. Pont.* 264–5; Ordericus, iv. 373–4.

27. *Carl*: son of (St.) Canute of Denmark by a daughter of Robert 'the Frisian' (*EHD* 999, also 1085/4); for his death, see 1127/13 n.

1120

1. *sehte*: partly, it is said, through the good offices of Calixtus II (Henry I's third cousin), see Hugh the Chantor, 75 et seq., and *Hist. Reg.* ii. 258. Louis now recognized William 'Adelinus' as duke of Normandy.

4. *se of Puntiw*: William, count of Ponthieu, son and heir of Robert of Bellême (Ordericus, iv. 163, also 347–8).

7. *adruncene*: in the White Ship, which had run on to rocks in the calmest weather, some said as divine chastisement of the vices of the court, some because the seamen were all drunk (Ordericus, iv. 410–20; *Gest. Reg.* ii. 496–8; *Hist. Reg.* ii. 258–9; Hen. Hunt. 242–3, 303–4; Hugh the Chantor, 99; Eadmer, 288–9, and, in similar wording, John of Worcester, 15). All agree that one eye-witness, of low degree, was saved.

Willelm 7 Ricard: that is, William 'Adelinus', Henry I's only legitimate son, and one of his countless bastard brothers. By an odd irony, the future King Stephen had been on the ship but had disembarked.

8. *Ricard eorl of Ceastre*: son of Hugh of Avranches (1094/38 n.; *Complete Peerage*, iii. 165–6).

Ottuel: the princes' tutor.

12. *feawa heora lichaman*: treasure was washed ashore, but not the bodies.

13. *þet leoht*: for this miracle, a supernatural lighting of the lamps in the Holy Sepulchre, see L. H. Vincent and F. H. Abel, *Jérusalem: recherches de topographie, d'archéologie et d'histoire*, 2 vols., Paris, 1914–26, ii. 288–9. A list of relics in Bodleian MS. Auct. D. 2. 16 M (about 1030) includes, *Of þære candele ðe Godes engel ontende mid heofenlicum leohte æt ures Drihtenes sepulchre on easteræfen* (Förster, *Sitzungsberichte der Bayerischen Akademie der Wissenschaften*, viii 8 (1943), 70).

16. *Turstein*: for this reconciliation, see Hugh the Chantor, 89–104; Eadmer, 258–9; *Gest. Pont.* 266; *Hist. Reg.* ii. 262.

1121

3. *Aðelis*: for this marriage, see Ordericus, iv. 422; John of Worcester, 15–16; *Gest. Reg.* ii. 495; Hen. Hunt. 243; Eadmer, 290; *Hist. Reg.* ii. 259. Apart from the obvious dynastic motive, it continued the policy begun by Matilda's marriage in 1110.

10. *fram Ierusalem*: from the pilgrimage he had undertaken the year before (Ordericus, iv. 423; compare *supra* 1110/22 n.).

11. *his dohter*: see 1119/12 n., also *Hist. Reg.* ii. 263. Her dowry proved harder to recover, see 1123/2, 37.

1122

3. *forbearn se burch on Gleawecestre*: see W. H. Hart, ed., *Historia et Cartularium Monasterii Sancti Petri Gloucestriæ*, 3 vols., R.S., 1863–5, ii. 14–15, also John of Worcester, 17.

5. '*Preteriens Iesus*': John ix, the Gospel for Wednesday in the fourth week of Lent.

1123

2. *sandermen*: sent to reclaim the dowry of Fulk's widowed daughter (see 1121/11 n.; *Hist. Reg.* ii. 267).

5. *derfald*: for Henry I's exotic menagerie at Woodstock, see *Gest. Reg.* ii. 485 and Hen. Hunt. 244, 300.

6. *Roger of Seresbyrig*: chief minister and the most powerful man in England after the king himself, see *Gest. Reg.* ii. 483–4; *Hist. Nov.* 37–9; *Gest. Steph.* 64–5; also West, *Justiciarship*, 16–19, and D. M. Stenton, 'Roger of Salisbury, Regni Angliae Procurator', *EHR* xxxix (1924), 79–80.

7. *Rotbert Bloet*: bishop of Lincoln since 1094, he is considered frivolous and worldly by William of Malmesbury, but by Henry of Huntingdon, who had lived in his household, praised warmly as one *quo non erat alter forma venustior, mente serenior, affatu dulcior* (*Gest. Pont.* 313–15, also xv–xvi; Hen. Hunt. 216, 244, 299–300; also *Hist. Reg.* ii. 268, and John of Worcester, 17).

13. *Rotbert Peccep*: otherwise *Peccatum* (*Gest. Pont.* 310–11; John of Worcester, 23), or *Peccator* (*Hist. Reg.* ii. 259); the origin of the cognomen seems unknown. Eadmer, 290–1, says he had formerly been in charge of the royal bread and wine.

19. *cesen hem ærcebiscop*: for other accounts of the proceedings, see *Hist. Reg.* ii. 268–9, 272–3; *Gest. Pont.* 146 and note 4; Hugh the Chantor, 108–11; see also D. L. Bethell, *EHR* lxxxvi (1969), 673–98.

32. *Willelm of Curboil*: William of Corbeil, see D. Bethell, *Journal of Ecclesiastical History*, xix (1968), 145–59. Modest and learned, he proved, in spite of this inauspicious beginning, an ascetic but kindly archbishop, see *Gest. Pont.* 146 (but compare *Gest. Steph.* 6).

33. *Cicc*: since the mid twelfth century known by the name of the priory of St. Osyth (P. H. Reaney, *The Place-Names of Essex*, EPNS xii, Cambridge, 1935, 347–8).

38. *rohton*: from *reccan* 'care about'; Whitelock *et alii* offer the interpretation: 'they had no reason to respect his liberality'.

39. *Henri* . . .: see 1127/22 to end and notes there to. This present appointment as legate seems not to be mentioned in any independent record.

47. *biscop of Lundene*: Richard of Belmeis (Beaumais-sur-Dive, *dép.* Calvados, see Loyd, *Origins*, 13–14); see *Gest. Pont.* 146. The archbishop of York's offer to perform the consecration had been rejected (Hugh the Chantor, 109–11; compare *Hist. Reg.* ii. 269).

49. *of Wales*: of St. David's.

50. *ferde se ærcebiscop to Rome*: see Hugh the Chantor, 111 et seq., and *Hist. Reg.* ii. 269.

51. *Sefred*: brother of Ralph of Canterbury; afterwards bishop of Chichester (Hen. Hunt. 245; *Hist. Reg.* ii. 269; John of Worcester, 18).

52. *Anselm*: see 1115/11 n. *Iohan*: see 1114/36 n.

54. *Đurstan*: although summoned to a Papal council, he had been forced by Henry I to wait until the new archbishop of Canterbury was also ready to set out; Hugh the Chantor, 111, says (but with some obscurity) that he arrived a week before the rival party, compare *Hist. Reg.* ii. 272.

57. *mid micel wurðscipe*: because of the friendship formed between Pope and archbishop when both were in exile in 1119 (Hugh the Chantor, 111).

61. *togeanes rihte*: for the objections made, see Hugh the Chantor, 112, and *Hist. Reg.* ii. 272.

62. *gold 7 seolure*: Hugh the Chantor, 112–14, attributes the granting of the pallium to Thurstan's intercession, and mentions bribery only, 115–16, in connection with the later airing of the primacy dispute ignored by our chronicler. The gibe at the venality of Rome was traditional, compare, for instance, Eadmer, 69.

72. *Alexander*: 'the Magnificent', to whom Henry of Huntingdon dedicated his *Historia Anglorum* and Geoffrey of Monmouth his *Prophecies of Merlin*; see Hen. Hunt. 246–7, 278–9, 280, and below 1137/8.

79. *unfrið*: a revolt partly aimed at making William 'Clito' duke of Normandy, see Ordericus, iv. 439 et seq.; *Hist. Reg.* ii. 273–4.

80. *Walaram*: son of Robert of Meulan (see 1118/14 n.) and his heir in France and Normandy (a twin brother taking the English lands and earldom), see G. H. White, 'The Career of Waleran, Count of Meulan and Earl of Worcester (1104–1166)', *TRHS*, 4th ser. xvii (1934), 19–48 (similarly, *Complete Peerage*, xii. 829–37).

Hamalri: Amaury of Montfort (Montfort l'Amaury, *dép*. Seine-et-Oise), brother of Bertrada and so uncle of Fulk of Anjou (see *Complete Peerage*, vii, Appendix D, 713–14). He instigated the revolt, having already in 1118 quarrelled with Henry I over the county of Évreux. Waleran married one of his daughters.

Hugo of Mundford: of Montfort-sur-Risle (*dép*. Eure), Waleran's brother-in-law.

81. *Willelm of Romare*: lord of Roumare (*dép*. Seine-Maritime), half-brother of Rannulf II, earl of Chester (see *Complete Peerage*, iii. 166–7, and 1140/9 n.), and himself later earl of Leicester (see *Complete Peerage*, vii. 677–60). He had earlier quarrelled with Henry I over his mother's estates. See also 1140/13.

83. *Punt Aldemer*: Pont Audemer (*dép*. Eure); for the siege, see Ordericus, iv. 444, 448–9.

86. *forbearn . . . se burh of Lincolne*: see also *Margam Annals* (*Annales Monastici*, i), *s.a.* 1122 (for 1123), and compare J. W. F. Hill, *Medieval Lincoln*, Cambridge, 1948, 173.

1124

6. *Belmunt*: Beaumont-le-Roger (*dép*. Eure). *Watteuile*: Vatteville (*dép*. Seine-Maritime).

7. *Hugo Gerueises sunu*: Hugh of Châteauneuf-en-Thimerais (*dép*. Eure-et-Loir), descended in the maternal line from the Montgomerys and also a brother-in-law of Waleran of Meulan's (White, *TRHS* (1934), 24 and note 4).

10. *fuhton*: at Bourgthéroulde (*dép*. Eure), see Ordericus, iv. 455–9; *Hist. Reg*. ii. 257; Hen. Hunt. 245; John of Worcester, 18.

21. *hefde numen Fulkes eorles . . . dohter*: but see 1127/17 ff.

27. *þet acersæd hwæte*: compare Hen. Hunt. 246, *s.a.* 1125, *Iste est annus carissimus omnium nostri temporis, in quo vendebatur onus equi frumentarium vi solidis*; and for the heavy death-rate in this famine, see also *Hist. Reg*. ii. 275. There is no evidence for normal prices at this time, but in the thirteenth century, when prices had risen considerably, the two bushels needed for sowing an acre are priced at twelve pence (E. Lamond and W. Cunningham, eds., *Walter of Henley's Husbandry*, 1890, 19).

36. *Dauid*: married to an Anglo-Norman heiress, daughter of Earl Waltheof and of the Conqueror's niece Judith, he had himself become Anglo-Normanized, see Ritchie, *Normans in Scotland*, 124 et seq.

40. *se Pape on Rome*: i.e. the true one, not the Antipope.

42. *Raulf Basset*: the justiciar; for his functions, see D. M. Stenton, *English Justice*, 60–2, and West, *Justiciarship*, 22–3. For the family, see Loyd, *Origins*, 12.

43. *Hundehoge*: the common identification with Huncote, Leics., (e.g. Poole, 404) is unsatisfactory. *Huncote* has a Domesday form *Hunecote*, whereas the form here seems to imply an etymology similar to the one O. S. Anderson [Arngart] suggested for the former East-Riding hundred-name *Huntow*, i.e. *Hunda haugr* (*The English Hundred-Names*, Lunds Universitets Årsskrift, N.F. Avd. 1, Bd. 30, Nr. 1, 1934, 12; but compare A. H. Smith, *The Place-Names of the East-Riding of Yorkshire and York*, EPNS xiv, Cambridge, 1937, 103).

50. MS. *Ful heui gær wæs hit se man þe æni god heafde. him me hit beræfode* . . .: the punctuation supplied in the text seems required by the sense; compare the similar construction at 1131/8–9, also *supra*, line 32, and 1125/5. Compare Matthew xxv. 39: *Omni enim habenti dabitur et abundabit; ei autem qui non habet, et quod videtur habere auferetur ab eo*, to which the annalist evidently intended an ironical allusion.

1125

3. *þa minetere*: see also Hen. Hunt. 246; John of Worcester, 18; *Hist. Reg.* ii. 281. Amputation of the guilty hand was the common Anglo-Saxon punishment for false moneyers (II Athelstan 14.1, IV Æthelred 5.3, II Cnut 8.1: Liebermann, *Gesetze*, i. 158, 234, 314; but compare III Æthelred 8, 8.1, 8.2: ibid. i. 230). For Henry I's practice, see his statute *De Moneta* (ibid. i. 523), also *Gest. Reg.* ii. 476, and Eadmer, 193. For the background to such laws, see D. M. Stenton, *English Society in the Early Middle Ages*, 1951, 159–62.

12. *fals*: in OE specifically associated with debasement of the coinage (Garmonsway, 255, n. 2).

13. *Iohan*: John of Crema. For the discrepancy between the canons he promulgated and the conduct attributed to him, see Hen. Hunt. 245–6.

25. *þa ilce lagas*: the canons dealt with simony and other disciplinary matters as well as with clerical marriage (*Hist. Reg.* ii. 279–81; John of Worcester, 20–2).

26. *for ofer sæ . . . 7 . . . Willelm . . . 7 . . . Turstein*: a further attempt to settle the primacy dispute, see Hugh the Chantor, 120–8, also John of Worcester, 22. Only the York party travelled with John of Crema, who, anxious about the *micele gife 7 mære*, led them by such pathless and difficult ways that, *vagabundi, disturbati, capti, redempti*, they were long in reaching Rome.

30. *Loþene*: the see of Glasgow lately restored by David of Scotland.

Gosfreið: the friend and protector of Christina of Markyate, see *Gesta Abbatum Monasterii S. Albani*, i. 72–105, and Talbot, ed., *Life of Christina of Markyate*, 134 et seq.

37. *Iohan of Burch*: this vacancy at Peterborough occasioned the 1125 survey of the abbey preserved in the Black Book (Stapleton, ed., *Chronicon Petroburgense*, 157–83; compare Hugo, 99; also *EHD* 829–30).

1126

4. *Kasere*: he had died in 1125 (Ordericus, iv. 466–7; *Hist. Nov.* 2; *Hist. Reg.* ii. 275; John of Worcester, 19; Hen. Hunt. 246).

12. *Rotbert*: to die in 1134 at Cardiff, still in captivity (John of Worcester, 38; *Hist. Reg.* ii. 285–6).

14. *Rotbert eorl*: one of Henry I's many bastard sons, see *Complete Peerage*, v. 683–6; during the Anarchy Matilda's chief supporter (1140 *passim*); and the patron to whom William of Malmesbury dedicated his *Historia Novella* (compare Patterson, *American Historical Review*, lxx. 983–97, and *Speculum*, xliii. 487–92).

1127

5. *Æðelic*: i.e. Matilda, the ex-Empress (see 1126/4 n.). For this oath of loyalty, see *Hist. Nov.* 3–6; John of Worcester, 22–3; *Hist. Reg.* ii. 281; it was repeated in 1130, see *Hist. Nov.* 10.

8. *Brian*: Brian 'FitzCount', Matilda's cousin (see table, *EHD* 985), and one of her most loyal supporters during the Anarchy, see *Gest. Steph.* 89: *Ipsa et Brienus . . . ut sicut sese antea mutuo et indiuise dilexerant, ita nec in aduersis, plurimo impediente periculo, aliquatenus separarentur.*

10. *Gosfreið Martæl*: otherwise 'Plantagenet' or 'the Fair'.
naþema: as Plummer noted (ii. 303), *naþeles* would give better sense.

12. *Willelm*: William 'Clito'. The consanguinity which Henry I invoked against the Clito's Angevin marriage would equally well have invalidated those of Henry's own son and daughter.

13. *Karle*: see 1119/27. For his murder, oddly like that of his father, see H. Pirenne, ed., *Histoire du meurtre de Charles le Bon, comte de Flandre (1127–1128), par Galbert de Bruges*, Paris, 1891 (compare J. B. Ross, trans., *The Murder of Charles the Good*, New York, 1960); also Suger, 240–50; Ordericus, iv. 474–5; Hen. Hunt. 247; *Hist. Reg.* ii. 282.

22. *Flandres*: William Clito's grandmother was Matilda of Flanders.

23. *Heanri*: see ' "This ecclesiastical adventurer": Henry of Saint-Jean d'Angély', *EHR* lxxxiv (1969), 548–60.

29. *7 ðurh þes abbotes of Clunni*: the abbey of Saint-Jean d'Angély belonged to the Cluniac Order.

33. *Scesscuns*: a Henry was bishop of Soissons from about 1087 to 1092 (*Gallia Christiana*, ix. col. 353). Having received the see by lay investiture, in 1088 he surrendered it to Pope Urban II but was reinstated on swearing to forsake all such practices (P. Ewald, 'Die Papstbriefe der Brittischen Sammlung', *Neues Archiv*, v (1880), 360).
on Clunni: a Cluny charter of 1093 is attested by *Heinricus olim Suessionensis episcopus, tunc Cluniacensis monachus* (A. Bernard and A. Bruel, eds., *Recueil des chartes de l'abbaye de Cluny*, 6 vols., Paris, 1876–1903, v. 26).

34. *prior on þone seolue minstre*: for a prior called Henry at Cluny between 1100 and 1103, see M. Chaume, 'Les grands prieurs de Cluny', *Revue Mabillon*, xxviii (1938), 151, also J. Richard, ed., *Le cartulaire de Marcigny-sur-Loire (1045–1144)*, Dijon, 1957, 95 and 170.

35. *Sauenni*: probably the Cluniac priory of Souvigny. If so, then before the priorate at Cluny itself: a prior called Henry held office there from 1095 until 1100 (L. Côte, *Contributions à l'histoire du prieuré clunisien de Souvigny*, Moulins, 1942, 127, also 38, 39); and the fifteenth-century *obituarium*, now Moulins MS. 13, lists Henry, abbot of Saint-Jean d'Angély, among the priory's benefactors (I am indebted to the Librarian at Moulins for verifying this reference for me).

35. *ðes kynges mæi*: Henry's family connections are not yet fully elucidated. A Montierneuf charter shows Hildegarde of Burgundy, widow of Guy-Geoffrey of Poitou, speaking of *Enrico, nepote meo, tunc Priore Cluniaci* (*Gallia Christiana*, ii. Instrumenta, cols. 355–6): a relationship which would conveniently make this Henry, apparently to be identified with ours, not only a first cousin of William VII of Poitou, Hildegarde's son, but also a second cousin of Henry I of England (see tables, *EHD* 983, 998, 999). But a Cîteaux charter shows *Haynricus angeliacensis servus indignus* referring to *fratre meo Hugone filioque ejus Gerardo*, whom other evidence fixes as lords of Pouilly-sur-Saône (*dép.* Côte d'Or) (J. Marilier, ed., *Chartes et documents concernant l'abbaye de Cîteaux, 1098–1182*, Rome, 1961, 89–90, com pare 95, 101, 104, 109; a reference for which I am indebted to Professor Giles Constable, of Harvard University); and that relationship would seem to preclude more than the most distant alliance with the Burgundian ducal house (I must also thank M. l'abbé Marilier for his generosity in enlightening me on the ramifications of Burgundian genealogy).

36. *geaf se eorl . . .*: for Henry's election to Angély in 1104, with the support of William, count of Poitou, and of Rannulf, bishop of Saintes,

see G. Musset, *Cartulaire de Saint-Jean d'Angély*, 2 vols., Paris, 1901–3, i. 398–9.

38. *Besencun*: there is no known record of any connection between Henry of Angély and this see.

41. *Seintes*: there is no direct evidence connecting Henry of Angély with this see. But verses in a mortuary roll of 1113 describe a Cluniac-inspired attack on the bishop of Saintes (L. Delisle, *Rouleaux des morts du ixe au xve siècle*, Paris, 1866, 24: for this reference also I have to thank Professor Constable); and also about 1113 Geoffrey of Vendôme accused the Papal legate, Girard of Angoulême, of conspiring with the abbot of Angély to depose *Rainaldum Chesnelli*, whom some have identified with the Rainald who became bishop of Saintes about 1111 (Migne, *P.L.* clvii, col. 65; compare M. l'abbé Maratu, *Girard, évêque d'Angoulême*, Angoulême, 1866, 100–2, and L. Compain, *Étude sur Geoffroi de Vendôme*, Bibliothèque de l'École des Hautes Études: sciences philologiques et historiques lxxxvi, 1891, 229 n.).

fif mile: in fact, over sixteen miles, so there seems some confusion between the mile and the *leuca* (compare *infra*, 656 E, 117, where *mile* occurs four times as the equivalent of *leugia*, Hugo, 11).

47. *ne mihte ðolen þa micele unrihte 7 þa micele unsibbe*: Geoffrey of Vendôme, some twenty years earlier admittedly, had described Henry of Angély as *discordiæ amatorem, seminatorem jurgiorum, pacis perturbatorem* (Migne, *P.L.* clvii, col. 146).

48. *þurh him 7 ðurh ealle his freond*: Hugo, 101, *per se et per suos amicos.*

49. *namcuðlice*: Hugo, 101, *nominatim.*

58. *eall þet he mihte tacen*: compare Hugo, 101, *et accepit homagium et pecuniam de militibus et de tota abbacia.* Dr. Edmund King, of Sheffield University, tells me that there is no evidence extant of Abbot Henry's alleged depredations.

62. '*Exurge, . . .*': the introit for Sexagesima Sunday, which in 1127 fell on 6 February.

64. *huntes*: the literary history of the Wild Hunt was traced by H. Flasdieck, 'Herlekin', *Anglia*, lxi (1937), 225–338, also ibid. lxvi (1942), 59–69, a well-known description of it is by Ordericus, iii. 367–77; see also Kemp Malone, 'Herlekin and Herlewin', in *Studies in Heroic Legend and in Current Speech*, Copenhagen, 1959, 193–6.

1128

3. *eorl of Flandres*: i.e. William 'Clito'. For this campaign and the count's fatal wound at Alost, see Ordericus, iv. 479–82; Hen. Hunt. 247–50; *Hist. Reg.* ii. 282–3; John of Worcester, 29. He was succeeded as count of Flanders by Thierry III of Alsace, a grandson of Robert 'the Frisian' (see table, *EHD* 999).

8. *Randulf*: for his death, see *Hist. Eccl. Dun.* i. 140.

17. *Hugo of þe Temple*: Hugo of Payns (*dép.* Aube), a founder of the Knights Templars; he had come to Europe to attend the Council of Troyes at which his Order was recognized and given a rule (see M. Melville, *La Vie des Templiers*, Paris, 1951, 13–25). For the abortive expedition described here, see also Hen. Hunt. 250, 251; and for other aspects of Hugo's visit, see B. A. Lees, *Records of the Templars in England in the Twelfth Century*, 1935, xxxviii–xxxix.

1129

3. *to his agen land to France*: Châteauneuf-en-Thimerais (see *supra*, 1124/7 n.) being in the French Vexin.

14. *þet mot*: see also Hen. Hunt. 250–1.

26. *Henri his nefe*: Henry of Blois, brother of Count Thibaut and of the future King Stephen; he played a great part in the politics of the Anarchy (see 1140/22 n.). He held the abbacy of Glastonbury and the see of Winchester in plurality until his death in 1171 (see Hearne, ed., *Adami de Domerham Historia*, i. 121–2 and ii. 303–31; and for a modern assessment of him, Knowles, *Monastic Order*, 286–93, and idem, *The Episcopal Colleagues of Archbishop Thomas Becket*, Cambridge, 1951, 36–7).

30. *twa papes*: Innocent II (*Gregorius*), and the Antipope Anacletus II (*Petrus*, i.e. Piero de Pierleoni, descendant of a family of Jewish usurers), see *CMH* v. 363 et seq. Contemporary accounts include Suger, 256–70, and *Hist. Nov.* 61. The recognition of Innocent by the kings in question did not take place until 1131.

32. *duc of Sicilie*: the Norman Roger II of Sicily, brother-in-law of Anacletus (Ordericus, v. 37).

34. *se Kasere of Sexlande*: now Lothar III, formerly duke of Saxony.

1130

1. *mynstre of Cantwarabyri*: the new Christ Church Cathedral, see *VCH Kent*, ii. 14 and compare 1087/69 n. See also John of Worcester, 30, for this consecration and the fire at Rochester.

3. *Iohan of Roueceastre*: the former archdeacon of Canterbury (see 1114/36 n., 1123/52; Hen. Hunt. 245; John of Worcester, 19).

Gilebert Uniuersal: so called probably on account of his 'universal' learning (Hen. Hunt. 307, *non fuit adusque Romam par ei scientia*), see B. Smalley, 'Gilbertus Universalis, Bishop of London (1128–34), and the Problem of the "Glossa Ordinaria" ', *Recherches de théologie ancienne et médiévale*, vii (1935), 235–62, and viii (1936), 24–60. For his consecration, see also John of Worcester, 26.

7. *Audoenus*: brother of Thurstan of York, see Hugh the Chantor, 123.

13. *Heanri*: his presence in Poitou until some time in 1130 is confirmed by a Maillezais document (M. l'abbé Lacurie, *Histoire de l'abbaye de Maillezais*, Fontenay-le-Comte, 1852, 248–50).

15. *Petrus*: Peter the Venerable. This may be the occasion referred to when, in an undated letter to Henry of Winchester, Peter himself speaks of a long stay in England the previous year (G. Constable, ed., *The Letters of Peter the Venerable*, 2 vols., Harvard Historical Studies lxxviii, 1967, i. 150).

1131

5. *orfcwalm*: see also *Hist. Nov.* 11.

23. *7 Se eorl . . .*: an Angély document tells how, on St. John's Day itself, William VIII of Poitou raided the abbey church; it makes no mention at all of Abbot Henry, but twice names 'Hugo, the abbot-elect' (Musset, *Cartulaire*, i. 270–2). Compare also Hugo, 102–3, and Ordericus, iv. 430.

38. *France*: since the sentence apparently summarizes the episode, referring to the visits to Normandy and to Poitou as well as that to Cluny (in French Burgundy), the sense here must be, not the narrow one previously noted (1076/7 n., 1087/38 n.), but a generalized one, equivalent to *Gallia*, for which no other English expression seems to have existed at this date (see *Leeds Studies in English*, N.S. iii. 35–45).

1132

1. *þa com Henri abbot*: similarly Hugo, 103–4.

2. *þe king*: well-disposed to the Cluniacs (Knowles, *Monastic Order*, 280–2).

3. *ðat*: here the full form is regularly *ðat* instead of the earlier *þet*.

6. *feorde mid swicdom*: 'was behaving treacherously', compare Laȝamon A 24294, *ferden mid þan crafte* (=B, *usede*), and *Gawain* 1282, *ferde with defence*, also the ON *fara með* 'to deal in'.

7. *nefe*: Hugo adds the name *Gerardus*.

10. *ut of lande*: Hugo finishes the story:

'Abbas autem Henricus cum suis mare transiuit et iterum abbaciam suam de Angeli recuperauit. Quicquid tamen fecit, bonus elemosinator omnibus diebus fuit, et ideo sicut dictum est bonum finem fecit. Nam non diu postquam ibi uenit uixit.'

Compare the obits quoted in *Gallia Christiana*, ii. col. 1101.

11. *Martin*: originally a monk of Bec: see 1137/57 to end and notes.

1135

6. *ilc gær*: although Henry died in 1135, the eclipse and his departure from England belong under 1133, see John of Worcester, 37–8, 39; *Hist. Reg.* ii. 285, also 295–6 (as John of Worcester); *Hist. Nov.* 11–12. Hugo, 104, agrees with E, compare *supra*, xxvii–xxviii.

warth þe king ded: for Henry I's death and funeral, see Hen. Hunt. 254–8; Ordericus, v. 49–54; *Hist. Reg.* ii. 286; *Hist. Nov.* 12–14, 16; John of Worcester, 40.

8. MS. *þestre sona*: for the emendation, see H. Bradley, 'Trȩson in the Anglo-Saxon Chronicle', *MLR* xii (1917), 72 et seq., and 492, and N. R. Ker, 'Some Notes on the Peterborough Chronicle', *MÆ* iii (1934), 136–7, where he quotes Hugo, 104, *Tunc contenebrata est terra.* For the disorders following Henry I's death, see *Gest. Steph.* 1–2; *Hist. Reg.* ii. 286; John of Worcester, 40; Rich. Hex. 139–40.

9. *sune*: i.e. the bastard son, Robert of Gloucester (see 1126/14 n., 1140 *passim*).

10. *Redinge*: Henry I's own foundation (*Gest. Pont.* 193; *Gest. Reg.* ii. 489; Rich. Hex. 141; also Knowles, *Monastic Order*, 281).

God man . . .: compare the identifications of Henry I with the Lion of Justice from *The Prophecies of Merlin* (Ordericus, iv. 493; Suger, 98–102). As Henry of Huntingdon said (255–6), comparison with what followed made Henry's reign seem good. For other contemporary assessments of him, see *Gest. Reg.* ii. 485, 486–8; *Hist. Reg.* ii. 286; Ordericus, iii. 267, iv. 237; Rich. Hex. 140–1. See also R. W. Southern, 'The Place of Henry I in English History', *PBA* xlviii (1962), 127–69.

12. . . . *7 dær*: i.e. in the well-policed royal forests; compare *Gest. Steph.* 2 on the indiscriminate slaughter of game during the Anarchy.

Wua sua . . .: compare 1087/91 n.

14. *Stephne de Blais*: see R. H. C. Davis, *King Stephen.* He was brother of Thibaut of Blois (see 1116/8 n.) and of Henry bishop of Winchester (see 1129/26 n.), and so a grandson of the Conqueror through his daughter Adela; count of Mortain by Henry I's gift, and count of Boulogne through his wife Matilda, the only child of Eustace III of Boulogne and of Mary of Scotland (Ordericus, iv. 189; *Hist. Nov.* 57). Both Stephen himself, and William of Canterbury who crowned him, had been prominent among those taking the 1127 oath of loyalty to Matilda (Hen. Hunt. 256; *Hist. Nov.* 4; also *Gest. Steph.* 6–8). For his reception in England, see *Hist. Nov.* 15–16; *Gest. Steph.* 2–4; *Hist. Reg.* ii. 286–7; Ordericus, iv. 54–6. His Coronation charter is no. 270 (p. 95) in H. A. Cronne and R. H. C. Davis, eds., *Regesta Regum Anglo-Normannorum*, III: 1135–1154, Oxford, 1968.

19. *Balduin de Reduers*: of Reviers (*dép.* Calvados), see *Complete Peerage*, iv. 311–12. For his revolt and the consequent siege of Exeter, see *Gest. Steph.* 20–30; Hen. Hunt. 259–60; Rich. Hex. 146–7; *Hist. Reg.* ii. 287–8; John of Worcester, 41.

21. *Dauid*: for this invasion and settlement, see *Hist. Nov.* 16; *Hist. Reg.* ii. 287; Hen. Hunt. 258–9; Rich. Hex. 145–6. Because of his oath to Matilda David refused to recognize Stephen, but he allowed his son Henry to do homage for the earldom of Huntingdon.

1137

1. *to Normandi*: apart from the general unrest there, Geoffrey of Anjou was attempting to take the duchy over in his wife's name (Ordericus, v. 56–92; also Hen. Hunt. 260; Rich. Hex. 150; *Gest. Steph.* 31).

4. *scatered sotlice*: for Stephen's foolish liberality and its consequences, see *Hist. Nov.* 17–18, also *Gest. Steph.* 30.

7. *æt Oxeneford*: in June 1139, see *Hist. Nov.* 26 et seq.

þar he nam . . .: see *Hist. Nov.* 27–34; *Gest. Steph.* 48–55; John of Worcester, 54–5; Ordericus, v. 119–21; Hen. Hunt. 265–6; *Hist. Reg.* ii. 301. The bishops were accused of fortifying castles in the Empress's interest. Roger of Salisbury died later the same year (*Hist. Nov.* 27; *Hist. Reg.* ii. 302; John of Worcester, 57–8; Hen. Hunt. 266).

9. *neues*: the chancellor Roger was not a nephew but a son (*nepos . . . uel plusquam nepos*, *Hist. Nov.* 27; compare Ordericus, v. 119).

10. *softe*: not derogatory, compare 1114/30 (of Ernulf), *swiðe god 7 softe man*. Stephen is invariably given this character, thus, *Gest. Steph.* 3, *humilis, munificus et affabilis*, and similarly at greater length, 14; *Hist. Nov.* 16, *lenis et exorabilis hostibus, affabilis omnibus*; so also Ordericus, v. 129 and Rich. Hex. 145.

na iustise ne dide: 'inflicted no punishment' (Hall, ii. 255; B. Dickins, 'The Peterborough Annal for 1137', *RES* ii (1926), 342); compare Hen. Hunt. 259, *vindictam non exercuit in proditores suos*.

11. *wunder*: 'atrocities'.

16. *castles*: see *Hist. Nov.* 40 et seq.

17. *deoules*: compare *Chronicle of Jocelin of Brakelond*, ed. H. E. Butler, 1949, 32, *demon nimis fuerat, inimicus Dei et excoriator rusticorum*.

þa namen hi . . .: compare *Gest. Steph.* 41, *sicubi pecuniosos uel opulentos audierant . . . aut ieiuniis macerare, aut suppliciis addictis usque ad nouissimum quadrantem quicquid possederant ab eis exigere*; *Hist. Nov.* 40–1, *Vauassores, rusticos, quicumque pecuniosi putabantur, intercipientes, suppliciorum magnitudine ad quoduis promittendum cogebant*; also *Liber Eliensis*, ed. Blake, 328, *captivos . . . miserabiliter cruciabant, . . . ut ab afflictis pecunias excutiant*.

19. MS. *diden heom ˡin prisunˡ ế̋fter gold 7 syluer ⁊́ pined heom / untellendlice pining*: for these diacritics, see Ker, *MÆ* iii. 137–8.

23. *hengen bryniges on her fet*: compare *Hist. Eccl. Dun.* i. 153, *Suspendebantur . . . homines, . . . collo atque pedibus immensis loricarum sive saxorum ponderibus alligatis.*

26. *crucethur*: for this reading, see J. Gerritsen, 'A Ghost-word: crucet-hūs', *ES* xlii (1961), 300–1, where the etymon suggested is Lat. *cruciator*. Compare *Hist. Eccl. Dun.* i. 153–4, *genus illud supplicii exquisitum, quo simul compressa in arctissimi loculi spatio membra collidebant.*

29. *lof 7 grin*: translate perhaps 'chain and halter' (see Dickins, *RES* ii. 342; F. P. Magoun, 'Two Lexicographical Notes', *MLN* xl (1925), 411–12, and O. F. Emerson, 'The Crux in the Peterborough Chronicle', *MLN* xli (1926), 170–2).

38. *æure um wile*: 'time and again'.

"*tenserie*": 'protection-money' (OFr. *tenser* 'to protect'), not noted elsewhere in an English context; compare *Wistasse le Moine* (W. Foerster and J. Trost, eds., Halle, 1891), 2111–13, *Wistasces vint a Bareflué. / .xxx. mars ot de tenserie / Es isles et en l'autre partie*; and for the practice, see *Gest. Steph.* 55. (The suggestion of *censerie* made by Davis, *King Stephen*, 84, is unacceptable, as the MS. has an unambiguous *t*.)

40. *wel þu myhtes . . .*: compare *Gest. Steph.* 101–2, *Videres famosissimi nominis uillas . . . solitarias stare et prorsus euacuatas*; also *Liber Eliensis*, 328, *Per viginti miliaria seu xxx non bos, non arator inventus est qui particulam terre excoleret.*

41. *corn dære*: compare *Liber Eliensis*, 328, *Vix parvissimus tunc modius emi poterat ducentis denariis, tantaque hominum clades de inopia panis secuta est, ut . . . centeni et milleni . . . exanimes iacerent*; also *Gest. Steph.* 101, *fames . . . in omni Anglia dirissime inualuerat*, etc.

44. *flugen ut of lande*: compare *Gest. Steph.* loc. cit., *Alii patriæ dulcedinem in nausientem amaritudinem intuentes conuersam, exteras magis regiones inhabitare eligere.*

46. *ouer sithon*: C. Sisam, 'Notes on Middle English Texts', *RES* N.S. xiii (1962), 385–6, questions the usual interpretation 'contrary to custom', suggesting instead an error for *of(t)sithon* 'often'. For marauding knights *nec ecclesiis nec cimiteriis parcentes*, see *Hist. Nov.* 40, and *Gest. Steph.* 68, 87, 102–3, and esp. 72–3.

50. *ouermyhte*: 'was the stronger' (see Dickins, *RES* ii. 342; compare *Vices and Virtues*, EETS 89, 13, line 13, and also *Owl and Nightingale*, line 64). Compare John of Worcester, 40, *Quisque in alterum caput elevat . . . Quisque alium rebus spoliat. Potens impotentem vi opprimit*;

and *Gest. Steph.* 1, *Nouo enim quisque sæuiendi raptus amore, in alterum crudele debacchari . . .*

Gif twa men . . .: compare *Gest. Steph.* 42, *Ubicumque alter alterum in itinere conspicabatur, totus protinus contremiscere, meticulose uisum effugere uel prope in silua uel in diuortio aliquo . . .* For people to be driven thus into hiding was no new thing, compare Eadmer, 192.

52. *cursede*: 'excommunicated', compare *Gest. Steph.* 103–4, 105, 111, 124, 141–2.

55. *al fordon*: compare *Hist. Eccl. Dun.* i. 153:

'Quicquid in agris natum erat conterendo calcibus, aut depascendo delebant; perque terram cultam iter agendo faciebant eam sterilem et vastitatis facie deformem videri. Et velut post locustas silva cerni solet floribus et foliis spoliata, sic quacunque transibant solitudinem a tergo relinquebant.'

Note also *Liber Eliensis*, 328 (with a Virgilian reminiscence), *Oppresserat enim fames universam regionem et egra seges victum omnem negaverat.*

58. *Martin abbot*: see 1132/11 and Hugo, 104–24 (closely related to E, but fuller).

60. *carited*: 'ceremonial almsgivings and commemoration feasts'.

61. *circe*: Abbot Martin's church largely survives, see Clapham, *English Romanesque Architecture after the Conquest*, 41–2, and Boase, *English Art, 1100–1216*, 123–5, also *VCH Northants.* ii. 432 et seq. For the 1140 inauguration ceremonies, see Hugo, 105–6, 108.

65. *Eugenie*: Eugenius III, a Cistercian, elected in 1145.

66. *priuilegies*: the texts, which refer to the places mentioned below as well as to many others, are given in Hugo, 109–16, 116–19, compare also 171–3; compare the 1125 Survey (*Chronicon Petroburgense*, 159–60, 166) and the thirteenth-century documents in C. N. L. Brooke and M. M. Postan, eds., *Carte Nativorum*, Northamptonshire Record Society xx, 1960, 123–6, 129–31, 136–43.

68. *horderwycan*: Hugo, 122–3, *redditus celerarii et camerarii.*

69. *Willelm Malduit*: Hugo, 123 and 173, *Willelmo Maleducto*; William Mauduit II, hereditary royal chamberlain and constable of Rockingham Castle (see *Regesta* III, no. 582, pp. 212–13; and G. H. White, 'Financial Administration under Henry I', *TRHS*, 4th ser. viii (1925), 60–2, 72–7; also Loyd, *Origins*, 62).

70. *Estun*: Great Easton, Leics. (*VCH Leics.* i. 288–9, 310–11 (Domesday); *Chronicon Petroburgense*, 172; *Carte Nativorum*, 136–43); Dr. Edmund King has pointed out to me that this Easton, the only one in which the abbey retained any interest after Henry I's day, was,

like Cottingham, so placed as to be especially vulnerable to a rapacious castellan at Rockingham.

Hugo of Walteruile: the Vatierville (*dép.* Seine-Maritime, see Loyd, *Origins*, 111) family were abbey tenants (Hugo, 112, 117, 163, 168).

71. *Hyrtlingbyri*: Irthlingborough (*EPNS Northants.*, 182–3).

Aldewingle: Aldwinkle; a record of this transaction survives (*VCH Northants.* iii. 160; for the Domesday valuation of this estate, compare ibid. i. 316).

73. *winiærd*: Hugo, 123, *uineam plantauit*; part of the cathedral precincts is still called 'The Vineyard' (*VCH Northants.* ii. 448, plan). At this time vineyards were not uncommon in Midland England, Thorney having a famous one (*Gest. Pont.* 326, compare 292); they are thought to have been made possible by a climate resembling that of present-day Touraine (H. H. Lamb, *The Changing Climate*, 1966, 7–10, 18, 188–92, and idem, 'Britain's Changing Climate', *Geographical Journal*, cxxxiii (1967), 455–6).

wende þe tun betere: Hugo, 122, *Portam monasterii et mercatum et portum nauium et uillam multo melius mutauit, et multa emendauit*; see also W. T. Mellows, ed., *Peterborough Local Administration*, Northamptonshire Record Society ix, 1939, ci–cii, and *VCH Northants.* ii. 424–5.

75. *God 7 gode men*: a traditional alliterative phrase current in Norse as well as in Old and Middle English (see C. T. Onions, *TLS*, 13 August 1931, 621; also E. S. Olsewska, 'Alliterative Phrases in the *Ormulum*: Some Norse Parallels', *English and Medieval Studies Presented to J. R. R. Tolkien*, Oxford, 1962, 125).

77. *an Cristen cild*: St. William of Norwich, see A. Jessopp and M. R. James, eds., *The Life and Miracles of St. William of Norwich*, Cambridge, 1896, and also M. D. Anderson, *A Saint at Stake*, 1964. This is the earliest known accusation of ritual murder brought against the Jews, see E. Vacandard, 'La question du meurtre rituel chez les Juifs', *Études de critique et d'histoire religieuse*, iiie sér., Paris, 1912, 313–77, and also C. Roth, 'The Feast of Purim and the Origins of the Blood Accusation', *Speculum*, viii (1933), 520–6. Compare the parodic version in *The Chronicle of Richard of Devizes*, ed. J. T. Appleby, 1963, 64–9.

1138

1. *com Dauid king*: for these Scottish invasions, marked by extraordinary brutality, see Rich. Hex. 151–67; *Hist. Reg.* ii. 288, 289–95; Hen. Hunt. 260–1, 261–5; John of Worcester, 46, 51; *Gest. Steph.* 33–7. The Scottish king professed to be animated by loyalty to his niece Matilda, compare 1135/21 n.

3. *Willelm eorl of Albamar*: lord of Holderness, afterwards earl of Yorkshire (*Complete Peerage*, i. 353).

5. *Standard*: for the Battle of the Standard, fought just north of Northallerton and so called because the English forces, organized by Archbishop Thurstan of York, rallied round the banners of St. John of Beverley, St. Peter of York, and St. Wilfrid of Ripon, see the references at 1 n. above and also Ailred of Rievaulx, *Relatio de Standardo* (Howlett, ed., *Chronicles of the Reigns of Stephen, etc.*, iii. 181–99).

1140

1. *Rodbert eorl*: although for a time he had made politic submission to Stephen (*Hist. Nov.* 17–18; *Gest. Steph.* 8), in 1138 he formally renounced his allegiance (*Hist. Nov.* 23); and in 1139 he landed at Arundel with his sister (ibid. 34–5; *Gest. Steph.* 58; John of Worcester, 55; compare *infra*, 19 n.). For Stephen's unsuccessful attempt to capture him, see *Gest. Steph.* 58, also John of Worcester, 55–6.

4. *abuton nontid dæies*: compare *Hist. Nov.* 42–3, *hora nona*.

6. *Willelm ærcebiscop*: William of Corbeil (see 1123/32 n.); his death occurred in 1136 (John of Worcester, 41).

7. *Teodbald*: see A. Saltman, *Theobald, Archbishop of Canterbury*, 1956.

9. *Randolf*: a son-in-law of Robert of Gloucester; see H. A. Cronne, 'Ranulf de Gernons, Earl of Chester 1129–1153', *TRHS*, 4th ser. xx (1937), 103–34, and also R. H. C. Davis, 'King Stephen and the Earl of Chester Revised', *EHR* lxxv (1960), 654–60. His present rebellion arose from the granting of lands he claimed to Prince Henry of Scotland (*Hist. Reg.* ii. 306).

11. *Lincol*: the siege of Lincoln took place early in 1141; see Hen. Hunt. 268–75; Ordericus, v. 125–9; *Hist. Nov.* 46–9; *Gest. Steph.* 73–5; *Hist. Reg.* ii. 307–8; Florence, ii. 129.

13. *Willelm de Romare*: see 1123/81 n.

16. *namen him*: see *Hist. Nov.* 49–50 and *Gest. Steph.* 75 et seq.

17. *Bristowe*: Robert of Gloucester's headquarters (*Hist. Nov.* 24–35; *Gest. Steph.* 37 et seq., 58–9).

18. *7 [in fe]teres*: see Ker, *MÆ* iii. 138; compare *Hist. Nov.* 50, Hen. Hunt. 275, and Florence, ii. 129.

19. *þe kinges dohter Henries*: Matilda had landed at Arundel in 1139; see *Hist. Nov.* 34 et seq.; *Gest. Steph.* 58 et seq.; Hen. Hunt. 266; *Hist. Reg.* ii. 302, 309–11; Ordericus, v. 121 et seq.; John of Worcester, 55.

21. *com to Lundene*: see the contrasting accounts in *Hist. Nov.* 56–7

and *Gest. Steph.* 80–5, also Florence, ii. 131–2 and Hen. Hunt. 275. Even *Hist. Nov.*, in spite of attempts to minimize Matilda's discomfiture, admits that she fled in such haste as to leave all her goods in her lodgings for looters to plunder.

23. *Henri*: offended in 1138 when passed over for the see of Canterbury and further alienated in 1139 by Stephen's treatment of the bishops, Henry of Blois had soon after Easter 1141 renounced allegiance to his brother, on grounds of unfitness to rule, and then proclaimed Matilda *Anglie Normannieque dominam* (*Hist. Nov.* 50–4; *Gest. Steph.* 78–9; Florence, ii. 130). This preceded the events in London. Later the same year Matilda's highhandedness moved him to renounce her (*Hist. Nov.* 57–8; *Gest. Steph.* 80, 83–4; *Hist. Reg.* ii. 145). The siege took place when she returned to Winchester in an attempt to reclaim it (*Hist. Nov.* 58–60; *Gest. Steph.* 84–9; Florence, ii. 133–4; Hen. Hunt. 275).

28. *kinges cuen*: Matilda of Boulogne, see *Gest. Steph.* 85; her forces had already played a part in the London attack on the Empress (ibid. 81–2, 83).

31. *namen Rodbert*: see *Hist. Nov.* 60–1, 66–7; *Gest. Steph.* 88; Florence, ii. 134–5.

34. *sahtlede*: see *Hist. Nov.* 61–2, 67–70; *Gest. Steph.* 90; Florence, ii. 136; Hen. Hunt. 275.

38. *him sithen nam*: the seizure of Randolf of Chester, on the pretext that he was trying to entrap the king, occurred in 1146 (*Gest. Steph.* 128–30; Hen. Hunt. 279).

42. *wærse þanne he hær sculde*: C. Sisam, *RES* N.S. xiii. 386, suggests the translation 'worse than he is said to have done before'; but compare Bennett and Smithers, 388, 'ever ought to have done'. Another possibility, but no easier than the others to support by parallels, seems to be 'than he would have done before' (i.e. before provoked by unwise treatment), with *sculde* as subjunctive auxiliary and ellipsis of the infinitive. For Randolf's hostility to Stephen after his release, see *Gest. Steph.* 131–2, 145–6.

46. *Oxenford*: one of Matilda's bases (*Hist. Nov.* 58, 62, 72; *Gest. Steph.* 83, 91; Florence, ii. 130). Stephen burnt the town and besieged the castle in the autumn of 1142 (*Hist. Nov.* 74, 76–7; *Gest. Steph.* 92–6; Hen. Hunt. 276; but *Hist. Reg.* ii. 317, dates it *s.a.* 1144).

48. *læt hire dun . . .*: not only *Hist. Nov.* 77 but even the hostile *Gest. Steph.* 94–5, calls her escape miraculous; see also Hen. Hunt. 276.

50. *Walingford*: a headquarters of Matilda's party (*Hist. Nov.* 74; *Gest. Steph.* 60), held by Brian FitzCount (see 1127/8 n.).

ferde ouer sæ: in 1148, after Robert of Gloucester's death the preceding autumn.

Hi of Normandi . . . to þe eorl of Angæu: Geoffrey of Anjou was recognized as duke of Normandy in 1144.

53. *Eustace*: *Gest. Steph.* 137–8 gives him a very different character, representing him as a paragon of chivalry (but compare 147–8; see also Hen. Hunt. 283–4, 288; *Hist. Reg.* ii. 331). His marriage took place in 1140 (John of Worcester, 61; Hen. Hunt. 265). He died in 1153, during Henry of Anjou's campaign (*Gest. Steph.* 158).

61. *Te eorl . . . ded*: for Geoffrey of Anjou's death in 1151 and its consequences, see Hen. Hunt. 283, and *Gest. Steph.* 149.

62. *Henri*: i.e. the future Henry II of England, already about 1150 invested with the duchy of Normandy (*Gest. Steph.* 148–9).

cuen of France: Eleanor of Aquitaine; see E.-R. Labande, 'Pour une image véridique d'Aliénor d'Aquitaine', *Bulletin de la Société des Antiquaires de l'Ouest*, 4e sér. iv (1952–4), 175–234, and H. G. Richardson, 'The Letters and Charters of Eleanor of Aquitaine', *EHR* lxxiv (1959), 193–213; also the more popular biography by Régine Pernoud, *Aliénor d'Aquitaine*, Paris, 1965.

63. *þe king*: i.e. Louis VII, who had succeeded Louis le Gros in 1137 (Suger, 282–6).

64. *ferde . . . into Engleland*: early in 1153, see *Gest. Steph.* 152–8, Hen. Hunt. 284–9, and *Hist. Reg.* ii. 324 et seq. (for abortive earlier visits, see *Gest. Steph.* 135–7, 146–8).

67. *ðat sahte*: for the Treaty of Westminster drawn up in November 1953, see *Regesta* III, no. 272, pp. 97–9, also *EHD* 404–7. Stephen's surviving son, William, was to hold from Henry all the estates which his father had held before becoming king, together with the Warenne lands belonging to his wife.

76. *herere*; 77. *her*: i.e. *æror*, *ær*. Hen. Hunt. 290, also says that, *adoptivi gratia filii*, Stephen now reigned in peace for the first time.

1154

1. *wærd . . . Stephne ded*: compare *Gest. Steph.* 159, *leui febricula tactus ex hac uita discessit.*

2. *Fauresfeld*: the Cluniac abbey which Stephen had founded at Faversham in 1148 (see *Regesta* III, nos. 300, 301, 302, pp. 113–14). The form of the name here is anomalous, see J. K. Wallenberg, *Kentish Place-Names*, Uppsala Universitets Årsskrift, 1931, 117.

8. *Martin*: for his death, see Hugo, 124.

10. *innen dæ̈is*: 'within the day', compare Hugo, 124, *Eodem uero die quo obiit . . . .*; see also S. Einarsson, 'Two Scandinavisms in the *Peterborough Chronicle*', *JEGP* xxxvii (1938), 20.

Willelm de Walteruile: for his election, see Hugo, 124–7. For the family, compare 1137/69 n.

12. *on [morg]en*: compare Hugo, 124, *Alio uero die post . . .*

13. *to Oxenforde*: see Hugo, 126.

16. *mid micel wurtscipe*: for the welcoming of a new abbot *cum debito honore et etiam processione*, see *Chronicle of Jocelin of Brakelond*, 24–5.

18. *7 F . . . .*: the most probable wording here is *7 For ham* (no likely religious house has a name which fits the traces in the manuscript), see Whitelock, *Facsimile*, 14, n. 7.

19. . . . *þus enden!*: after a reign described as profitable for the abbey, William of Waterville was deposed in 1175, apparently on false charges (see Hugo, 127–32).

APPENDIX

THE PETERBOROUGH INTERPOLATIONS

FOR bibliographical information about the charters on which most of the Interpolations are based and for summaries of scholarly opinion, see P. H. Sawyer, *Anglo-Saxon Charters: An Annotated List and Bibliography*, 1968, Nos. 68 (p. 88), 72 (pp. 89–90), 787 (pp. 251–2), 1377 (p. 390), 1412 (p. 397), and 1448 (p. 406). See also especially F. M. Stenton, 'Medeshamstede and its Colonies', *Historical Essays in Honour of James Tait*, Manchester, 1933, 313–26, W. Levison, *England and the Continent in the Eighth Century*, 219–20, and Robertson, *Anglo-Saxon Charters*, VII, XXXIX, and XL.

654. On his time þa comon togadere heo 7 Oswiu, Oswaldes broðor cyningas, 7 sprecon þ*et* hi wolden an mynstre areren Criste to louc 7 Sancte Petre to wurðminte. And hi swa diden, 7 nama hit gauen Medeshamstede, forþan þet ðær is an wæl þe is gehaten Medeswæl; 7 hi ongunnan þa þ*et* grundwalla, 7 þæron wrohten. Betahten hit þa an munec, SAXVLF wæs gehaten; he wæs swyðe Godes freond 7 hi*m* luuede al þeode, 7 he wæs swyðe æþelboren on weorulde 7 rice—he is nu mycelne riccere mid Criste. Oc se kining Peada ne rixade nane hwile, forþan he wæs beswicen þurh his agen cwen on Estrentide. f. 14r 5 10

656. On his time wæx þet abbodrice Medesha*m*stede swiðe rice þ*et* his br[o]ðor hafde ongunnen. Þa luuede se kining hit swiðe for his broðer luuen Peada, 7 for his wedbroðeres luuen Oswi, 7 for Saxulfes luuen þes abbodes; cweð þa þ*et* he wolde hit wurðminten 7 arwurðen be his broðre ræd Æðelred 7 Merwala, 7 be his swustre red Kyneburges 7 Kyneswiðes, 7 be se ærcebiscopes ræd, se wæs gehaten D*eu*sdedit, 7 be al his gewiten ræd, læred 7 lawed, þe on his kynerice wæron; 7 he swa dide. Ða seonde se kyning æfter þone ab[b]ode þet he æuestelice f. 14v 5

654/4 *MS.* nama *followed by erasure of one letter.* 656/2 *MS.* brðor
9 *MS.* abdode

10 scolde to him cumon; 7 he swa dyde. Ða cwæ[ð] se kyning to þan abbode:

"La, leof Sæxulf, ic haue geseond æfter þe for mine saule þurfe; 7 ic hit wile þe wæl secgon forhwi. Min broðor Peada 7 min leoue freond Oswi ongunnen an mynstre Criste to loue 7 15 Sancte Petre; oc min broðer is faren of þisse liue swa swa Crist wolde. Oc ic wile ðe gebidden, la, leoue freond, þ*et* hii wi˹r˺ce æuostlice on þere werce, 7 ic þe wile finden þærto gold 7 siluer, land 7 ahte, 7 al þet þærto behofeð."

Ða feorde se abbot ham, 7 ongan to wircene. Swa he spedde, 20 swa him Crist huðe, swa þet in feu[u]a geare wæs þ*et* mynstre gare. Ða þa kyning heorda þæt gesecgon, þa wærð he swiðe glæd; heot seonden geond al hi[s] þeode æfter alle his þægne, æfter ærcebiscop, 7 æfter biscopes, 7 æfter his eorles, 7 æfter alle þa þe Gode luuedon, þ*et* hi scoldon to him cumene; 7 25 seotte þa dæi hwonne man scolde þ*et* mynstre gehalegon. Ða / f. 15ʳ man halgode seo mynstre, þa wæs seo kyning Wulfere þær, 7 his broðer Æðelred, 7 his swustre Kyneburg 7 Kynesuuith; 7 seo mynstre halgode seo ærcebiscop D*eu*sdedit of Cantwarbyrig, 7 seo biscop of Rofecæstre Ithamar, 7 seo biscop of Lundone, 30 þe wæs Wina gehaten, 7 seo Myrcene biscop, Ieruman wæs gehaten, 7 Tuda biscop, 7 þær wæs Wilfrid preost þe siððon wæs biscop, 7 þær wæron ælle his ðegnas þe wæron on his kynerice. Ða seo mynstre wæs gehalgod on Sancte Petres nama 7 S*ancte* Paules 7 S*ancte* Andr*eas*, þa stod seo kyning up 35 toforen ealle his ðægna, 7 cwæ[ð] luddor stefne:

"Ðancod wurð hit þon hæge ælmihti God þis wurðscipe þ*et* her is gedon; 7 ic wile wurðigen þis dæi Crist 7 S*anct*e Peter, 7 ic wille þ*et* ge ealle getiðe mine worde. Ic, Wulfere, gife to dæi S*anct*e Petre 7 þone abbode Saxulf 7 þa munecas of þe mynstre 40 þas landes 7 þas wateres 7 meres 7 fennes 7 weres, 7 ealle þa landes þa þærabuton liggeð, ða of mine kynerice sindon, freolice swa ðet nan man na haue þær nan onsting buton seo abbot 7 se muneces. Ðas is se gife: fra*m* Medeshamstede to Norðburh, 7 swa to ðet stede þet man cleopeð Folies, 7 swa æl se feon riht to

10 *MS.* cwæd 20 *MS.* feuna 22 *MS.* hi 35 *MS.* cwæd

Esendic, 7 fra Esendic to þ*et* steode þe man cleopeð Feðermuðe, 45
7 swa þ*et* rihte weie x mile lang to Cuggedic, 7 swa to Raggewilh, 7 fra Raggewilh v mile to þe rihte æ þe gað to Ælm 7 to Wisebece, 7 swa abutan iii mile to Þrokonholt, 7 fra Þrokonholt riht þurh al ðe fen to Dereuorde, þ*et* is xx mile lang, 7 swa to Græte Cros, 7 fra Græte Cros þurh an scyr wæter Bradanæ 50
hatte, 7 þeonon vi mile to Paccelade, 7 swa forð þurh ælle þa meres 7 feonnes þa liggen toward Huntendene porte, 7 þas meres 7 laces, Scælfremere 7 / Witlesmere, 7 ælle þa oþre þa f. 15v
þarabutan liggan, mid land 7 mid huses þa sindon on æsthalfe Scælfremere, 7 þeonen ælle þa feonnon to Medeshamstede, 7 55
fra Medesha*m*stede al to Welmesforde, 7 fra Welmesforde to Cliue, and þeonen to Æstune, 7 fra Æstune to Stanford, 7 fra Stanford swa swa þ*et* wæter renneð to seo forensprecone Norðburh."

Ðis sindon þa landes 7 ða feonnes þe seo kyning gef into 60
S*anct*e Petres mynstre. Ða cwæð seo kyning:

"Hit is litel, þeos gife; ac ic wille þ*et* hi hit hælden swa kynelice 7 swa freolice þ*et* þær ne be numen of na geld ne gaule, buton to þa munecan ane. Ðus ic wille freon þis minstre þet hit ne be underþed buton Rome ane. 7 Hider ic wille þ*et* we secan 65
S*anct*e Petre, ealle þa þa to Rome na magen faren."

Betwix þas worde, þa geornde seo abb*od*e þet he scolde him tyþian þet he æt him geornde; 7 seo kining hit him tydde:

'Ic haue here Godefrihte muneces þa wolden drohtien here lif on ankersetle, gif hi wisten hwere; oc her is an igland þ*et* 70
man cleopeð Ancarig, 7 wile þes geornen þ*et* we moten þær wircen an mynstre S*anct*e Marie to loue, þet hi moten þær wunen, þa ða here lif wilen læden mid sibbe 7 mid reste."

Ða andswerode seo kyning, 7 þus cwæð:

"Saxulf la leof, ne þet an þ*et* ðu geornest, oc ealle þa þing 75
þ*et* ic wat þet ðu geornest on ure Drihtnes halfe, swa ic lufe 7 tyðe. And ic bidde þe, broðer Æðelred, 7 mine swustre Cyneburh 7 Cynesuuith, for iure sawle alesednesse, þet ge beon witnesse, 7 þ*et* geo hit write mid iure fingre. And ic bidde ealle þa ða æfter me cumen—beon hi mine sunes, beon hi mine 80

breðre, ouþer kyningas þa æfter me cumen—þ*et* ure gyfe mote
standen, swa swa hi willen beon delnimende on þa ece lif 7
f. 16r swa swa hi wilen ætbeorstan / þet ece wite. Swa hwa swa ure
gife ouþer oðre godene manne gyfe wansiaþ, wansie him seo
85 heofenlice iateward on heofenrice; 7 swa hwa swa hit eceð, ece
him seo heofenlice iateward on heofenrice."

Ðas sindon þa witnes þe þær wæron 7 þa þ*et* gewriten mid
here fingre on Cristes mele 7 ietten mid here tunge. Ðet wæs
f'i'rst seo kyning Wulfere þe þ*et* feostnode first mid his worde,
90 7 siððon mid his fingre gewrat on Cristes mel, 7 þus cwæð:

"Ic, Wulfere kyning, mid þas kyningas 7 mid eorles 7 mid
heorotogas 7 mid þægnas, þas gewitnesse mines gifes, toforan
þone ærcebiscop D*eu*sdedit ic hit festnia mid Cristes mel ✝."

"And ic, Oswi Norþhimbre kyning, þeos mynstres freond 7
95 þes abbotes Saxulf, hit loue mid Cristes mel ✝."

"And ic, Sighere kyning, hit tyðe mid Cristes mel ✝."

"And ic, Sibbi kyning, hit write mid Cristes mel ✝."

"And ic, Æðelred þes kyningas broðer, þet ilce ty[ð]e mid
Cristes mel ✝."

100 "And we, þes kyningas swustre Cyneburh 7 Cynesuith, we
hit louien."

"And ic, Kantwarabyrig ærcebiscop D*eu*sdedit, hit tyðe."

Siððan þa getton hit ælle þa oðre þe þær wæron mid Cristes
mel ✝. Ðet wæron be nam: Ithamar biscop of Rofecestre, and
105 Wine biscop of Lundene, 7 Ieruman se wæs Myrcene biscop,
7 Tuda biscop, 7 Wilfrid preost seo wæs siððon biscop, 7
Eoppa preost þe seo kyning Wul[fh]ere seonde to bodian
Cristendome on Wiht, 7 Saxulf abbot, 7 Immine ealdorman, 7
Eadberht ealdorman, 7 Herefri[ð] ældorman, 7 Wilberht ældor-
110 man, 7 Abon ældorman, Æðelbold, Brordan, Wilberht, Ælh-
mund, Freðegis—þas 7 feola oþre þa wæron þær kyninges
þeonestmen hit geotton ealle. Ðes writ wæs gewriton æfter
f. 16v ure Drihtnes acennednesse dc.lxiiii, / þes kyningas Wul[fh]eres
seoueðende gear, þes ærcebiscopes D*eu*sdedit ix gear. Leidon

84 *hole in parchment under* n (? ꞃ) *of* godene   85 *A particularly emphatic pointing hand in the margin.*   98 *MS.* tyde   107 *MS.* Wulhfere
109 *MS.* Herefrid   113 *MS.* wulhferes

þa Godes curs 7 ealre halgane curs 7 al Cristene folces þe ani 115
þing undyde *þet* þær wæs gedon: swa beo hit, seiþ alle, Am*en*.
Þa þis þing wæs gedon, þa seonde seo kyning to Rome to seo
Papa Uitalian*us* þe þa was, 7 geornde *þet* he scolde tyðian mid
his writ 7 mid his bletsinge eal þis forsprecene þing; 7 seo Papa
seonde þa his writ þus cwæðend: 120

"Ic, Uitalian*us* Papa, geate þe, Wul[fh]ere cyning, 7 D*eu*sdedit
ærcebiscop 7 Saxulf abb*ot* ealle þe þing þe ge geornon. 7 Ic
forbede þet ne kyning ne nan man ne haue nan onsting buton
þon abb*ot* ane, ne he ne hersumie nan man buton þone Papa on
Rome 7 se ærcebiscop on Cantwarbyrig. Gif hwa þis tobrekeþ 125
æni þing, S*anct*e Petre mid his sweord him adylige. Gif hwa
hit hælt, S*ancte* Petre mid heofne keie undo him heofenrice."

Ðus wæs seo mynstre Medesha*m*stede agunnen, *þet* man
siððon cleopede Burh. Siððon com an oþre ærceb*iscop* to Cantwarbyrig, seo wæs gehaten Theodor*us*, swiðe god man 7 wis; 130
7 heold his sinoþ mid his biscopes 7 mid þe lerede folc. Þa wæs
Winfrid Myrcene biscop don of his biscoprice, 7 Saxulf abb*ot*
was þær gecoren to biscop, 7 Cuðbald munec of þe selue mynstre
wæs coren to abbot. Þis sinað was gehalden æfter ure Drihtnes
acennednesse seoxhundred wintra 7 iii 7 hundseofenti wintra. 135

675. On his time þa seonde he to Rome Wilfrid biscop to þa*m* f. 17[v]
Pape þe þa wes—Agatho he wæs gehaten—7 cydde him mid
writ 7 mid worde hu his breðre Peada 7 Wulfhere 7 se abbot
Saxulf heafden wroht an minstre, Medesha*m*stede wæs gehaten,
7 *þet* hi hit heafden gefreod wið kyning 7 wið biscop of ealle 5
þewdom; 7 bed him *þet* he scolde *þet* geten mid his writ 7 mid
his bletsunge. And seo Papa seonde þa his gewrite to Englalande þus cweðende:

"Ic, Agatho Papa of Rome, grete wel seo wurðfulle Æþelred
Myrcene kyning, 7 se ærcebiscop Theodoru*m* of Can'*t*'war- 10
byrig, 7 seo Myrcene biscop Saxulf seo ær wæs abbot, 7 alle
þa abbotes þa sindon on Englalande, Godes gretinge 7 minre
bletsunge. Ic haue geheord seo kyninges Æðelredes geornunge,

121 *MS.* Wulhfere

f. 18r / 7 þes ærcebiscopes Theodor*us* 7 þes biscopes Saxulfes 7 þes
15 abbotes Cuthbaldes; 7 ic hit wille, *þet* hit on ælle wise beo swa
swa ge hit sprecon hauen. And ic bebeode, of Godes half 7
S*ancte* Petreˡsˡ 7 ealra halgan 7 ealre hadode heafde, þet ne
kyning ne biscop ne eorl ne ˡnˡan man ne haue nan onsting, ne
gafle ne geold ne feording, ne nanes cinnes ðeudom ne nime
20 man of *þet* abbotrice of Medeshamstede. Ic beode æc *þet* þe
scyrbiscop ne seo swa dyrstlece *þet* he ne hading ne haleging ne
do on þis abbotrice, buton seo abbot hit him bidde; ne biscop-
wite ne sinað ne nanes kinnes þing na haue þær nan onsting. 7
Ic wille *þet* seo abbot beo gehealden for legat of Rome ofer eal
25 *þet* iglande; 7 hwilc abbot þe beþ þær coren of þe munecan, *þet*
he beo gebletsad of þan ærcebiscop of Cantwarbyrig. Ic wille
7 tyðe *þet* hwilc man swa haue[ð] behaten to faren to Rome, and
he ne muge hit forðian, ouðer for untru*m*nisse, ouðer for
lauerdes neode, ouðer for haueleste, ouðer for hwilces cinnes
30 oðer neod he ne muge þær cumon, beo he of Englelande ouðer
of hwilc oðer igland beo he—cume to *þet* mynstre on Medeshamstede, 7 haue *þet* iˡlˡce forgiuenesse of Criste 7 S*ancte*
Peter 7 of þone abbot 7 of þone muneca *þet* he scolde hauen gif
he to Rome fore. Nu bidde ic þe, broðer Theodorus, *þet* þu
35 lete bedon geond æl Englelande þet seo sinað wurðe gegaderod
7 þis write wurðe geredd 7 gehealdon. Alswa ic beode þe,
Saxulf biscop, *þet* swa swa þu hit geornest, *þet* seo mynstre beo
freo, swa ic forbeode þe 7 ealle þe biscopas þe æfter ðe cumon,
of Criste 7 of ealle his halgan, *þet* ge nan onsting ne hauen of
40 *þet* mynstre, buton swa micel swa þone abbot wile. Nu wille ic
f. 18v hit segge mid worde, *þet* hwa swa halt þis write 7 þis / bode, þa
wurðe he efre wuniende mid God ælmihti on heuenrice; 7 hwa
swa hit tobreceð, þa wurðe he amansumed 7 aniðrod mid Iudas
7 mid ealle deofle on helle, buton he cume to dedbote. AMEN."

45 Ðas writ seonde seo Papa Agatho, 7 an hundred 7 fif 7 twenti
biscopes, bi Wilfrid ærcebiscop of Eoferwic to Englalande. Þis
wæs gedon æfter ure Drihtnes acennednesse dc.lxxx, þes
kininges vi gear Æðelredes. Ða heot seo kining þone ærce-

22 *Another emphatic pointing hand.* 27 *MS.* haued

biscop Theodor*us* þ*et* he scolde setton ealle gewitene mot æt þone stede þ*et* man cleopeð Heatfelde. Ða hi wæron þær gegaderod, þa leot he rædon þa gewrite þe seo Papa þider seonde; 7 ealle hit getton 7 fulfeostnodon. Ða seide se kyning: 50

"Ealle þa þing þe min broðer Peada 7 min broðer Wulfere 7 mine swuster Kineburh 7 Kynesuith geafon 7 getton S*anct*e Peter 7 þone abbot, þa wile ic þ*et* stande. 7 Ic wile on min dæi hit æcon for here sawle 7 for minre sawle. Nu gife ic S*anct*e Peter to dæi into his minstre Medeshamstede þas landes 7 eal þ*et* þærto ligge[ð]: þet is, Bredune, Hrepingas, Cedenac, Swineshæfed, Heanbyrig, Lodeshac, Scuffanhalch, Costesford, Stretford, Wætelleburne, Lufgeard, Æþelhuniglond, Barþanig. Ðas landes ic gife S*anct*e Peter eal swa freolice swa ic seolf hit ahte, 7 swa þ*et* nan min æftergengles þær nan þing of ne nime. Gif hwa hit doð, þes Papa curs of Rome 7 ealre biscope curs he habbe, 7 here ealre þe her be gewitnesse. 7 Þis ic festnie mid Cristes tacne ✠." 55 60 65

"Ic, Theodor*us* ærcebiscop of Cantwarbyrig, am witnesse of þas gewrite of Medeshamstede, 7 ic festnie mid min gewrite, 7 ic amansumie ealle þa þær ani þing / of breke, 7 ic bletsie ealle þa þe hit healden ✠." f. 19r

"Ic, Wilfrid ærceb*iscop* of Æferwic, ic eam witnesse of þas gewrite, 7 ic gæte þæs ilce curs ✠." 70

"Ic, Saxulf, þe wæs first abbot 7 nu eam biscop, ic gife hi min curs 7 ealle min æftergengle þe þis tobreket."

"Ic, Ostriðe, Æðelredes cwen, hit tyðe."

"Ic, Adrianus legat, hit iete." 75

"Ic, Putta biscop of Rofecestre, ic hit write."

"Ic, Waldhere biscop of Lundene, hit festnie."

"Ic, Cuðbald abbot, hit geate swa þet hwa swa hit breket, ealre biscope cursunge 7 eal Cristene fo[l]ces he hafe. Am*en*". 79

686. Þæs Cædwala gef into S*anct*e Petres minstre Medeshamstede Hoge: þ*et* is in an igland Heabureahg hatte. Þa wæs abbot f. 19v

675/52 seide *corrected from* seonde 58 *MS.* ligged 79 *MS.* fo/ces *divided between two lines.*

on þære minstre, Egbalth wæs gehaten; heo wæs se þridde abbot
4 æfter Saxulfe. Þa wæs Theodor*us* ærceb*iscop* on Cent.

f. 24r 777. On þas kinges dæi Offa wæs an abbot on Medeshamstede Beonne gehaten. Se ilca Beonne, þurh ealle þa muneke red of
f.24v þere minstre, þa let he Cuthbriht ealdorma[n] x bonde land / at Swinesheafde mid læswe 7 mid mædwe 7 mid eal þ*et* ðærto læi,
5 7 swa þ*et* seo Cuðbriht geaf þone abbote l punde þærfore, 7 ilca gear anes nihtes feorme ouðer xxx scyllinge penega; swa eac þ*et* eafter his dæi scolde seo land ongean into þa mynstre. At þis gewitnesse wæs seo kining Offa 7 seo kining Egferð 7 seo ærceb*iscop* Hygeberht 7 Ceolwulf biscop 7 Inwona b*iscop* 7 Beonna
10 abbot 7 feola oþre biscopes 7 abbotes 7 feola oðre rice men. On þes ilca Offa dæi wæs an ealdorman, Brordan wæs gehaten. He geornde at se kyning þ*et* he scolde for his luuen freon his ane mynstre, Wocingas het, forþi ðet he hit wolde giuen into Medeshamstede 7 S*anct*e Peter 7 þone abbote þe þa was (he was
15 Pusa gehaten; seo Pusa wæs æfter Beonna, and seo kining hine luuede swiðe); 7 seo kyning freode þa þ*et* mynstre Wocingas wið cining 7 wið biscop 7 wið eorl 7 wiþ ealle men, swa þ*et* nan man ne hafde þær nan onsting buton S*ancte* Peter 7 þone ab*bot*. Ðis
19 wæs don on þe cininges tune Freoricburna hatte.

f. 29r 852. Her on þis tima leot Ceolred abb*ot* of Medeshamstede 7 þa munecas Wulfrede to hande þet land of Sempigaham to þ*et* forewearde þ*et* æfter his dæi scolde þ*et* land into þe minstre; 7 Wulfred scolde gifen þ*et* land of Sliowaforda into Medesham-
5 stede, 7 he scolde gife ilca gear into þe minstre sixtiga foðra wuda, 7 twælf foður græfan, 7 sex foður gearda, 7 twa tu[nn]an fulle hlutres aloð, 7 twa slægnæt, 7 sex hund hlafes, 7 ten mittan wælsces aloð, 7 ilca gear an hors, 7 þrittiga scillinga, 7 ane næht gefeormige. Her wæs wið se cining Burhred 7 Ceolred ærce-
10 b*iscop* and Tunberht b*iscop* 7 Ce[n]red b*iscop* 7 Alhh[un] b*iscop* 7 Berhtred b*iscop* 7 Wihtred abb*ot* 7 Werhtherd abb*ot*, Æðelheard ealdorman, Hunberht ealdorman, 7 feola oðre.

777/3 *MS*. ealdorma 5 s(eo *altered from* h(eo 852/6 *MS*. tunnnan 10 *MS*. ceured; *MS*. alhhim

870. . . . 7 fordiden ealle þa mynstre þa hi to comen. On þa ilcan tima, þa comon hi to Medeshamstede; beorndon 7 bræcon; slogon abbot 7 munecas; 7 eall þ*et* hi þær fundon, macedon hit þa þ*et* ær wæs ful rice, þa hit wearð to nan þing. f. 30v 4

963. Her ˡfra*m*ˡ Eadgar cyning to ðe biscopdome on Wintanceastra wes gecoren S*anct*e Aðelwold, 7 þe arc*e*biscop of Cantwarbyrig, S*anct*e Dunstan, him gehalgod to biscop on þe fyrste Sunnondæg of Aduent, þ*et* wæs on iii K*alendarum* Decemb*ris*. On þes oðer gear syððon he wæs gehalgod, þa makode he feola minstra; 7 draf ut þa clerca of þe biscoprice forþan þ*et* hi noldon nan regul healden, 7 sætta þær muneca. He macode þær twa abbotrice, an of muneca, oðer of nunna: þ*et* wæs eall wiðinnan Wintanceastra. Syððan þa com he to se cyng Eadgar; bed him þet he scolde him giuen ealle þa minstre þa hæðene men heafden ær tobrocon, for[ð]i þet he hit wolde geeadnewion; 7 se kyng hit bliþelice tyðode. And se biscop com þa fyrst to Elig, þær S*ancte* Æðel[ð]rið lið, 7 leot macen þone mynstre; geaf hit þa his an munac, Brihtnoð wæs gehaten, halgode him þa abbot, 7 sætte þær munecas Gode to þewian þær hwilon wæron nun[na]; bohte þa feola cotlif æt se king 7 macode hit swyðe rice. Syððon com se biscop Aðelwold to þære mynstre þe wæs gehaten Medeshamstede, ðe hwilon wæs fordon fra heðene folce; ne fand þær nan þing buton ealde weallas 7 wilde wuda. Fand þa hidde in þa ealde wealle writes þet Headda abb*ot* heafde ær gewriton, hu Wulfhere kyng 7 Æðelred his broðor hit heafden wroht, 7 hu hi hit freodon wið king 7 wið b*iscop* 7 wið ealle weoruldþeudom, 7 hu se Papa Agatho / hit feostnode mid his write, 7 se arc*ebiscop* De*us*dedit. Leot wircen þa þ*et* mynstre, 7 sætte þær abbot se wæs gehaten Aldulf; macede þær munecas þær ær ne wæs nan þing. Com þa to þe cyng, 7 leot him locon þa gewrite þe ær wæron gefunden; and se kyng andswerode þa 7 cwe[ð]: f. 36v 5 10 15 20 f. 37r 25

"Ic, Ædgar, geate 7 gife to dæi toforen Gode 7 toforen þone ærceb*iscop* Dunstan freodom S*anct*e Petres mynstre Medesha*m*- 30

963/11 *MS.* fordi 13 *MS.* æðeldrið 16 *MS.* nun *followed by erasure of two or three letters.* 28 *MS.* cwed

stede of kyng 7 of b*iscop*, 7 ealle þa þorpes þe ðærto lin: þ*et* is,
Æstfeld, 7 Dode˹s˺thorp, 7 Ege, 7 Pastun; 7 swa ic hit freo þet
nan biscop ne haue þær nane hæse buton se abbot of þone
minstre. And ic gife þone tun þe man cleopeð Vndela, mid eall
35 þet þærto lið: þ*et* i˹s˺ þet man cleopeð Eahtehundred, 7 market 7
toll swa freolice þ*et* ne king ne b*iscop* ne eorl ne sc[i]rreue ne
haue þær nane hæse, ne nan man buton se abbot ane 7 þam þe
he þærto sæt. And ic gife Crist 7 S*anct*e Peter, 7 þurh þes
b*iscopes* bene Aðelwold, þas land: þ*et* is, Barwe, Wermi*ng*tun,
40 Æsctun, Ketering, Castra, Egleswurðe, Waltun, Wiðringtun, Ege,
Thorp, 7 an myneter in Stanfor[d].* Ðas land 7 ealla þa oðre
þe lin into þe mynstre, þa cwe[ð]e ic scyr—þ[*et* is] saca 7 socne,
toll 7 team, 7 infangenþef. þas rihting 7 ealle oðre ða cweðe ic
scyr Crist 7 S*ancte* Peter. And ic gife þa twa dæl of Witlesmere
45 mid watres 7 mid wæres 7 feonnes, 7 swa þurh Merelade on an
to þ*et* wæter þ*et* man cleopeð Nen, 7 swa eastweard to Cynges
Dælf. And ic wille þ*et* markete beo in þe selue tun, 7 þ*et* nan
oþer ne [beo] betwix Stanford 7 Hu[n]tandune. 7 Ic wille þet
þus be gifen se toll: fyrst fra Witlesmære eall to þe cynges toll of
50 Norðmannes Cros hundred, 7 eft ongeanward fra Witlesmære
f. 37v þurh Merelade on an to Nen, 7 swa swa þ*et* wæter / reonneð to
Crulande, 7 fra Crulande to Must, 7 fra Must to Cynges Dælf
7 to Witlesmære. And ic wille þ*et* ealle þa freodom 7 ealle þa
forgiuenesse þe mine forgengles geafen, þet hit stande. 7 Ic
55 write 7 feostnige mid Cristes rodetacne ✝."

36 *MS.* scrreue 39 *MS.* Ƿermiȝ/tun *divided between two lines.* 41 *MS.* stanforð 42 *MS.* cwede; *MS.* þ *followed by space for two or three letters.* 48 *MS.* ne betwix; *MS.* hutandune

* *7 an myneter in Stanford*: what seems to be a striking confirmation of the accuracy of this statement was discovered by Mr. R. H. M. Dolley, now of Queen's University, Belfast. This is a fragment of a coin, datable *c.* 985–*c.* 988, which bears on the reverse the inscription:

HILDE MO*NETARIUS* MEÐ . . . . . .

The letters MEÐ correspond to the name of no mint previously known, and *Hild*(*e*) is recorded as a moneyer's name only from Stamford: probably, therefore, this was a *Medeshamstede* coin minted at Stamford under the provision set forth here. (See 'A New Anglo-Saxon Mint—Medeshamstede', *British Numismatic Journal*, xxvii (1954), 263–5.)

Ð'a' andswerade se arcebiscop Dunstan of Cantwarbyrig 7 sæide:

"Ic tyðe þ*et* ealle þa þing þe her is gifen 7 sprecon 7 ealle þa þing þe þin forgengles 7 min geatton, þa wille ic þ*et* hit stande. 7 Swa hwa swa hit tobrecoð, þa gife ic him Godes curs 7 ealra halgan 7 eallre hadede heafde 7 min, buton he cume to dædbote. 7 Ic gife tocnawlece S*anct*e Peter min messehacel, 7 min stol, 7 min ræf, Criste to þeuwian."   60

"Ic, Oswald arcebiscop of Eoferwic, geate ealle þas worde þurh þa halgo rode þet Crist wæs on þrowod ✝."   65

"Ic, Aðelwold biscop, blætsige ealle þe þis healdon, 7 ic amansumie ealle þe þis tobræcon, buton he cume to dædbote."

Her wæs Ælf's'tan biscop, Aþulf b*iscop*, 7 Escwi abbot, 7 Osgar abb*ot*, 7 Æþelgar abb*ot*, 7 Ælfere ealdorman, Æðelwine ealdorman, Brihtnoþ, Oslac ealdorman, 7 feola oðre rice men; 7 ealle hit geatton, 7 ealle hit writen mid Cristes mæl ✝. Ðis wæs gedon syððon ure Drihtnes acennednesse dcccc lxx°ii°, þes kinges xvi gear. Ða bohte se abbot Aldulf landes feola 7 manega, 7 godede þa þ*et* mynstre swiðe mid ealle. 7 Wæs þær þa swa lange þ*et* se arcebiscop Oswald of Eoferwic wæs forð gewiton; 7 man cæs him þa to erceb*iscop*. 7 Man cæs þa sona oðer abbot of þe sylfe minstre, KENVLF wæs gehaten, se wæs syððon biscop in Wintanceastre. 7 He macode fyrst þa wealle abutan þone mynstre; geaf hit þa 'to' nama Burch þe ær het / Medeshamstede. Wæs þær swa lange þ*et* man sette him to biscop on Wintanceastre. Þa cæs man oðer abbot of þe silue minstre, þe wæs gehaten Ælfsi. Se Ælfsi wæs þa abbot syððon fiftig wintre. He nam up S*anct*a Kyneburh 7 S*ancta* Kynesuið, þe lægen in Castra, and S*ancta* Tibba, þe læi in Rihala, 7 brohte heom to Burch, and offrede heom eall S*ancte* Peter on an dæi; 7 heold þa hwile þe he þær wæs.   70 75 f. 38r 80 85

1013. 7 Ða hwile þe seo læfdige mid hire broþer wæs begondon sæ, Ælfsige abb*ot* of Burh, þe þær wæs mid hire, for to þone mynstre þe is gehaten Boneual, þær S*anct*e Florentines lichama læg; fand þær ærm stede, ærm abbot, 7 ærme muneces, forþan   f. 46v

5 þe hi forhergode wæron; bohte þa þær æt þone abb*ot* 7 æt þe muneces S*anct*e Florentines lichaman eall buton þe heafod, to v hundred punda; 7 þa þe he ongean co*m*, þa offrede hit Crist 7 S*anct*e Peter.

f. 51r 1041. 7 On þis ilcan tyme forðferde Ælf[sige] abbot of Burh; 7 man ceas þa Arnwi munec to abb*ot*, forðan þe he wæs swiðe god man 7 swiðe bilehwit.

f. 56r 1052. 7 On þis ilcan tyme forlet Arnwi abb*ot* of Burh / abbotrice be his halre life, 7 geaf hit Leofric munec be þes cynges leafe 7 b[e] þære munece; 7 se abbot Arnwi lifode syððon viii wintre. 7 Se abbot Leofri[c go]dede þa þ*et* mynstre swa þ*et* man hit
5 cleopede þa Gildene Burh; þa wæx hit swi[ðe] on land 7 on gold 7 on seolfer.

f. 57v 1066. 7 Ða wæs Leofric abbot of Burh æt þ*et* ilca feord, 7 sæclode þær, 7 co*m* ham, 7 wæs dæd sone þæræfter on Ælre
f. 58r Halgan mæsseniht—God / are his saule! On his dæg wæs ealle blisse 7 ealle gode on Burh; 7 he wæs leaf eall folc, swa þ*et* se
5 cyng geaf S*anct*e Peter 7 hi*m* þ*et* abbotrice on Byrtune, 7 se of Couentre þ*et* se eorl Leofric, þe wæs his eam, ær heafde macod, 7 se of Crulande, 7 se of Þorneie. 7 He dyde swa mycel to gode into þ*et* mynstre of Burh, on golde 7 on seolfre 7 on scrud 7 on lande, swa nefre nan oðre ne dyde toforen hi*m* ne nan æfter
10 hi*m*. Þa wearð Gildene Burh to wrecce Burh. Ða cusen þa munecas to abbot Brand p*ro*uost, forðan þ*et* he wæs swiðe god man 7 swiðe wis; 7 senden him þa to Ædgar æðeling, forðan þet þe landfolc wendon þ*et* he sceolde cyng wurðen; 7 se æðeling hit hi*m* geatte þa bliþolice. Þa þe cyng Willelm geherde
15 þ*et* secgen, þa wearð he swiðe wrað, 7 sæde þ*et* se abbot hi*m*

1041. *The original annal ends at the bottom of the page and the interpolation is added in the same hand and ink, but with a fresh rubrication, in the margin beneath, running over into the side-margins.* 1 *the end of* Ælf[sige] *is lost through margin-cutting.* 1052. *This interpolation* (*as far as* Burh) *is added, with a fresh rubrication, by the same hand at the end of the original annal, and is continued in the lower margin, running over into the side-margin.* 3 b[e]; 4 Leofri[c go]dede; 5 swi[ðe]: *letters in brackets supplied to fill lacunae caused by margin-trimming* (*instead of* godede *Thorpe more picturesquely suggests* gildede).

heafde forsegon. Þa eodon gode men heom betwenen, 7 sahtloden heo*m*, forðan þ*et* se abbot wæs goddera manne; geaf þa þone cyng xl marc goldes to sahtnysse. 7 þa lifede ˡheˡ litle hwile þæræft*er* buton þry gear. Syððon comen ealle dræuednysse 7 ealle ifele to þone mynstre—God hit gemyltse! 20

1069. 7 On þisu*m* ilcan geare forðferde Brand abb*ot* of Burh, f. 58v
on v K*alendarum* Decembr*is*.

INDEX OF PROPER NAMES

Names are listed under the forms in the text; with most place-names these represent oblique cases.